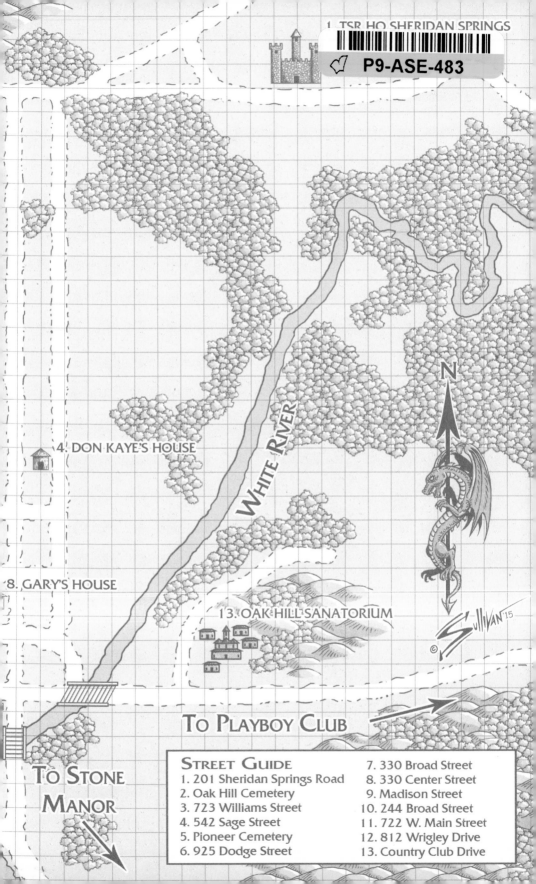

1. TSR HQ SHERIDAN SPRINGS

P9-ASE-483

N

WHITE RIVER

4. DON KAYE'S HOUSE

8. GARY'S HOUSE

13. OAK HILL SANATORIUM

To PLAYBOY CLUB

To STONE MANOR

Sullivan '15

STREET GUIDE
1. 201 Sheridan Springs Road
2. Oak Hill Cemetery
3. 723 Williams Street
4. 542 Sage Street
5. Pioneer Cemetery
6. 925 Dodge Street
7. 330 Broad Street
8. 330 Center Street
9. Madison Street
10. 244 Broad Street
11. 722 W. Main Street
12. 812 Wrigley Drive
13. Country Club Drive

Empire of Imagination

Empire of Imagination

GARY GYGAX AND THE BIRTH OF DUNGEONS & DRAGONS

Michael Witwer

BLOOMSBURY

NEW YORK · LONDON · OXFORD · NEW DELHI · SYDNEY

Bloomsbury USA
An imprint of Bloomsbury Publishing Plc

1385 Broadway	50 Bedford Square
New York	London
NY 10018	WC1B 3DP
USA	UK

www.bloomsbury.com

BLOOMSBURY and the Diana logo are trademarks of Bloomsbury Publishing Plc

First published 2015

ISBN: HB: 978-1-63286-279-2
ePub: 978-1-63286-204-4

LIBRARY OF CONGRESS CATALOGING-IN-PUBLICATION DATA

Witwer, Michael.
Empire of imagination : Gary Gygax and the birth of Dungeons & dragons / by
Michael Witwer.
pages ; cm
Includes bibliographical references and index.
ISBN: 978-1-63286-279-2 (hardcover) / 978-1-63286-204-4 (ePub)
1. Gygax, Gary. 2. Dungeons and Dragons (Game)
I. Title.
GV1469.62.D84W57 2015
794.8—dc23
2015016223

2 4 6 8 10 9 7 5 3 1

Typeset by RefineCatch Limited, Bungay, Suffolk
Printed and bound in the U.S.A. by Thomson-Shore Inc., Dexter, Michigan

To find out more about our authors and books visit www.bloomsbury.com. Here you
will find extracts, author interviews, details of forthcoming events and the option to
sign up for our newsletters.

Bloomsbury books may be purchased for business or promotional use.
For information on bulk purchases please contact Macmillan Corporate and
Premium Sales Department at specialmarkets@macmillan.com.

For Kalysta, Vivienne & William

Contents

Author's Note
Telling the Story of a Storyteller

EMPIRE OF IMAGINATION: *Gary Gygax and the Birth of Dungeons & Dragons* is the dramatic story of the creator of one of history's most influential games. While the story's narrative is based on an extensive research and interview process, I have also used a bit of imagination and informed judgment to fill in the gaps of this dynamic yet largely unknown story, making it as complete and cohesive as possible. In many cases, scenes and dialogue have been re-created, combined, and in some instances imagined to best support the known documentary record. Many of the events described are controversial and told from personal perspectives that reflect the beliefs of the individuals involved, and are not necessarily shared or endorsed by this author. Ultimately, it is my hope that the reader will come away not just with a clear picture of Gary Gygax's achievements but also with a sense of his personality—a picture of his life. Nonetheless, a great effort was made to be as conceptually accurate and precise as possible in the descriptions of these events, and in all factual details of this work.

I have, however, provided a way for those who would like to be able to distinguish actual quotes and writings from those that have been editorialized, re-created, or imagined in the course of this work. Quotes or strings of quotes that are immediately followed by a note reference number are derived from actual comments and writings; the associated note provides relevant source and contextual information. Notes are also used to provide source information on particular accounts (especially those that are otherwise controversial or contested), to credit sources for various information, or to provide further details on a particular topic. A more extensive bibliography with complete information on the sources cited in the notes is provided at the end. The quotes that appear without an accompanying citation are, as acknowledged above, editorialized, re-created, or imagined within a factual context. Out of respect for those who were present at the time of these events, I feel it is important to reiterate that great lengths were taken to be as factually accurate as possible, but I also believe the dramatic aspect of the narrative is fully in line with detailing a remarkable life such as Gary's.

One challenge of gathering accurate information about and from such a creative and imaginative group of individuals is that in many cases recollections of events tend to be just that, creative and imaginative. This, coupled with a range of personal feelings around these people and events, not to mention many years of distance, no doubt explains the significant discrepancies that exist in the historical record. Gary himself was known to speak off the cuff, probably not foreseeing that his words might someday be chronicled and assembled as part of historical research. For example, he was often inexact—and sometimes inconsistent—with dates, facts, and figures in interviews conducted at different times about the same event. To this end, and as part of the research process, I used primary sources wherever available and practicable in order to eliminate factual conflicts, especially those that occurred in later interviews and in poorly controlled published sources. In this respect, Jon Peterson's *Playing at the World* proved especially helpful and deserves special recognition, as its research is largely based on hard-to-find primary sources and effectively functioned as a factual control for my research. This is not to leave out all the individuals who generously donated their time in the form of interviews and other correspondence for this effort, a complete list of which is available in the acknowledgments and bibliography.

This is a story—the story of the vibrant and dynamic life of Ernest Gary Gygax. From all I have come to understand of my subject, I believe he would want his story told in precisely this way.

Introduction

In 1974, a small-town Wisconsin cobbler stumbled on an idea that would forever change the face of popular culture: a role-playing game. The cobbler was Gary Gygax, and the game was *Dungeons & Dragons* (*D&D*). Within a few years, this geeky counterculture game had become a worldwide phenomenon, but it was ultimately stifled amid chilling accusations of psychological dangers, allegations of Satan worship, costly lawsuits, broken partnerships, and suspect business decisions, forever relegating the game to the fringes of the mainstream. But perhaps this often overlooked and misunderstood game had a larger impact than previously believed . . .

When I first started looking into Gary, I was stunned to find that a complete biography had not already been written. Beyond his creating *D&D*, the first role-playing game—a hobby enjoyed by roughly six million people in the United States alone—one can argue that his creation led to some of today's most important pop culture phenomena. If you have ever played a first-person shooter video game like *Call of Duty*, a massively multiplayer online role-playing game (MMO) like *World of Warcraft*, or a computer role-playing game like *Final Fantasy*; if you have ever logged on to an online virtual world like *Second Life* or experienced the wildly popular *Game of Thrones* television series and books, then you are already tangentially familiar with the work of Gary Gygax. Simply put, his seminal game made these later multibillion-dollar pop culture phenomena possible. But unlike other innovators who laid the foundations of today's popular culture—luminaries such as Steve Jobs and Walt Disney—Gygax and his esoteric game are relatively unknown to the mainstream, yet revered by the geeky faithful.

Gary changed the world, but in ways far more abstract than his better-recognized peers. His game assembled and inspired an early group of nerds who became the computer programmers, fantasy writers, video game designers, and film stars of today—the leaders and masters of the Information Age. And that is just the tip of the iceberg.

Having grown up a role-playing gamer, it was Gary's work that led me to the idea of taking on a biography. But I soon discovered that his personal life was equally intriguing. It had all of the high-concept elements of a rags-to-riches-to-rags story: small-town man makes it big, forgets who he is, falls hard, and finds redemption late in life. It was also the close examination of his childhood that helped me realize that *D&D* didn't begin on a single day in 1974 when Gary's company, TSR, published its first one thousand copies. It began when Gary played his first game of chess, experienced his first haunting, read his first pulp novel, roamed the tunnels of the local abandoned insane asylum, and so forth. This is largely why the biography is comprehensive, spanning from Gary's early days to his death in 2008.

So who was this man so admired by the likes of Stephen Colbert, Vin Diesel, Jon Favreau, Anderson Cooper, the late Robin Williams, and scores of other pop culture icons and innovators, not to mention millions of role-playing gamers around the world? Perhaps more important, why does any of this matter?

I hope *Empire of Imagination* will answer these questions and others about the man who was ranked number one on *Sync* magazine's list of the fifty biggest nerds of all time. And in an era when it is chic to be geek, Gary Gygax is king, making his story as relevant today, arguably more so, as it was when *D&D* was "the great game of the 1980s."

Memory Lane

DUNGEON MASTER: *You stand aboard the deck of a pirate ship. You've just vanquished several brigands, who lay slain at your feet. What do you do?*

PLAYER (SIR EGARY): *I search the bodies, starting with the captain.*

DUNGEON MASTER: *You make your way over to the edge of the deck, where the body of the brigand captain is lying. As you rummage through his things you find a number of your effects that had been stolen, including the Key of Revelation. Just as you pick up the key from the captain's pouch, an arrow shoots down from the crow's nest of the front mast and . . .* [DM looks down at the character sheets in front of him and rolls a twenty-sided die] *hits you square in the chest, penetrating your platemail armor.* [DM rolls a six-sided die] *This, on top of the wounds you sustained earlier, leaves you very badly injured.*

PLAYER (SIR EGARY): *I take cover behind the crates on deck.*

DUNGEON MASTER: *You try to make your way over to the crates . . .* [DM rolls a twenty-sided die] *but you are losing a lot of blood and your vision is starting to tunnel. Before you make the crates, you stumble back and begin to fumble the key off the side of the ship.*

PLAYER (SIR EGARY): *I try to recover and catch the key before it falls into the water.*

DUNGEON MASTER: [DM rolls a twenty-sided die] *You look over the side of the ship just in time to see the key hit the surface of the water and sink. The Key of Revelation is lost to the depths of Shadow Lake . . .*

IT WAS A BLEAK and blustery October evening as a graying, portly man hastily exited a light-industrial office building in Lake Geneva, Wisconsin. He stood motionless for several moments, his bearded face expressionless, his steely brown eyes glazed through his thick, horn-rimmed glasses.

How could I let this happen? he thought.

He wanted to shout at the top of his lungs, but he couldn't seem to move at present. He felt numb, empty, and entirely speechless.

As the man stood in the building's portico recovering from his temporary paralysis, he noticed something of a commotion behind him. Regaining his focus, he turned to peer into the building's entrance, from which emanated an unnatural fluorescent glow. It was no surprise that more than one shadow stood in the lobby returning his gaze. These were his former employees and friends.

As if by instinct, he drew a pack of Camel unfiltered cigarettes and a small plastic lighter from his coat pocket. He quickly lit his cigarette and lumbered away from the entrance with his first exhalation, all the while pondering questions of how and why. He was not a man of ambition, at least not in a worldly sense. He certainly wasn't a "corporate type." He just wanted to create and play games. He just wanted others to love and play games, as he did. How had his love of gaming led to this?

The year was 1985, and the man was Ernest Gary Gygax, creator of the world's first role-playing game, *Dungeons & Dragons*. He was also, up until minutes ago, the president and CEO of TSR Inc., the publisher and owner of *Dungeons & Dragons* and many of his other creations. His leadership at TSR had ended, however, as he had just been ousted by its board of directors in a takeover orchestrated by the company's new majority shareholder, Lorraine Williams.

By 1985 *Dungeons & Dragons*, commonly referred to as *D&D*, had become a worldwide phenomenon, with distribution in twenty-two countries and annual sales peaking at $30 million. The subject of both a monthly magazine and popular CBS cartoon, *D&D* had created a unique category of table game known as a role-playing game (RPG). *D&D*, now one of many RPGs on the market, paired the tactical qualities of tabletop miniature war games with the flexibility and imagination of group storytelling. Led through these imaginary adventures by a referee called the Dungeon Master, each player in *D&D* developed a customized "character," complete with a unique persona and set of tangible attributes, to be guided through the adventure cooperatively with other players. Furthermore, unlike common board games that were meant to be played and concluded in one sitting, in *D&D* both your character and the adventure were ongoing and upgradable, creating a more intense and lasting sense of continuity for players and Dungeon Masters alike.

Gary plodded over to the driver's side of a blue Cadillac Seville with tinted windows that was parked nearest the entrance. The car's license plate read TSR 1.[1] He didn't enter the car, but knocked on the driver's-side window. As the dark window descended it revealed the rugged face of Gary's former gardener turned driver and bodyguard, Jim Johnson.

"You can go home, Jim. I'm gonna take a walk into town. I'll call you when I need a pickup," said Gary, mustering as much coolness and indifference as he could manage in the face of the humiliation he had just experienced.

To this, Jim nodded and closed the car window.

Usually Johnson would have asked for further direction, as these were very unusual instructions from his employer, but Jim had worked for Gary for several years and could sense that he was not in the mood for explanation. In fact, it was well understood by all of Gary's employees that he was not to be crossed when in a mood, as he clearly was now.

What struck Jim as particularly unusual, though, was that Gary rarely walked anywhere these days, whether for leisure, exercise, or otherwise. A bad knee, paired with a slightly overweight physique and smoker's lungs, precluded Gary from taking the frequent walks he had been accustomed to as a younger man. In fact, before Gary had achieved extraordinary success with TSR and *Dungeons & Dragons*, walking was often his mode of transportation, since he had never been issued a driver's license. Thus the need for Johnson's chauffeuring services.

Gary slowly made his way through the parking lot and its remarkable fleet of more than seventy cars and trucks owned or leased by TSR. The vehicles had once been used by a local staff that numbered nearly four hundred, but had since dwindled to a skeleton crew of ninety-five. This oversupply of vehicles served as a poignant reminder to Gary of where things had started to go wrong on the business front.

He swore under his breath as he began to head down the hill of the wooded Northeast Business Park, on which TSR's headquarters was located. As he arrived at the bottom, where Sheridan Springs Road intersected the much busier Williams Street, he thought about how much the town had changed since he first moved there as a boy. Once a sleepy and woodsy fishing town, located just within Wisconsin's southern border, Lake Geneva had become a hugely popular resort and weekend getaway for Chicago executives and regional vacationers. It had, however, always been a summer destination for Chicago's elite, with its shores notably punctuated by ornate mansions owned by the ultrawealthy, such as appliance magnate Frederick Maytag or the Wrigley family—of chewing gum, Chicago Cubs, and Wrigley Field fame. But the volume of tourism had never been so great as it was now. Still, the locale did retain its rustic, small-town charm, with its beautiful historic business district surrounded by charming brick bungalows and grand Victorian homes along tree-lined streets.

Gary had returned to his hometown full-time within the last year, when he became aware of severe financial difficulties and, what he deemed to be, "gross mismanagement"[2] of the company he had founded, TSR. His majority business partners, brothers Kevin and Brian Blume, had been running the company while Gary was living in Hollywood growing the brand through Dungeons & Dragons Entertainment Corporation, a subsidiary of TSR responsible for the company's media products, including the popular cartoon series. The previous year, Kevin had been removed as CEO amid Gary's allegations of poor performance, but now it seemed it was Gary's turn.

Even worse, Gary knew that his present crisis was largely self-created. It was, after all, the person he brought in to help stabilize and manage the company who had turned against him. That person was Lorraine

Dille Williams, the sister of Gary's close friend and business associate Flint Dille. Although Williams had boasted some prior management experience, she proved more to be a wealthy entrepreneur looking for a project. Funded by the affluent Dille estate, which owned the rights to the Buck Rogers character, among other things, she found in TSR a unique opportunity to assert her control and seized it. She quickly made a deal with the Blume brothers to acquire their controlling interest in TSR. By this time the Blumes were more than happy to acquiesce; they wanted out after many turbulent years with Gary and, most recently, Gary's aggressive removal of Kevin as CEO.

Gary thought about the turmoil TSR had been through over the last ten years, and how he had always managed to come out on top, until now: the death of his friend and original business partner, Don Kaye; lawsuits from *D&D*'s co-creator, Dave Arneson; the extraordinary mismanagement by the Blume brothers; the defamatory tales of the alleged *D&D*-related disappearance of a young Michigan State University student and the ensuing claims that *D&D* was even psychologically dangerous to teens. All this, not to mention the accusation that the game served as a recruitment tool for devil worship! Such unflattering depictions of the game had been detailed in a recent *60 Minutes* segment with Ed Bradley, in which both Gary and his creation, *D&D*, were vilified.

As Gary pondered these things, he suddenly stopped dead in his tracks.

"The devil!" he said chuckling to himself.

He had finally come to the conclusion that his critics were right. TSR had indeed been in league with demonic forces, Gary thought. First in the form of the Blume brothers, and now in the form of president and current majority owner Lorraine Williams. This humorous notion lightened his mood a bit as he made his way toward Lake Geneva's business district.

Fortunately, traffic was light today, as it was off-season, and the leaves had begun to turn to the stunning reds, browns, and yellows typical of fall in southern Wisconsin. As he followed the curve of Williams Street, he observed the rise of scenic Oak Hill Cemetery in the near distance. This was the final resting place of many of the most important people of his life: his father, Ernest; TSR co-founder, Don Kaye; and most recently, his beloved mother, Posey.[3]

Seeing the treetops of the cemetery made Gary wonder what Don would have thought if he could be there now. *He's probably turning over in his grave*, he thought.

Gary had made it only another few hundred yards before he came upon a large gray house at 723 Williams Street. Somehow Gary hadn't expected to bump into it today during his walking tour of Lake Geneva, though he certainly hadn't forgotten where it was. This residence turned place of business was the first permanent headquarters of TSR, once owned jointly with Brian Blume. The ground floor of this home had also played host to TSR's first retail location, appropriately called the Dungeon. Later, the house served as one of TSR's six locations around Lake Geneva, this one dedicated to the company's house organ magazine, the *Dragon*, before TSR had consolidated its operations at the Sheridan Springs facility.

It appeared, however, that the building was once again being used as a residence.

Good, Gary mused. *At least someone's getting some use out of it.*

Gary looked up at the second-floor window that was once his office and probably now a bedroom. He thought to himself how simple things used to be with TSR, how good things had once been with his former partner Brian Blume. At this, Gary hastily pressed on, as he wanted to get his mind off TSR, not get buried in recollections of the past.

But only a few short blocks later, he came upon Dodge Street—the street where he had grown up. He usually paid no mind to passing by Dodge, or any other street in Lake Geneva, for that matter, but the realization that it had been years since he had done so on foot made him pause. Gary stopped on the corner and gazed at the impressive turn-of-the-century Victorian homes that accented the neighborhood, one of the most prominent being the large green house at number 925, where he had lived so happily as a boy.

Just beyond the house, Gary could faintly make out the gate of Pioneer Cemetery. Unlike Oak Hill Cemetery, Pioneer was not a place of sentimental memories for Gary but humorous ones. This was where Gary's friend and fellow prankster Tom Keogh had on one full-mooned summer evening disguised himself as a wolfman using "an aged Russian bearskin coat" and "reversed a pair of fur-lined gloves for paws."[4] Tom had hidden behind a gravestone near the sidewalk while Gary observed from a short distance away. When an unsuspecting young waitress passed by the graveyard on her way home from her shift, "Tom emitted a low growling sound, slipped his 'paws' into view atop the stone, then peered over the monument, growling louder as he stood."[5] This scared the poor waitress out of her wits, and she wasted no time getting the hell *off* of Dodge. Gary had been so "weak from laughter"[6] as they sprinted back to his home that he tore his jeans and cut his leg as he tried to jump the cemetery's cyclone fence.

Tom had lived just a few blocks away, and his father had been a freelance artist who worked for Walt Disney in his heyday. In fact, Mr. Keogh even looked a little like Disney, making him oddly intimidating to young Gary. As for Tom, he had inherited his father's great artistic talents and had shown a great imagination for fantasy, so much so that Gary had used one of his early sketches in the first edition of *Dungeons & Dragons*. Ironically, it was Tom's pen sketch of a werewolf. Unfortunately, Tom's talents would go largely unrealized when he died of a rare illness just a few years after their wolfman escapade.

Gary sighed and moved on, reflecting on the fact that Tom was yet another soul in his life who had passed into the ages.

A block later he came upon another monument of his past—the Lake Geneva Horticultural Hall. This modest Tudor-style hall was the site where he had hosted the first Lake Geneva Wargames Convention, or "Gen Con" for short. Of course, Gen Con had long since outgrown the humble space limitations of the Hall and was now a huge national gaming convention held at the Milwaukee Exposition and Convention Center in its eighteenth year. Gary smiled as he remembered the small, disorganized gathering of eclectic gamers, mostly just kids, who had descended upon Lake Geneva in 1968. And only a block east was the place where several of those gamers stayed that first Gen Con weekend— Gary's home on Center Street.

The small white house at 330 Center Street hadn't changed much since he lived there. In fact, the concrete step that he had once poured many years prior still bore the initials of his young family. The home was unremarkable and would otherwise warrant little attention except for the fact that it was considered, from a role-playing game perspective, ground zero. If Lake Geneva was the "Holy City of Gaming,"[7] this unassuming home was its temple. It was here that *D&D* was born, the place where TSR had operated, and—perhaps most important to Gary—the place where he had lived for many years with his wife, Mary Jo, and his five children.

Of course, his kids were all grown up, and he and Mary Jo had since divorced, but were both still mired in the messy legal proceeding.

"Twenty-four highly unhappy years for both people is a long time,"[8] he whispered—a sentiment he had expressed in a recent interview. Sure, he had embellished a bit, as there had certainly been good times, but the relationship had been tumultuous, to say the least, and both he and Mary Jo were still in recovery. In fact, Mary Jo's recovery had included a recent six-week stay at the Dewey Center in Wauwatosa for the treatment of alcoholism.

Gary, on the other hand, had moved on. Since returning from his time in Hollywood he had become seriously involved with his former TSR assistant Gail Carpenter. They lived together in a lavish four-room condominium on the second floor of Stone Manor, a converted mansion on the shores of Lake Geneva. Gary loved the old-world elegance of the estate, with its high ceilings, broad stairways, and grand sitting rooms, although he also felt pretty certain the place was haunted. Gary had some expertise in this area, based on a couple of unexplained occurrences in his childhood home on Dodge Street, so he took it in stride.

Seeing his modest home on Center Street stirred up feelings of ambivalence in Gary. It somehow served not only as a reminder of his many triumphs throughout the years but also as a reproach for his many mistakes, both personal and professional.

Once again, not wanting to face the mountain of emotions that bubbled inside him, he lit another cigarette and moved on toward town center. But Gary hadn't cleared a city block before he encountered new, bittersweet memories: the Geneva Theatre, with its grand marquee overhanging Broad Street, where he had watched countless serials and films that inspired his imagination; the once-lavish Hotel Clair, which had served as TSR's second headquarters when the company reached prominence. Gary just couldn't seem to avoid his past.

By now his gait had slowed and his breathing had grown labored. The distance, terrain, and memories were catching up with him, leaving him physically and emotionally exhausted. Of course, Gary always carried with him a heavy load of memories, both pleasant and painful. He claimed to have "a most unusual memory," noting that he could "recall incidents from before I could walk, the time I first walked (ran rather, as I tried to do that and made it about three steps), and so forth."[9]

"Maybe this wasn't such a good idea," he muttered to himself as he picked up his pace and headed toward the lake. He had thought a walk along the lakefront might clear his mind and calm his nerves. The usually beautiful and sparkling Lake Geneva looked murky and gray as the last light of day faded from the horizon—a perfect reflection of Gary's mood. Worse, just like seemingly everywhere else in town, the lake brought with it a new array of memories, both good and bad: fishing with his kids from the piers of the Riviera, a big-band-era supper club located just a block from town center; the lakeside Prairie-style library built by Frank Lloyd Wright's apprentice James R. Dresser, the place where Gary had originally injured his knee as a teen during its construction.

Gary so badly wanted to escape this day, without thought, feeling, or memory. But no matter where he went he couldn't clear his mind of the thoughts, feelings, and memories that surrounded him. Every rock, tree, and building seemed to have an associated story, and it seemed that this collection of stories had somehow made up his life. Lake Geneva was his home, and his past lingered inescapably all around him.

The minutes passed very slowly for Gary as he walked along the lake. He felt alone and at a total loss about what to do. Usually when corporate emergencies erupted for Gary, as they did regularly at TSR, he would respond with breakneck activity and frantic phone calls to lawyers and consultants in an effort to put out the fire. But this was not the case today; there was simply nothing to be done.

Gary did, however, make one phone call when he returned home that evening, but it wasn't to a lawyer or anyone else who might help him out of this situation. Instead it was made to his now ex-wife, Mary Jo, an ever-present part of Gary's past:

"Mary, you're not gonna believe this!" Gary fumed. "Those bastards took TSR!"

Mary Jo was speechless for a few moments. She had not expected to hear from Gary today, at least not in this context.

"What happened, Gary?" she asked. "Who took TSR?"

"I'm not sure . . . where to start . . ." Gary answered, his anger quickly surrendering to tears.

Mary Jo knew this was serious. This was only the second time she had ever heard Gary cry in a relationship that spanned over forty years.[10]

She sighed. Although they were now divorced and still embroiled in a contentious legal proceeding, she still cared for the man and hated to see him in pain.

"Gary, why don't you start from the beginning . . . ?"

Level 1

DUNGEON MASTER: *You have been walking now for several hours on the rough mountain path. Your father is riding ahead, fully armored and keeping a lookout. Your mother is driving the wagon, which is tethered to two oxen. The wagon holds all of your worldly possessions except for the sword, gifted by your father, which you always carry on your person. You come up over a ridge, revealing a vast valley before you, anchored by a massive black lake. A tattered wooden sign reads, appropriately,* SHADOW LAKE. *There is a settlement on the opposite bank, far off in the distance. Smoke emanates from the chimneys of the thatch-roofed wood, stone, and plaster dwellings. This must be the village of Shadow Lake, which your parents have spoken of. Surrounding the lake is dense forest, which your eyes cannot penetrate more than a few feet; immense mountains rise high in all directions. This is your new home. What do you do?*

PLAYER (PAGE EGARY): *What can I do? My parents have made their choice. I move on . . .*

+1

Midwestern Mischief

THE YOUNG BOY COULD hear his heart pounding as he stared into the eyes of his opponent. His eyes welled with tears while his stomach grew sick with adrenaline. The time had come, and in fact was long past, for this showdown. His "gang," if it could be called that, numbered about a dozen neighborhood boys, most of whom came from good, hard-working immigrant families. They called themselves the "Kenmore Pirates" because most of them lived on Chicago's Kenmore Street, and *pirates* sounded more dangerous than *kids*. Their rivals, however, had come from the wealthier far north side of Chicago and outnumbered them by more than two to one.[1]

Little Gary thought, *This must be how Roland felt when he fought the dreaded giant Ferracutus.*

The story of Roland the Paladin was one of Gary's favorites, a story he'd known for as long as he could remember. Since his earliest days it had been a nightly ritual for his father to tell him fantastic stories of "giants and dragons" and "wise old wizards with magic rings,"[2] and Gary had acquired a true passion for these tales of swords and sorcery.

Would Roland have backed down? he wondered. *Hell, no!*

And with this thought Gary launched himself at his nearest adversary, unleashing all sixty pounds of his force toward these bullies who had caused them so much distress. Chaos ensued, and if not for the leader of Gary's gang, Jerry Paul, and Jerry's BB gun and strong throwing arm, all would have been lost.

The Kenmore Pirates had managed to hold off this fighting force from the north, but the battlefront had receded all the way back to the porch of the Paul home. Just as it appeared that the Kenmore Pirates would be forced to make a last stand, worthy of Butch Cassidy or the Alamo boys, Jerry "beaned their leader, one Rex, with a clinker [cement rock]" that "knocked him cold."[3] The rock "dropped Rex and his pals carried him off, the lot of them running away."[4] It had surely been a close one. It was dusk by the time Gary arrived on the front porch of the two-family brownstone his parents shared with his aunt and uncle Elsie and Ed Hohensee and his grandmother Elise Zumkher Gygax, who lived upstairs. He had never been so battered and bruised. He had spent the last hour on a swing at a nearby playground trying to decide what to tell his parents. What would his parents say when they saw him? What would Roland do?

This notion gave him just enough courage to crack the front door and quietly slip inside. His black eye throbbed as it came into contact with the warmth of his home. The intense aroma of stewed beef emanated from the kitchen and stirred in Gary one part anticipation and two parts anxiety. He was hungry and it was almost dinnertime, after all, but there would also be no place to hide. The melodious sound of violin music on his father's phonograph, a sound that usually gave Gary comfort, seemed to intensify the already gloomy atmosphere.

Gary took a deep breath and, without further consideration, headed straight for the kitchen. No sooner did he enter the room than his mother's screech filled the house, silencing the phonograph and sending chills through all the inhabitants.

His mother's howl spread alarm through the house like wildfire, and moments later his father burst into in the kitchen, visibly agitated. He took one look at Gary and realized what all the commotion was about. As Gary met his father's stern gaze he sensed that things were about to change.

AND CHANGE WAS NOT limited to the Gygax household. In a global sense, change was rampant; some of it good, some daunting. The year was 1946, and Gary's hometown of Chicago was thriving. Emerging from the Great Depression and World War II, Chicago—with its 3.5 million residents—was alive again, buzzing with elevated trains, streetcars, and heavy American-made automobiles. Glass-and-steel skyscrapers were going up in the metropolitan area to the south, while somewhat unimaginative single-family ranch homes were being constructed in the surrounding suburbs in every direction to accommodate those returning from the war.

Times hadn't been this good since the Prohibition era of the 1920s, when Chicago was one of the most powerful cities in the world, dominated by the legendary Al Capone and his vast ring of organized crime and corruption. Now, with perhaps the exception of being a hard-luck Cubs fan like Gary, it was a good time to live in Chicago.

Seven-year-old Ernest Gary Gygax lived with his parents in a modest two-family house, known in the region as a "two-flat," at 4113 N. Kenmore Avenue on the outskirts of Chicago's Lakeview neighborhood, just blocks away from Wrigley Field. Today an up-and-coming area known as Buena Park, it was at that time a working-class neighborhood full of industrious immigrant families like Gary's.

It was an exciting neighborhood, as both the Chicago Cubs and the Chicago Bears shared the use of Wrigley Field, making the area a hotbed for all sorts of stimulating activity. It was not uncommon for Gary to hear the spirited roar of Wrigley's crowds from his front yard.

Gary's father, Ernest Gygax, was a Swiss immigrant and talented violinist who had allegedly played with the world-renowned Chicago Symphony Orchestra. In fact, it was rumored that he had been second chair but quit because he could not be the concertmaster. Other hardluck stories circulated about Ernest. As a young man, he had been offered a chance to buy a quarter interest in a soda-water venture that later morphed into the Coca-Cola Company. Later, as the story goes, he had refused the advice of his stockbroker to sell his stock portfolio the day before the crash of 1929.[5] Whatever the case, Ernest had finally settled into a job as a suit salesman at Rothschild & Co. to make ends meet. Gary himself would later understand the tenuous balance between passion, artistry, and work.

Gary's mother, Almina "Posey" Burdick Gygax, was a housewife, now on her second marriage. She came from a prominent Lake Geneva, Wisconsin, family and had two children from her previous marriage, Nancy and Hugh, eleven and nine years older than Gary, respectively.

Even from his earliest days, Posey held a special affection for Gary and spent ample time with the young boy reading him fairy tales, myths, and folklore. It wasn't long before Gary and Posey were competing against each other in *Reader's Digest*'s "It Pays to Increase Your Word Power" tests, "and I hated to lose,"[6] Gary would recall. Driven to outscore his mother on these weekly vocabulary quizzes, Gary quickly developed language skills well beyond his years and education level—a quality that would no doubt prove essential when articulating new and complex gaming concepts.

Gary, as the only biological child of the complex and at times melancholy Ernest Gygax, was truly the apple of his father's eye. Unsurprisingly, Gary's given first name was also Ernest. Gary's middle name, however, was the name he commonly went by; this name was given not after a relative but after the great American film actor Gary Cooper. Gary's mother, Posey, had been a huge fan of the actor, and Ernest, being a middle-aged man of considerable pragmatism and wit, had given in to the middle name under the condition that Posey would never have an affair with anyone other than himself or Mr. Cooper.[7]

Perhaps most interesting, though, was Gary's unusual family name. Gygax was a derivative of a Greek word meaning "giant." Family tradition held that they were descendants of the biblical Philistine champion Goliath. These Philistines had supposedly relocated to Greece during biblical times and finally settled in Switzerland during the Middle Ages. Young Gary loved to daydream about his giant ancestors wandering in a world long past, a world of swords and sorcery. At the time, however, he could scarcely imagine the part he would later play in these same worlds of fantasy.

+2

Fright Night

EIGHT-YEAR-OLD GARY lay motionless on his bottom bunk, wide awake. This was nothing new, as he always had trouble sleeping. There was just too much to think about, to imagine, and this was the time of day where Gary's mind did its best work. Only a few minutes earlier Gary's top bunk had also been occupied by his guest and former Kenmore Pirate companion, Dave Dimery. But Dave had since been relocated across the hall by his father to ensure that the sleep part of this sleepover would indeed be fulfilled.[1]

Less than a year had passed since the "fracas"[2] involving the Kenmore Pirates, and Gary's father had hastily made preparations to move the family to Lake Geneva. Apparently the fight had been the straw that broke the camel's back, and Ernest, at the behest of his wife, decided that her small Wisconsin hometown would be a safer, more wholesome environment to raise the family. By late summer of 1946 the family had moved not just to Gary's mother's hometown but into her childhood home with her parents. Gary's maternal grandparents, Hugh and Grace Burdick, owned a towering, six-bedroom green-and-white Victorian home with a generous porch and a chalet-like second-story balcony situated among similar homes at 925 Dodge Street. The home reeked of character and intrigue—it was certainly one-of-a-kind. In fact, it so resembled the stuff of fantasy that Gary liked everything about it. It definitely beat their cramped and noisy Chicago apartment. Even better, Gary now had his own room—the first door on the left at the top of the stairs. Gary had even had a choice of rooms, as Nancy, his teenage half sister, had recently married, moved out, and given birth to a baby boy.

Even before the move, Lake Geneva was well known to young Gary, as he had visited Grandpa and Grandma Burdick there every summer for as long as he could remember. He loved the scenic outdoorsiness of the lake town. He also had friends in Lake Geneva—good friends. These extended summer trips had allowed him to become close with the sons of his grandparents' neighbor, John and Jim Rasch. As was his nature, he had also befriended other kids in the neighborhood, including the genial Don Kaye and the attractive, red-haired hellion Mary Jo Powell. In fact, Powell kept up so well with the neighborhood boys that Gary's father often teased her, pretending he thought she was a boy and expressing surprise when she would tell him otherwise.

As Gary lay in bed without the distraction of his sleepover guest, his mind finally began to settle and his eyelids became heavy with sleep.

Boom!

The loud crash had shaken the whole house. Gary's heart stopped cold; his hair stood on end. The noise had come from overhead—from the attic.

Are we under attack? Gary thought as he sat up in his bed. *No, the war's over . . . Maybe an earthquake? Or . . . my imagination? No way!*

Gary was imaginative, to be sure, but he certainly knew the difference between the real and the imaginary.

Before Gary could come up with more theories, he heard, *Thump . . . thump . . . thump . . . Thump, thump, thump, thump!*

Gary had gone from being simply startled and alarmed to outright terrified. All he could think to do was to retreat the safety of his sheets and count the sounds—a total of "seven such pounding sounds,"[3] was the tally. To Gary, the sound in the attic had been distinct, "as if some very tall and heavy person was striding from the south front of the place, where the initial crash came from, to the north rear of the attic."[4]

After only a few seconds, the hall light turned on. He heard a muffled scamper heading quickly for his room. Gary, for lack of a better alternative, slowly pulled the sheets up to his face.

Gary's door swung open and the light from the hallway temporarily blinded him, allowing him to only make out a faint shadow.

"Gary, what did you do?" bellowed the shadow.

Much to Gary's relief, it was the voice of one of his caretakers that evening, Mrs. Dimery. Gary's parents and grandparents were vacationing in California, and the Gygaxes' former Chicago neighbors, Joe and Jean Dimery, had agreed to bring their son and stay with Gary in the Lake Geneva house during their absence.

"Wasn't me," said Gary sheepishly as he lowered his sheets. But then Gary quickly came to the realization that the sound must not have been Mr. or Mrs. Dimery either.

I'll bet it was Dave, Gary thought. This kind of hoax was right up his alley. But Gary dismissed this premise almost instantly when he heard Mr. Dimery waking his son in the room across the hall.

As Mrs. Dimery turned on the light, Gary rose from his bed and scanned the room to find an element of protection. His board games, chess set, and toy soldiers were scattered about the floor—a remnant of his entertaining evening. Meanwhile, numerous books and comics littered his shelves and lay in stacks next to his armchair, giving the room an appearance that drew into question whether he had ever entirely moved in. In only a moment, he spotted the items he was looking for: his baseball bat and penlight. He grabbed the equipment and joined the other three unlikely adventurers in the hallway, who were seeking a plan of action.

"So you two had nothing to do with this?" whispered Mr. Dimery, trying to maintain his composure.

"Nothing, I swear," Gary whispered back.

Dave, who had evidently slept through the whole event, just rubbed his eyes and shook his head in confusion.

"OK . . . Gary, give me the bat and the light," said Mr. Dimery.

Led by Mr. Dimery with bat and flashlight in hand, the group huddled together and slowly made its way down the long hallway toward the attic door. The floorboards creaked with every careful step. Finally they arrived at the entrance to the attic.

Slowly Mr. Dimery cracked the attic door and flashed his light inside. The staircase up to the attic was, thankfully, unoccupied.

"You stay here," whispered Mr. Dimery.

His companions only nodded in agreement.

Mr. Dimery stayed on his toes as he slowly walked the steps, but any attempt to be stealthy was hindered by the creakiness of the wooden stairs. The group waited breathlessly as Mr. Dimery disappeared into the darkness. He returned just a few seconds later.

"Nothing there that I can see," he said, no longer in a whisper. "Probably just an animal or something"—a premise that neither he nor the group believed. "OK, everyone, back to bed." Mr. Dimery hastily closed and locked the attic door.

The next morning, the light of a new day emboldened the whole group to join Mr. Dimery in an investigation of the attic. Gary was surprised to see that "all window screens were locked, nothing was disturbed or broken, and there was no trace of any animal."[5]

Although Gary never had another unusual experience with the attic, he distinctly had the impression that he was unwelcome there. Whether it was an animal, a poltergeist, or an overactive imagination, it had been an evening that Gary would never forget.

+3

Checkmate

TEN-YEAR-OLD GARY was sweating profusely as he contemplated his next move. This would be one of critical importance and potentially dire consequences. Many good lives were at stake, and his kingdom's future hung in the balance.

His grandfather's steely eyes burned into him from across the table, eyes that were usually impenetrable, but today there was something different behind them—a touch of fear, perhaps? He had never beaten his grandpa in chess, but this time he was close . . . if he could just make one or two more good moves.[1]

Aha! Gramps has made his queen vulnerable, he thought.

Without any further consideration, Gary smiled and moved his white knight to the space that had formerly occupied his grandpa's queen.

"I've got you this time, Grandpa!" exclaimed Gary as he menacingly rubbed his hands together.

Grandpa Burdick's eyes shot down at the chess board and then slowly lifted to Gary. There was no longer any fear in them. A slow Cheshire-cat grin began to develop across his wrinkled face. Gary knew his goose was cooked.

"Checkmate," said his grandpa matter-of-factly as he moved a knight of his own.

Gary had been so hell-bent on offensive maneuvers that he had effectively forgotten to play defense. He had allowed his king to be trapped!

"You'll get me one of these times Gary, I'm sure of it," his grandfather reassured him.

Gary moped as he slowly rose and cleared the chess set from the grand library table in the living room where they played. Games were not allowed to be left out; the table's only permanent fixture was the massive 1890 *Webster's Unexpurgated Dictionary*, a source of Gary's already extensive, if not antiquated, vocabulary.

In truth, Gary didn't take this defeat very personally. At only ten years old, he was but an amateur, having only been playing chess since he was six, and card games like pinochle since age five.[2] More recently, games like *Clue* had gotten his attention, which he thought to be a fun and innovative combination of board gaming and imaginative interaction. He liked playing Colonel Mustard and particularly enjoyed taking on a persona as part of a game. Grandpa Burdick, on the other hand, was an outstanding chess player and often let Gary retract moves for teaching purposes. Although Gary was a competitive sort, as he had shown today, it was really the playing of the game and the time spent with his grandpa that he liked best. The moping was merely a pose to get attention and possibly some ice cream if he performed it just right.

By 1948, Gary's home life largely revolved around these highly interactive yet simple activities. Whether it be cards, chess, or board games, there was almost always someone in the house willing to play. Of course, like all kids, he also had to deal with unpleasant daytime interruptions, like school, that distracted him from the important things in life. While Gary had some tolerance for topics such as history, school just wasn't for him. As he would later explain in blunt terms, "I hated school, didn't like the discipline."[3]

It was nearing dinnertime, and the light of the early-spring evening was beginning to fade. No sooner did he hear his mother entering the back door from the garden than he heard the rumble of his father's 1939 Nash Ambassador sedan as it pulled into the garage. This was an exciting time of day for young Gary, as his father always seemed to have a good story or two up his sleeve, but he could also "make them up on the spur of the moment."[4] Perhaps it was the long hours that his dad spent traveling that led to such creativity. Since moving to Lake Geneva, Ernest had retained his position as a suit salesman at Rothschild & Co. in Chicago and made the hour-and-a-half commute twice daily, often by train, but sometimes by car, as he had today. Gary suspected that his father enjoyed this time alone, but he always seemed happy to be home.

Gary ran out to the garage to greet his father, who was already limping down the garden path. Ernest Gygax had been victim of an accident as a young man, which had left him with one leg shorter than the other.[5] He wore a built-up shoe to compensate for the four-inch difference, but he still walked with a noticeable limp. His age of sixty-four contributed to his run-down demeanor, although he still had a twinkle in his eye.

"Hey, Dad, any good stories today?" asked Gary.

"Actually, now that you mention it, I do have a good one . . . in here," said his father as he reached into his worn brown leather briefcase and withdrew a brightly colored magazine. On the cover was an illustration of a barbarian equipped with nothing but sword, boots, and loincloth engaged in battle with a giant green serpent. It did not escape Gary's attention that a scantily clad vixen appeared prominently in the foreground. The title read *Weird Tales*.

"This, Gary, is for you," said Ernest as he handed Gary the flimsy magazine and ruffled his sandy hair.

"Wow . . . Thanks, Dad! What is it?"

"I think you'll like this one. It's got a story about a barbarian named Conan . . . but if your mother finds it, I'll deny having ever seen it," said Ernest. He winked through his round, horn-rimmed glasses and limped into the house.

Gary's eyes widened as he flipped the pages. He was captivated by its provocative illustrations and graphic writing style. It was a new type of fantasy—one more dangerous, more real.

Tracing their lineage from the serial fiction of Edgar Allan Poe, Sir Arthur Conan Doyle, and Edgar Rice Burroughs (who wrote the Tarzan and John Carter series), pulp magazines of the 1920s through the 1940s were compilations of sensational and sometimes racy fictional stories of intrigue, frequently set within the esoteric realms of fantasy or science fiction. Named for the cheap wood-pulp paper they were printed on, these eye-catching 130-page magazines featured highly illustrative, full-color covers that often left little to the imagination.

Despite sales of more than one million copies per issue for some of the largest publications, such as *Argosy* and *Blue Book*, pulp magazines were not well respected in serious literary circles, largely because of their explicit content, which came to be known as "pulp fiction." But at less than half the cost of glossy magazines, these publications targeted younger audiences and dreamers on the fringes of society—both categories that Gary already fit into. Smaller publications, like the Chicago-based *Weird Tales*, topped out at roughly fifty thousand copies per issue.

The used pulp that Gary now perused featured a heroic, if not savage, barbarian named Conan—one of seventeen *Weird Tales* issues from the 1930s featuring this character. It wasn't long before Gary began spending much of his time at a local gas station wearing out a copy of *Conan the Conqueror*—a posthumous printing of Robert E. Howard's Conan saga. Gary had found himself a new hero.

$\overset{+}{\underline{4}}$

Here, There Be Dragons

IT WAS A DARK and misty spring evening as twelve-year-old Gary rounded the corner of Broad Street onto Dodge. It was late, and he was walking briskly with his head down and hands in his pockets. Though summer was around the corner, there was a chill in the air, which felt oddly thick, and shadows seemed to lurk around every corner. He had chosen Broad Street this evening because it was the more populated route home, which was important because . . . he was being followed![1]

He wasn't sure who was following him or when this had begun, but ever since he had exited the Geneva Theatre a few minutes earlier, he'd felt certain he was being watched. Tonight's feature, *The Thing from Another World*, starring Kenneth Tobey and Margaret Sheridan, had scared Gary out of his wits. Now his sole focus was getting home in one piece.

His heart began to pound as he picked up his pace. The usually reliable gas streetlights seemed to do nothing but create ominous shadows at their bases this evening, and Gary knew that nothing good could be waiting for him there.

"Just a few more blocks," he said to himself, but the words gave him little comfort.

Suddenly, out of the corner of his eye, Gary saw movement in the shadows—he was sure of it. And he finally knew who his pursuer was. It was the Thing from Another World! It had come right out of the movie screen and was following him home.

Gary went into an all-out sprint. The Thing wouldn't catch him if he didn't look back, but then, out of nowhere, another one peered out at him from around a shadowy shrub. He made a hard turn and deserted the sidewalk for the street. At least in the street there would be fewer places for his foes to jump out and surprise him.

Two Things! he thought as his legs began to burn from exhaustion. But again Gary had underestimated the number of his adversaries. In fact, in Lake Geneva on that particularly cool May evening in 1951, there was a monster in every shadow, crevice, and crack all over town.

With his last breath, Gary lunged onto the brightly lit porch of his home, just out of the reach of his nearest attacker. He was completely out of breath, but safe. Monsters could not come into the light. An illusion? Perhaps, but for him it had been a very close call.

And while tonight's adventure had been purely an exercise in imagination, and a humorous one at that, Gary was convinced that not all such occurrences were of his own making.

A year earlier, Gary had experienced a second ghostly encounter in his Dodge Street home, this time while he was home alone reading Edgar Allan Poe's "The Fall of the House of Usher" in the parlor. Just as "the strange sounds were issuing from the burial vault below the House of Usher,"[2] Gary's beloved cat Queball, who lay in his lap, drew his attention to a door that led to the unlit sewing room off the parlor. The door was already ajar, and Gary and his cat witnessed the door open further into the darkness, "a full foot and a half,"[3] and heard the distinct sound of disembodied footsteps entering and approaching before stopping abruptly next to his armchair. "I was sitting in fear-frozen terror as Queball hissed and spat savagely,"[4] he wrote about the occurrence.

After a few very tense moments, Queball relaxed, but that didn't stop Gary from immediately retreating to his room to retrieve his machete, hunting knife, and lemonwood bow with arrow. He returned to the living room and monitored the sewing room door from a distance—lying in wait to launch a missile attack at a moment's notice—until his mother's arrival. The footsteps did not return.

This was Gary's last ghostly experience in the house, but others claimed to have encountered similar episodes there, including his friends Bill Fleming and Tom Keogh. Neither boy would stay overnight in

Gary's top bunk, each declaring he had been pushed into the mattress by "something unseen with a huge hand."[5]

This occurrence, combined with his earlier attic incident and the accounts of his friends, solidified Gary's belief in the paranormal. He would later say, "Of course there is the paranormal. To deny it is to flout reason . . . I do know, for example, that things have happened to me that have no rational or scientific explanation and those I consider as outside the known."[6]

Whether real, imagined, or misunderstood, one thing is clear: These encounters were formative for Gary and no doubt added fuel to an already overactive imagination. For him, adventure—whether self-created or of external origins—seemed to follow him wherever he went.

And for those familiar with Gary's early adventure modules, from *Tomb of Horrors* to *The Temple of Elemental Evil*, it may come as no surprise that Gary Gygax grew up in a haunted house.

+5
Tomb of Horrors

YOUNG GARY LAY CROOKEDLY on the bottom bunk of his bunk bed reading a brightly colored pulp magazine. He wore army fatigues from head to toe, which his parents foolishly thought were just for "play," along with his leather hiking boots. He knew he wasn't supposed to wear his boots on the bed, or even in the house, but his parents weren't home.

Surveying the room, one might find a five-tier bookshelf full of pulp novels and magazines; a worn copy of *The Practical Joker's Handbook*; toy soldiers sprawled across a drop-front desk, an area clearly used more for play than study; a box of blocks and Tinkertoys carelessly thrown together; a ragged stamp book sitting open on a shelf; a number of board games stacked in an oversized armchair; a pair of badly bent Johnson-Smith fencing foils resting haphazardly in the corner; an abused backpack on the floor; colorful posters taped to the wall; and an array of fireworks poorly hidden under the bed.[1] This thirteen-year-old's bedroom was, for lack of a better term, normal.

The room's most prominent exhibit, however, was a bolt-action Winchester .22 caliber rifle hanging over Gary's bed. Gary had exhausted his savings to buy the firearm but had still needed an equal match from his grandfather to complete the purchase. As a condition of the subsidy, Gary's grandfather had shrewdly removed and kept the gun's bolt until Gary had learned proper safety measures.

With only the warning of heavy steps bounding up the stairs, in burst his best friend, Don Kaye, panting from his sprint. Don, like Gary, was not the most athletic or fit of young men. Gary, pretending that he wasn't startled, slowly looked up from his magazine, *Startling Stories*.

"Well, are you ready?" huffed Don. "I've got the stuff," he said, gesturing to the bag slung over his shoulder.

"Yes, I'm ready. Where's John?" Gary calmly inquired.

"Grounded," muttered Don.

Gary's next-door neighbor John Rasch was a usual contributor to their collective mischief. Like Gary, John was quite imaginative. This behavior he had learned from his older brother, Jim, who often directed the neighborhood boys in "realistic cops & robbers type games" and other types of "Let's Pretend"[2] activities. Unfortunately, today neither John nor Jim's involvement was to be.

"Screw him," Gary replied resolutely. "What did you bring?"

At this Don dropped his bag with a thud onto Gary's bedroom floor and began tearing into its contents.

"Let's see . . . I've got my pocket knife, hatchet, my dad's flashlight, matches, candy, pellet gun, and my mom's camera . . . Now, let's go before my folks realize that this stuff is missing!" exclaimed Don.

"Sounds good," said Gary as he reached under his bed for his own Daisy pellet rifle and bag of Yankee Boy firecrackers.

The boys sprinted the block from Gary's home on Dodge Street to Broad Street, continuing to Main Street. On Main, they cut across the corner of a lawn to head east and up Catholic Hill. The journey got harder as the elevation rose, but it was only a short time before they arrived atop the wooded hill, where they were halted by a fence.

It was spring and the day was brisk. The boys stood in a driveway off Main Street that hadn't seen use for many years. The rusty chain-link fence was in poor condition, having been compromised numerous times over the last many years. A crude sign on the fence advised KEEP OUT— NO TRESPASSING. This, paired with a more formal but tattered sign inside the fence's perimeter reading OAK HILL SANATORIUM, served as a clear invitation for the boys to enter.[3]

Lake Geneva was not only a country retreat for Chicago's elite and a rustic fishing community. Beginning in the late nineteenth century, it had also become home to a disproportionately high number of sanatoriums and mental institutions, featuring no fewer than a half dozen such facilities for a town with only 2,300 permanent residents. To be sure, some of these facilities were little more than weekend bed-and-breakfasts where wealthy patrons with "nervous disorders" could unwind, but some of these facilities were certainly of the more "institutional" variety, keeping many of their committed clientele under lock and key.

The natural beauty of Lake Geneva was no doubt considered therapeutic to those with mental illness, which may explain the prevalence of such institutions, usually given business names less ominous than *asylum*. The now abandoned and decaying buildings at Oak Hill were a perfect backdrop for an imagination as fertile as Gary's, given fuel by circulating folk tales about escaped madmen and urban legends about prosthetic hooks found dangling from car doors by teenage lovers. Such tales would have hit very close to home for the population of Lake Geneva in the mid-twentieth century, to say nothing of a boy with Gary's fascination with danger and intrigue.

The boys wandered the perimeter, both in order to find a weak place in the fence and to avoid detection by any potential onlookers from Main Street. It wasn't long before they found the opening Gary knew about on the north side, adjacent to the White River ravine. It was obvious that this entrance spot had been used by numerous would-be adventurers in the past.

After exchanging a look, the boys hesitantly squeezed through the fence and entered the heavily forested and overgrown grounds. They walked slowly, as if trying not to make a sound. Their hearts pounded as they came nearer to the clearing around the buildings.

The towering complex of five-story buildings seemed to grow taller as they studied them up and down. The great redbrick facades were cracked and moss-covered; the wind seemed to howl through the broken windows and rickety bell tower. Or was that the howl of mad spirits, forever trapped in this worldly prison? If ever a building was haunted, it was this one.

Legend held that Oak Hill, unlike many of its local counterparts, was for "very disturbed"[4] patients who were subjected to an array of experimental and inhuman treatments. Adding to its intrigue, the doctor who owned and operated the facility allegedly went insane himself around 1910, which brought about the institution's demise.

Gary was paralyzed for a moment as he studied the compound. He always seemed to forget how classically terrifying the "abandoned insane asylum"⁵ was, even though this was not his first visit. That had occurred shortly after to moving to Lake Geneva, when he had gone with his parents on an uneventful police-guided tour of the first floor. A couple of years later, Gary had embarked on an unsupervised visit with a couple of school friends who had dared him to join in catching pigeons in the main building's bell tower. But this was Gary's first self-led expedition, and there was still much to explore—he was more than a little anxious.

Looking for a bit of guidance, he glanced over at Don, who had drawn his hatchet somewhere along the way. It quivered in his hands. This would have made Gary laugh, if not for the dead seriousness of the situation—Gary wholeheartedly believed in the supernatural, largely based on his paranormal encounters in the Dodge Street house. This added an obvious level of gravity to the adventure.

After surveying the building and grounds for a few more moments, Gary spotted what he was looking for, an entrance inside. It was a large garden-level window that lacked both board and window pane—a perfect access point. Beyond this, the remainder of the ground-level windows were boarded up, and the doors were chained shut.

I wonder if those chains are meant to keep people out . . . or keep something else in, he thought. His hesitation was short-lived—he was pushing onward.

Without looking back, he made his way to the opening. He was relieved to see that Don had accompanied him there, perhaps going through the same internal struggle and anxiety. The boys peered deep into the blackness. There was nothing to see, but definitely something to smell and hear: A powerful sewerlike odor emanated from the darkness, and the slow drip of water could be heard in the distance. To Gary, these were the smells and sounds of adventure.

Don quickly drew his flashlight out of his backpack and probed the blackness. Very little was visible, as the darkness and dust seemed to envelop his dim beam of light. They could, however, see that the table below the window was still there, which allowed for comfortable access to the lower level.

"You first," said Don. "I'll man the flashlight so you can see."

Gary thought to retort, but he could see by Don's expression that he would have to lead this operation. Without further hesitation, Gary lowered himself in, legs first, facing the outside. Fortunately, the table was not far down, and when he landed, it seemed to be just sturdy enough to support him. Don handed him the flashlight and made the same descent; then they pushed onward.

In the bowels of Oak Hill, the boys explored the "maze of tunnels,"[6] crawl spaces, claustrophobic rooms, and secret passages that made up this veritable dungeon—a place, they thought, more appropriate for dragons, monsters, ghosts, and treasures than patients. Gary would later make it clear that there shouldn't be "any doubts about where much of the inspiration for castle ruins and dungeon adventures came from . . ."[7]

Hours later, with the afternoon sun low in the sky over Lake Geneva, the town was still, except to the east up the hill on Main Street. There, one might notice two boys of thirteen, white as ghosts, bounding full speed down the hill toward Center Street with the thunder and sharp reports of pyrotechnics echoing behind them. A townsperson might recognize them as the Gygax boy and the Kaye boy.

Gary and Don's adolescence and early teen years in Lake Geneva would be full of similar adventures. Whether hunting rabbits in the forest, fishing off the shores of the lake, camping, hiking or returning for another round of exploring at the sanatorium, these formative and Rockwell-esque childhood experiences would fuel Gary's growing and unfettered imagination.

THIS WAS GARY'S SIMPLE and happy existence during his early years, but before long, things would get more complicated. Soon high school would be upon him and choices—hard choices—would have to be made.

+6
___

No One at the Wheel

"KEEP IT DOWN, DAMN IT!" said the teen in the brown leather jacket as he worked his way around to the front of the car in the small barnlike garage.

"Sorry, man. I tripped!" the other replied.

"Did you get 'er in neutral?"

"Yeah, I think so, but I can't really see."

It was a moonless and humid summer night in Lake Geneva. The free-standing garage faced an unlit alley adjacent to a large green Victorian house.

"OK. Come around front," said the jacket-clad teen as he positioned his body in front of the old Nash, his chest to the grille.

The teen's leather collar was turned up, his blue jeans cuffed, the look completed with a white T-shirt, duck-tailed greased hair, and a cigarette dangling from his mouth. If not for the few extra pounds he was carrying and his thick Coke-bottle glasses, one might mistake the boy for James Dean. But it was instead the fifteen-year-old Gary Gygax, who had found a style icon.[1]

"OK, on three. One . . . two . . . three— Push!" said Gary in a hoarse whisper.

For a moment the car sat like a tank, unmoved. In fact, it was a bit of a tank, as were many cars of the time: broad and solid steel.

"Are you sure it's in neutral?" Gary puffed.

"Yes, Gary, it's in neutral!" growled his usual companion, Don Kaye.

Gary wedged his feet against the back cabinet and pushed as hard as he could. This maneuver gave him just enough leverage to move the heavy car, which slowly creaked backward.

"OK, keep pushing—I'll steer her out!" gasped Gary.

This seemed a logical division of labor, as Don was the larger and stronger of the two, and it was Gary's father car, after all. The pudgy, glasses-wearing version of James Dean reached his arm through the driver's-side window to turn the wheel and provide a straight trajectory down the alley and away from his home.

"OK, Don, to the end of the block—we don't want my folks to hear," Gary said as he helped push the car from the driver's side.

Don was laboring like a tired mule, but he nodded, put his head down, and pushed. The car gained momentum and quickly approached the end of the alley, where they typically started it up, but tonight the boys had consumed one too many beers. Or maybe it was the promise of an exciting Lake Geneva summertime Saturday night cruising the strip, looking for ladies, and finishing up with a game of mailbox base-ball on Snake Road with a two-by-four they kept in the trunk.[2] Whatever the case, they pushed a little too hard and a little too fast, and as the car approached the slight downslope leading to the street, they lost control of its momentum. Coming up North Street was a car not expecting a surprise entrance from a blind alley, let alone a car that had neither lights nor running motor.

Events seemed to enter slow motion as Gary dove through the open window of the car, trying to get to the brake, while Don watched help-lessly. The car in the street clearly hadn't seen them and it approached quickly. Don covered his eyes.

Whoosh!

As events snapped back to real-time, somehow the car in the street zoomed by without being touched. Gary's father's car didn't have a scratch, but it also didn't appear to have a driver. When Don came over he found Gary sprawled across the seat, white as a ghost, with his hand still pressed hard on the brake.

A moment passed, and then Don burst forth in laughter. "Wow, that was a close one," he chortled.

"Shut up and get in the car," growled Gary as he shifted the car into park and sat up. They were now out of earshot and could start the noisy engine.

Don got in on the passenger side while Gary started the car. They sat for a moment in silence and listened to the engine rumble. Both were breathing heavily, but they were safe. They had avoided certain disaster and could now proceed with their plan to drag Main. Gary lit a fresh cigarette, having lost his during the chaos.

"Let's go," said Gary as he shifted the car out of park.

The two drove slowly down North Street to Broad Street, not speaking. After a minute had passed, Gary finally seemed ready to communicate again.

"I guess that was a pretty close one," Gary said with a smirk as he turned onto Main.

Don, still uncertain as to the extent of Gary's desire for conversation, just nodded and said, "Mmm-hmmm."

Then, without warning came a *crunch*, followed by the sickening sound of breaking glass and falling chrome. The world spun and tires screeched while smoke and fumes billowed into the night.

They had been hit squarely in the side by an oncoming vehicle. Gary, with little driving experience exacerbated by a beer buzz, hadn't seen the oncoming traffic on Main Street, which doubled as State Highway 50. His father's car was totaled, but worse still, he knew that *he* was totaled—screwed. His father was indulgent, to be sure, and usually let him off easy, but Gary was certain that he wouldn't be able to get out of this one.

When his father did find out, Gary's driving privileges ended even before they had officially begun.

Perhaps it was the accident or his poor eyesight—or maybe a belief that driving is boring, as he would later claim before confessing, "I think I'd be a terribly dangerous driver"[3]—but whatever the reason, Gary would never drive again.

+7

Low Times at Lake Geneva High

SEVENTEEN-YEAR-OLD GARY GYGAX stood in the bustling halls of Lake Geneva High School with a great feeling of anxiety. In his hand was an oversized yellow envelope that would determine his fate for at least the coming weeks. It was his report card, and if it showed another lackluster performance, he would be in deep with his parents. His academic performance had never been stellar, or even good, but lately he had been trying to block out all of his many distractions and make a stronger effort in school. This was from the fear of his parents' reaction to his poor grades and at the behest of Don Kaye, who was a far better student.

Unfortunately, one of the distractions that had Gary preoccupied was his father's illness. Ernest, now seventy-one, had been diagnosed with an aggressive form of cancer and had been bedridden for some time; it was uncertain how long he had left. Instead of spending more time around the house, as might have been expected, Gary spent much of his time out. His father's age and illness distressed him—a cause, no doubt, of Gary seeking more and more escapes, whether they be physical adventures or in the form of an immersive game or fantasy novel.

Gary clumsily tore open the envelope in the midst of a swarm of passing students who were busily accessing their lockers and heading to their next activities. As he began to study the card, his face dropped. He didn't understand it. He was way smarter than this, much smarter than many of his classmates whose grades far exceeded his. He had even put forth a bit of effort these past few months. How could his grades be so low?

Gary even had a taste for *some* academic pursuits. He was an incessant reader, among other things, although he had little interest or patience for the nonsense they assigned in school. He was more interested in the pulp fiction of Robert E. Howard, Jack Vance (the Dying Earth series), Fritz Leiber (the Fafhrd and the Gray Mouser fantasy series), H. P. Lovecraft ("The Call of Cthulhu"), and Edgar Rice Burroughs, or an occasional article in a history periodical. Howard's Conan the Cimmerian series was his favorite. When it came to this type of literature, Gary was certainly an addict and a formidable scholar of the genre. As he would explain, "From 1950 through 1956 I read about every book and magazine of [fantasy] & [science fiction] published in the US, and I bought used pulps so as to read back through the entire 1940 era . . . I read and enjoyed, was inspired by, a large number of authors."[1] Even at this time Gary could read five hundred to six hundred words per minute, capable of completing as many as two books per day. Unfortunately for him that day, they just weren't schoolbooks.

As Gary was taking in the entirety of his report card and contemplating the consequences that he would face at home, Don came bouncing up the hallway, smiling and carrying an envelope of his own.

"Hey, numbnuts, how did you do?"

"Not good, Don . . . I'm in deep shit," replied Gary as he handed the card to Don.

Don's brows knit as he quickly scanned the document.

"Oh, c'mon, Gary, you're too damned smart for this! Are you even trying?"

"Sort of," replied Gary. "It doesn't much matter now. It's over . . . So, how did you do?"

"Never mind," said Don, not wanting to compound his friend's misery. "It'll be all right. I'm sure your dad will let you off the hook. How is he, anyway?"

"Pretty sick . . . I don't know, Don. I'm really not sure if this school thing is for me . . ."

Level 2

DUNGEON MASTER: *You sit upon your warhorse equipped head to toe in heavy platemail, a shield in one arm, and a lance in the other. Your horse stands ready on one end of the jousting list—what do you do?*

PLAYER (SQUIRE EGARY): *Heyaw! I dig my heels into the horse and go full tilt.*

DUNGEON MASTER: *The black-armored knight at the other end initiates his run and is coming at you full speed, his lance aimed squarely at your shield.*

PLAYER (SQUIRE EGARY): *I hold firm to my shield and aim my lance squarely at his.*

DUNGEON MASTER: *In what seems like no time at all, your lances make contact simultaneously with each other's shields and . . .* [DM looks down at the character sheets in front of him and rolls a twenty-sided die twice] *you feel all of your momentum change direction. The world seems in slow motion for a moment, your body turns a perfect ninety degrees, and then bam! You hit the ground flat on your back for . . .* [DM rolls a four-sided die] *three hit-points damage.*

PLAYER (SQUIRE EGARY): *Zounds! I try to gather myself and get up. I look on the other side of the jousting rail.*

DUNGEON MASTER: *There is no one there. You hear loud laughing at the other end of the list. "Looks like you may need a bit more practice, Squire!" The black-armored knight removes his helmet, revealing your father displaying a warm smile. "Remember, boy, someday it won't be practice . . ."*

+8

The Real World

THE GYGAX HOUSE WAS quiet except for the rustle of newspaper eman-
ating from the kitchen. There, the restless seventeen-year-old Gary sat
wrinkling his nose as he scanned the *Lake Geneva Regional News*. In
front of him were a half dozen newspapers and magazines, carelessly
stacked next to his coffee on the large oak kitchen table. His right leg
bounced nervously as his eyes danced back and forth on the page.
Usually Gary found himself immersed in fantasy novels or pulp
magazines, but not today. Today he was reading the classified ads, a job
seeker looking for opportunity. He grimaced as he took a sip of his
black coffee, which had by now grown cold and stale.

It was Wednesday morning, but Gary wasn't in school. In fact, he
hadn't been to school in weeks and wouldn't be going back at all. The
high school junior had dropped out, and now he had some big decisions
to make. Gary wanted to play games, but games wouldn't pay the bills.
His mother had made it abundantly clear that if he was going to quit
school, he was going to have to find a "real job."

Compounding Gary's stress was the void now present in his household. Gary's father had died of cancer just a few months prior, in
January 1956. Gary, for his part, felt remorse about how he had treated
his father in his final years. Ernest had been bedridden for some
time, but Gary had been in denial and gone on like business as usual.
He had, on some level, even resented his father for being so old and
sick. It wasn't until the very end that Gary fully understood his father's
terminal condition, and now he wished that he had spent more
time with the man who had loved and spoiled him so much. Most of
all, though, Gary wished he could have made sure that his father

knew how much he was loved. But Gary had taken his father for granted.[1]

Gary had repaid his father's leniency with little more than trouble, starting around the beginning of high school. Ernest had been fifty-four when Gary was born, and he had found it increasingly difficult to keep up with his hellion son over the last few years. And even though Ernest had slowed down considerably as a result of his age and the cancer that had taken control of his body, his loss made for a very quiet, very lonely home.

Much of Gary's trouble clearly stemmed from his poor performance in school and his near obsession with games instead of doing his chores or homework. The little matter of the wrecked car when he was fifteen certainly hadn't helped, and of course Gary hadn't driven since. In short, the seventeen-year-old was more than an unusual or eccentric case; he was a small-town "bad boy" who clearly marched to the beat of his own drummer and appeared to have no future.

Finally something caught the eye of the impetuous teen, making him draw the newspaper close to his face. SERVE YOUR COUNTRY, the ad read. JOIN THE U.S. MARINES.

The Marines, Gary thought.

All of a sudden the picture of a dapper fellow in uniform went through Gary's mind. The man looked like Gary, but a little leaner—a little more dangerous. He wore a saber on his side, with a white captain's hat and a striking navy blue coat with shiny gold buttons. This man was a hero—the man Gary wanted to be. Even then Gary understood that "Every man wants to be the hero of his own life,"[2] but little could he have guessed at the time that he would provide a means for himself and many others to achieve this goal—though not through military service.

A little discipline might do me good, he thought.

The irony was that for years Gary's parents had threatened to send him to the nearby military school on the shores of Lake Geneva because of the trouble he was always in. In response, he had usually threatened to run away, which seemed to hold their threats at bay. Now it seemed that he would voluntarily choose a military track. Gary was a patriot and a staunch supporter of the U.S. military, and he didn't have any better prospects on the horizon. The military seemed an elegant solution, matching many of his interests, including his taste for adventure.

Gary hastily circled the ad with a red marker and closed the newspaper, setting it on the table.

"All in a day's work," he said to himself as he rose.

Gary had already decided that he would spend his last day as a carefree teenager reading his pulps. He would visit the recruitment office first thing the next day.

The young man entered his bedroom and sighed as he reflected on his surroundings. Not much had changed since he was about thirteen, he realized, except that everything that was there before now existed in greater quantity: more miniature soldiers, more board games, more fireworks. The one notable difference was that his prized pulp magazines and novels were conspicuously missing from his bookshelves. Instead, they lay stacked in boxes on the floor. Now that Gary was "growing up," he had decided that maybe he needed to put such childish things behind him. This started with getting rid of his pulps, among other things. He had made a deal to sell his entire collection to a former classmate, but he already regretted it. These were treasures—his escape to other worlds, to adventure and excitement—but he had to put all of these things behind him now. He would, however, take this last chance to get some reading in before "life" took hold of him.

He drew an issue off the top, featuring a "beautiful redhead in— would you believe skin-tight armor wielding a huge, double bitted black axe."[3] This fantasy cover girl reminded him of someone, but he couldn't place her.

Probably someone from the movies, he thought as he dropped onto his bed and cracked open the magazine.

Change was imminent for young Gary, which made him both excited and uneasy. The next morning he would visit the Marines recruitment office, marking his entrance into the "real world." But Gary would soon realize that not everyone is cut out to be a living, breathing, real-life hero.

+9

Dueling Passions

GARY STOOD STIFF AS a board, with beads of sweat dripping down his face and soiling the perfectly starched collar that was squeezing his neck. He reached in a finger to loosen it, but his tie was too tight. His breath was shallow due, in part, to his constricted airways, but probably more related to his frayed nerves.[1]

He quivered a bit as he stared into the eyes of his bride-to-be. He could hardly believe it, but she was his—the prettiest girl in town. With her striking red hair and voluptuous figure, Mary Jo had been the object of affection of many would-be suitors around Lake Geneva, including his best friend, Don. As a result of this competition, Gary and Don were temporarily estranged, which explained Kaye's absence at the event; he was playing the part of the "sore loser."[2] Ironically, it was this same competitive nature that made Don such a great gaming companion.

Of course, this rift between friends would pass, and Don's absence was probably for the best. No one at the wedding would have looked more out of place than him; dress clothes tended to wear him and not the other way around. Don worked at his father's sheet metal shop, and despite his strong academic record in high school, he was about "as blue-collar as they come—a sort of young Ralph Kramden."[3] Certainly not someone who enjoyed dressing up in suits, or any outfit with sleeves, for that matter.

Gary, looking around the room for much-needed support, shot a glance over at a friend who was there—his best man, former neighbor, and fellow Kenmore Pirate, Dave Dimery. Dave's smile helped calm Gary's nerves.

"Do you, Gary, take this woman to be your lawfully wedded wife, to have and to hold, in sickness and in health, till death do you part?"

Gary broke Dave's gaze and quickly returned his attention to the officiant, and then to Mary Jo. Gosh, she was beautiful! And something about the way she looked reminded him of someone else, but he couldn't place her.

"Gary?" said the officiant.

"I do," said the nineteen-year-old Gary, his voice cracking with nerves.

"And do you, Mary Jo, take this man to be your lawfully wedded husband, to have and to hold, in sickness and in health, till death do you part?

"I do!" proclaimed Mary Jo with a smile.

As Mary Jo smiled at him, all of the pieces fell into place—she looked like the girl from the pulp cover, the one with the skintight armor and double-bitted black axe! Gary chuckled to himself as he realized that this pulp magazine, which he had sold not long ago, might well have shaped his taste in women—Mary Jo bore an uncanny resemblance to this cartoon fantasy woman. He later admitted that this pulp cover probably "influenced me subconsciously in my choice of a wife."[4]

"Then by the power vested in me by the State of Wisconsin, I now declare you husband and wife! Gary, you may kiss the bride!"

Without further thought or hesitation, Gary eagerly kissed his new wife in front of the oversized fireplace in the parlor of his grandparents' large Dodge Street home. Just as their lips touched, Gary was mobbed by his friends and family, who began to razz him about the ills of marriage. In the crush, Mary Jo was gradually pushed to the perimeter, left awkwardly holding her bouquet—a moment that would prove symbolic for the young couple.

It was September 14, 1958, and Gary had just married Mary Jo Powell, a local girl he had known through visits to Lake Geneva since he was five. As children they had been regular playmates, and had even traded crushes on each other at one point, but when Mary Jo was nine her family relocated to Texas. Mary Jo and Gary had not stayed in touch during that period, and by the time she returned a few years later, they were more or less strangers. They had virtually no contact in high school, she being a good student and God-fearing, and he being a greaser and full-time troublemaker.

Since high school, their paths had continued to diverge. Mary Jo had joined the local branch of AT&T as a switchboard operator, and Gary had enlisted and been subsequently discharged from the Marines. His medical discharge was officially related to a bout of walking pneumonia, though his bum knee and terrible eyesight no doubt played a role as well. These medical issues, paired with a not so great attitude, had punched his ticket out. Gary wasn't disappointed, though. Between the subhuman treatment he'd experienced in boot camp and having soured on the idea of engaging in *real* physical warfare, he realized that joining the Marines had been a mistake. As such, he was secretly delighted that there were good objective reasons for his discharge.

When Gary's mother, Posey, ran into Mary Jo one day in town just before Christmas of 1957, she was amazed to see how beautiful the former tomboy had become. Posey seized the opportunity to set up a meeting between the two on the day after Christmas, pitched to Mary Jo as a casual visit and not pitched to Gary at all. She knew Gary wouldn't have gone for it if the meeting was arranged, but she also knew that the now grown-up Mary Jo would get his attention. When they did meet, Gary got Mary Jo's attention too. Since returning from his short stint in the Marines, Gary, who had once been a pudgy greaser, was now a lean, well-groomed, handsome man. Within days, Mary Jo broke up with the boy she had been dating since high school, and she and Gary became an item.

Still, Gary's courtship of Mary Jo didn't come without significant effort on his part. She was much sought after around town and had attracted the affections of many suitors, including a dangerous-looking man who had been following her to and from the switchboard where she worked. Gary had been so concerned about this stalker that he took a week off from his own job as a shipping clerk at Kemper Insurance in Chicago and walked Mary Jo to and from her work in the dead of winter with a pistol in his pocket. Gary's commitment paid off—they were engaged on Valentine's Day 1958.

Now, no matter how unlikely the match, it was their wedding day, and thirty or so wedding attendees were packed into the spacious interior of the Burdick home. These guests were mostly members of the Burdick and Gygax families, Gary's mother's and father's sides, respectively. In contrast, Mary Jo's modest representation consisted of her mother, a few friends, and her uncle, a justice of the peace who had officiated at the ceremony.

In spite of the scant representation, Mary Jo felt right at home. She had always loved Gary's family, even as a little girl, and viewed them as the archetypal functional, loving family—the kind she always wanted and now had. Unlike Gary, Mary Jo came from a broken home, her father having left when she was young. Perhaps it was this experience that prevented Mary Jo's mother from warming up to Gary. In fact, she had fervently tried to talk Mary Jo out of the marriage, even as recently as their arrival at the Dodge Street house earlier that morning. But it was no use. The twenty-year-old was in love and not going to change her mind—she was now a Gygax.

Little did Mary Jo know, however, was that Gary was *already* married—or at least engaged—to a new, all-consuming activity.

Just weeks earlier, Gary, who had always loved board and strategy games, had been introduced to a wargame published by the Avalon Hill company called *Gettysburg*. Gary had never played anything quite like it. As much as the Marines and real-life warfare not been his cup of tea, he found this tabletop version of combat simulation life-changing. To be sure, it was just a board game featuring a square grid and simple rectangular cardboard counters representing combat units, but the tactical battle theme, coupled with the historical reenactment elements, not to mention the chance to rewrite history, intrigued Gary to the point of obsession. And Gary wasn't the only one who was so taken with the game.

FOUNDED IN 1954 BY U.S. Army Reserve Infantryman Charles S. Roberts, the Baltimore-based Avalon Hill Company had taken off.

Roberts had designed his first combat simulation board game in 1952 in an effort to better understand the army's Principles of War, but quickly realized the commercial appeal of the game. He began operating the mail-order Avalon Games Company out of his garage, releasing its first game, *Tactics*—largely considered the first commercial wargame—in 1954. By 1958, the company, now called Avalon Hill, released a successful revision to *Tactics* called *Tactics II* and the first historically based wargame in *Gettysburg*, meant to re-create the Civil War battle and commemorate its centennial.

Far smaller and more specialized than its board game counterparts Parker Bros. and Milton Bradley, Avalon Hill's niche was wargames, specifically war simulation games. It was important for the company's fan base that the games be not only fun but also a realistic simulation of battle as far as probabilities and strategy were concerned. This was such an important facet of games like *Gettysburg* that the front of its box reads, NOW YOU FIGHT THE CIVIL WAR BATTLE IN THIS REALISTIC GAME BY AVALON HILL.[5] Perhaps most appealing to wargamers, though, was that these wargames were highly competitive and had virtually infinite variability within each contest, unlike their traditional board game counterparts.

By the time of his wedding, Gary was already wargaming at least one night a week for sessions that lasted anywhere from two hours to marathon all-nighters. For Christmas of that year, Gary finally bought himself a copy of the addictive *Gettysburg* game for the "hefty sum" of $4.98, which according to him was "the best five buck investment I ever made!"[6]

Gary's usual *Gettysburg* accomplice was a friend named Mike Magida, who, according to Mary Jo, was vastly preferable to some of his other friends. "Potheads,"[7] she had called them, and they often had little trouble convincing Gary to partake. These long and increasingly frequent gaming sessions did, however, begin to arouse Mary Jo's suspicions. She couldn't understand how anyone could put so much time and effort into a game. It wasn't long before she began to think something was up—another woman.

+10

Another Woman?

BANG, BANG, BANG!

"I know you're in there, Ernest Gary Gygax! Open up! It's your wife, and I know what you're up to, you snake!"

It was a Saturday evening in January 1961, and an angry, newly pregnant Mary Jo was standing on the snow-covered doorstep of a small, unfamiliar home, holding a screaming one-year-old child in her arms. Gary had been spending many long weekends out of the house, and by now she was convinced that her husband was up to something—today she had tracked him here. He, of course, had denied any wrongdoing and insisted instead that he had simply been playing wargames with friends. But she suspected he was playing games of a more insidious variety with "friends" of the opposite sex.[1]

More than two years had passed since their wedding, and Gary and Mary Jo had moved to a small apartment on Chicago's North Side. Gary was still working as a shipping clerk at Kemper Insurance and had managed to find Mary Jo a position there as well. This had been short-lived, however, as it was discovered just a few months after she started that she was pregnant with their first child. Once she started showing, and it being 1959, she was no longer welcome to work at Kemper. Things were further complicated by the fact that their previous apartment had not been baby-friendly, and so they had recently moved. All the while, Gary was attending night school at Wright Junior College, at Mary Jo's insistence, where he was actually excelling academically.

Between demanding work and school schedules, Gary's time at home was already sparse, but lately he had been spending more and more of his free time away. First it was commitments he had taken on with the

Young Republicans, along with longtime friend Dave Dimery. This had led to Gary serving as a Republican precinct captain during the 1960 presidential election. Coincidentally, the friendly Jewish man who lived downstairs served as the Democratic captain; Gary had witnessed him taking part in outright voter fraud during the balloting, bribing men with pints of whiskey and women with a dozen eggs in exchange for their votes. In contrast, Gary took rules seriously, whether it was with games or elections. When he threatened to report these infractions he was allegedly offered a surprisingly lucrative bribe of his own by his Young Republicans boss, a political strategist who had himself already defected to the winning Democrat team: a full scholarship to the University of Chicago.[2]

Gary, true to his nature, turned down the scholarship. He also decided not to report the voter fraud, as he was convinced that nothing could or would be done. His instincts were correct: Illinois, and specifically the political machine in Gary's own Cook County, would go down in infamy as the linchpin of the "stolen" election of 1960.

These political matters, however, were all a transitory sideshow for Gary. His latest diversion had been his increasingly frequent "game nights."

The anxious young housewife at the doorstep waited several moments, but she could hear no movement inside.

Of course not, she thought. *They're probably asleep . . . or in the shower!* This enraged her and she started a fresh and more violent series of knocks. Just then, the door swung open.

"Mary . . . Hi! What are you doing here?"

"Mike! Uh . . . is Gary here?" said Mary Jo sheepishly.

The man who answered the door was Mike Magida, one of Gary's best friends and a regular dinner guest at their home. This made him unique, since Gary and Mary Jo barely had enough food for themselves, let alone for dinner guests. After Mary Jo's departure from Kemper, there was very little money for anything beyond basic necessities. Ernie, the couple's first child, was born in September 1959, and beyond baby food and macaroni and cheese, the cupboards were bare in their forty-eight-step walk-up at 5740 N. Winthrop. Their neighborhood was, at best, up and coming, and if not for the compassion of the Jewish family who lived downstairs, life might have been untenable for the young couple. It was not uncommon for pots of matzo ball soup to show up on their doorstep, along with other treats and gestures of concern. Of course, Mary Jo had lately found herself enjoying these neighborly gifts alone most nights.

Mary Jo stood frozen for a moment, collecting herself. She had not expected to see Mike—or any male for that matter. She had more expected a blonde in a short silk robe.

Maybe Gary was telling the truth after all, she thought. Her mind, however, quickly dismissed this improbable premise. What sane person could spend this many hours, even days, playing board games with his friends? *Mike's a cover . . . He must be in on it!*

As Mary Jo began to conjure up more conspiracy theories, Mike answered, "Yeah, he's downstairs—c'mon in." He cheerfully moved aside and gestured toward the back of the house.

The young mother brushed past him, still convinced that this must be a trick. She was no fool, and she was going to call their bluff. She passed through a modest living room with orange shag carpet to a basement door that had been left open.

This must be it, she thought.

At this point baby Ernie, sensing his mother's displeasure, began to wail more vigorously. Mary Jo, realizing that her cover had been blown and clinging to an intense desire to catch Gary in some illicit act, quickly made for the stairs. The plywood under her feet creaked loudly as she descended into the dank, semifinished cellar. Her eyes widened as the space came into view. She couldn't believe what she saw.

The room was filled with a thick haze of cigarette smoke. Empty Pepsi cans and Mars bars wrappers littered almost every inch of the claustrophobic cell. And Gary, a man whom she thought she had known well, was . . . leading the Confederate Army to victory in battle?

Gary, Mike, and a couple of nerdy-looking accomplices had been playing Avalon Hill's *Gettysburg* on a fold-out card table in the basement. Gary had been telling the truth, but this was somehow cold comfort.

His frequent late-night excursions continued to be an ongoing point of contention between him and Mary Jo. As Gary would later explain, "After much disputation, I agreed to have the games played at our place despite the children's presence (noisy) and her [Mary Jo] wanting to talk."[3]

With this concession by her husband, the untrusting Mary Jo may have gotten more than she bargained for. Their home quickly became the center of gaming operations for him and his group. And once the floodgates had been opened, they proved very hard to close.

✝11

The One That Got Away

GARY'S FISHING ROD WAS almost yanked straight out of his hands as he fought for what seemed like hours with a determined yet unknown adversary on the other end of the line. He struggled, but still couldn't seem to outmaneuver his opponent in this game of aquatic chess that he was determined to win. This was the big one—he could feel it.[1]

Since moving back to Lake Geneva in late 1963, it had been a regular occurrence for Gary to take his young children—his firstborn, Ernie, and the family's newest addition, three-year-old Elise—fishing off the piers of Lake Geneva's "Riviera." Though Gary still worked in Chicago, now as an insurance underwriter at Fireman's Fund Insurance of Chicago, he found that the lower cost of living in Lake Geneva more than compensated for the three hours he spent commuting by train every day. Here in his hometown he could enjoy the outdoors, as he always had as a kid, while living in a home they wouldn't have been able to afford in the congested and overpriced metropolis of Chicago. The modest white house they rented at 330 Center Street was small, to be sure, but the hundred-year-old building had character.

Usually Gary and his kids returned home from the Riviera empty-handed. *Today will be different*, he thought.

Gary loved all things outdoors, including hunting, fishing, and camping, but he was not a very physical man and certainly not a skilled angler. As was his nature, he visualized himself the hero of this story as well—a man for all seasons. In real life, however, the spirit was willing but the flesh was weak.

"Watch out, Ernie! Give me some room!" Gary shouted as he maneuvered along the pier, trying to avoid having his line break.

Ernie, whom Gary had asked to hold his can of Special Export while he fought the beast, quickly relocated farther down the pier.

"See here, kids, I'm going to relax the rod and lull him to sleep, and then make my move," Gary said as a sly smile formed across his face. For at least a moment Gary felt like the captain of a whaling ship, imparting great wisdom to his crew, who stood at attention.

Gary waited a few seconds or perhaps a minute. Things were still.

"Ready?" he said gently to Elise.

The excitement was simply too much for her, and she began to clap and giggle uncontrollably.

That's the signal, he thought. *Go!*

Gary began to violently pull up on his rod while furiously turning the reel. It was coming! He had gotten the beast off guard, and now he could smell blood, at least from a fishing perspective. Ernie and Elise cheered on their father as he struggled to reel in the great fish—it was almost there! Gary's rod was bent like a strung bow and his line was straining, clearly close to the breaking point.

Just a few more seconds, he thought as his arms burned from exhaustion.

Then, just as he thought his line would snap, out of the water came the biggest smallmouth bass Gary had ever seen on Geneva Lake.

Gary quickly pulled the fish in to his body and secured it under his arm. She was a beauty! Gary could already see this trophy stuffed on his wall, hanging prominently in his dining room. He had done it—he had finally gotten his fish. He felt justified—he was a real fisherman, and now he had proof!

"Ernie, grab the stringer," he ordered.

His first mate, Ernie, quickly put down his father's beer can and ran to the tackle box. Gary held tight to the squirming trophy in his arms.

"Here it is, Elise! What do you think?" asked Gary.

"Wow! Cute fishy, Daddy! Don't hurt da fishy, Daddy. Put da fishy back!"[2]

"No, baby, Daddy's going to keep this one. That's why Daddy worked so hard to get it," said Gary gently.

"No, Daddy! Don't hurt da fishy, put it back! Put it back!"[3] screamed Elise as she broke into tears.

Gary's smile slowly vanished from his face. He looked at his daughter, and then at the writhing sea creature in his arms. He might have defeated the fish, but now he had been defeated, and by a three-year-old, no less. He was disarmed, feeling a lot like the fish now flopping and frantically gasping from its gills. Sighing, Gary worked his hook out of the fish's mouth and brought it back down to the water's edge.

"OK, OK, baby! Here we go. Say bye to the fishy!" Gary said reluctantly.

True to the roller coaster of emotions that is a toddler girl, Elise suddenly stopped crying and a smile erupted as she said farewell to her aquatic friend. As the fish sprang out of Gary's hands and descended into the blackness of Geneva Lake, so too did Gary's trophy and proof of his fishing prowess.

The walk home from the waterfront was a particularly long and painful one for Gary that day. Of course, Gary would distinguish himself in things other than fishing in the years to come, but letting the "big one" get away proved especially distressing. Nonetheless, the victory with his daughter proved to be bigger than any victory over a fish could be.

When he arrived home and went to the kitchen to tell Mary Jo what had happened, he suddenly realized that he was without credible adult witnesses to his valor. All of his efforts on the dock had netted him nothing but a good anecdote, making him just another Lake Genevan with a big-fish story to tell.

+12

Sunday in the Park with Gary

GARY STOOD WITH HIS arms fully extended in front of him winking through a square made with his fingers. He had finally found his view—a perfect combination of sunlight, trees, and meadow. Or it would have been perfect if not for the distraction provided by his eighteen-month-old daughter Heidi, who was eagerly chasing butterflies and disturbing the serenity of the scene.

"Mary, can you grab Heidi—she's in my view!"

As Mary Jo ran to wrangle her thirdborn, Gary stood completely still in the picturesque meadow clearing, so as to not lose his precious view. That Sunday afternoon, he was absorbed with his easel and canvas, along with a sawhorse that held his brushes, paints, and palette. The rest of his family—six-year-old Ernie, four-year-old Elise, and Gary's mother, Posey—sat on a blanket picnicking about fifty yards away, just out of his periphery. Gary needed the distance while he worked—he was in his element. He imagined himself a painter of the French Impressionist period, painting the world as he and only he could see it.[1]

Of course Gary wasn't living in France or in the era of Monet, but in mid-1960s America. No time he could remember had been so complex and polarized. In New York it was the era of sleek skinny suits, neat pomaded hair, Canadian Club whiskey, Madison Avenue hype, and scandalous office affairs, while on the opposite coast it was a time of social revolution, free love, and cheap LSD. But in Gary's small Midwestern hometown, nothing much had changed. Gary himself, though, had become a bit of a paradox: a pragmatic businessman meets freethinking hippie. Both his personality and appearance matched the

geography—somewhere between the two coasts. His tidy, coiffed hair
and thick black-rimmed glasses seemed in stark contrast to his side-
burns, handlebar mustache, and the few extra pounds he sometimes
carried.

Gary began making swift brushstrokes on the blank canvas, as if he
were a master painter. He painted aggressively and with vigor, unafraid
to make mistakes. He held that no mistake would be too big to correct
and any errors that might occur were indeed part of the creative process.
This "go big or go home" attitude toward his creative works would
serve him well.

The land on which Gary stood and painted was known as the "Back
40."[2] This particularly scenic parcel of Lake Geneva land had been in
Gary's mother's family for some time, and it was now owned by an
uncle. Gary loved to visit with his family for picnics and other outdoor
activities, which occasionally included dynamiting boulders with friends
John Kohn and Joe Fabian. Today, however, Gary's creative juices were
flowing and oil painting was on his mind. With painting, as with so
many things, Gary showed unusual aptitude. Though self-taught, he
seemed to know instinctively how to capture the mood of a moment—
no doubt a consequence of the countless hours he spent poring over
highly illustrative pulp magazines and books. Gary's familiarity with
and admiration for such illustrations would surely influence the artistic
stylings of his future game work—a hallmark of all TSR products.

Gary loved these Sundays, as they represented a steep departure from
the usual hustle and bustle of his workweek. In fact, earlier that summer
Gary had dragged his family out on a similar journey to picnic on Lake
Geneva's lakefront path so he could set up his easel and paint the town's
most impressive mansion, Stone Manor. It had been awkward for his
family, to say the least, as the path was a narrow, unpaved public
walkway through what was otherwise private property. Fortunately for
the Gygax family, Stone Manor's guard dogs were trained to attack only
those who wandered off the path. Mary Jo was kept especially busy
watching her young ones that day.

These increasingly rare outings proved special for Gary's family also,
as they were among the few times they could have his nearly undivided

attention. More than ever, Gary's free days were spent in long wargaming sessions, often playing Avalon Hill's *Gettysburg*, but sometimes venturing into new avenues of wargaming that featured the use of miniature figurines and terrain. Gary's relationship with Mary Jo had become gradually more difficult, and his children often found him distant and aloof. Some nights he would be a fun-loving dad full of energy and playfulness, eager to tell suspenseful stories to his children before bed, but others were spent in silence at the dinner table so as to not interrupt Gary as he read his mail. Some evenings he would abruptly rise from the table and enter the parlor, where he would spend the remainder of the evening planning and typing his next move in whatever play-by-mail game he was engaged in at the time. These games ranged from run-of-the-mill chess to *Diplomacy*, a game of political maneuvering that could be played entirely through the mail. In yet another odd contradiction, Gary showed the capacity to be both a great father and an absent one, depending on his mood and how things were progressing personally and professionally—perhaps reflecting the conflict of a carefree child living inside a man full of adult responsibilities.

On the surface, however, Gary was very much a maturing adult. Now a midlevel underwriter at the Fireman's Fund of Chicago, he continued to make the long train ride to Chicago daily during the workweek. Though he had a decent position, money was still extremely tight for the young family, in part due to its ever-expanding size. Compounding the issue was that Gary was not particularly shrewd with money. Though he had an unusual talent for calculating and managing insurance risks professionally, when it came to his own finances, he was impulsive and short on planning. Mary Jo was tasked with being tremendously frugal with the available resources. This included clipping coupons, growing vegetables for subsistence, and making and repairing the children's clothes as needed. It was not uncommon for the holes in their shoes to be patched with cardboard or for torn-up jeans to be recycled into denim shorts.

As the sun began to set on the family's Sunday outing, Gary was putting the finishing touches on his masterpiece of the day. It really was a strikingly good landscape, especially for a self-taught amateur artist. The day's activities had worn out his children, Heidi in particular, and it was time to go home.

As with so many things in Gary's life, it wasn't long after that summer day that Gary's idyllic view of the Back 40 would be vastly changed. Within a few short years, the land adjacent would be acquired and developed by the Lake Geneva Playboy Club, and later the Grand Geneva Resort. Gary's painting of the Back 40, however, remained prominently hung in the family's dining room, often drawing the admiration of their guests. It was so admired, in fact, that one day it was bought by a family friend who thought it a great find. True to Gary's reputation as a less than spectacular money man, he used the proceeds to buy a bottle of Château Margaux wine.

Thus Gary's efforts to capture the Back 40 on canvas that particular summer day yielded nothing lasting. Unfortunately, this would not be the last time Gary's significant efforts left him with little or nothing to show for them. In fact, this event would foreshadow an impetuous nature that he would carry with him through his professional life, even as the stakes grew higher.

Level 3

DUNGEON MASTER: *You can see a legion of orcs in the horizon hastily marching in your direction. Your stronghold lies mostly burned and broken around you. You can see a few of your unit shivering as they observe the oncoming throng. It is evident that morale is low. You've already lost three-quarters of your men, and those who are left (about twenty) are mostly injured and hungry. The keep that you defend, however, is the last human stronghold in orc territory and strategically very important to the lord and surrounding farms and villages. The orcs are closing in about a half mile away and outnumber you three to one. What do you do?*

PLAYER (SIR EGARY): *I try to rouse the troops, Braveheart style . . . "Freedom!"*

DUNGEON MASTER: [DM checks the player's charisma score and rolls a twenty-sided die] *There is silence. A pikeman stands. "To the end, sir!" "To the end!" cries another, and another: "To the end!" Soon they have all voiced their support.*

+13

Playing Games

"THIS WAS A MISTAKE, Mary Jo!" Gary fumed as he burst into the dimly lit kitchen. "This was a huge mistake, and I'll be damned if I ever do this again!"

"It's going to be all right, Gary. You're going to make it work . . . you always do," she said softly as she rose from her chair and placed her nearly empty coffee cup in the sink.

She rubbed her eyes as she went into the hallway. "I'm turning in, dear . . . Tell your guests to keep it down—Cindy is trying to sleep . . . And try to get some rest, OK?"

It was past midnight and Gary had hardly slept for days. He had just come home from Lake Geneva's Horticultural Hall, where he had spent the last several hours setting up for the inaugural Lake Geneva Wargames Convention, "Gen Con" for short. However, the way Gary felt at this moment, it would be both the first and last convention where he was in charge.[1]

It was Friday, August 23, 1968, and the one-day convention was supposed to open early the next morning with a _Fight in the Skies_ tournament, a popular World War I aerial combat wargame. A founding member of the International Federation of Wargaming (IFW) in 1967, Gary currently served as vice president and was responsible for all aspects of the event from food to setup, logistics to circulation, vendor and venue management to breakdown. As impressive and resourceful as the "International Federation of Wargaming" may sound, it was in actuality little more than a modest fan club of gamers, with roughly thirty members. As such, the conference would live or die based on Gary's efforts. He had even ponied up fifteen dollars of his own money (of the fifty dollars total) to rent the space and make the financial ends meet. He was in deep on this one. The pressure was on, and he didn't like it.

How the hell did I get talked into this? he thought as he doused his cigarette in the sink and removed his corduroy sport coat.

In spite of his rhetorical self-questioning, Gary had known precisely what he was getting into when he'd volunteered a few months earlier to host the convention. Though this was the first Gen Con, it was not the first attempted convention of this type. That had occurred one year prior, in July 1967, at General Wayne Junior High School in Malvern, Pennsylvania. It had been a dismal failure and had almost caused the collapse of the IFW altogether, whose membership had dropped from over one hundred members to its current thirty. Gary had been involved as an organizer of that event too, but he had not been in charge. That was left to the Malvern local and IFW president, William Speer, who had resigned from his position after getting stuck with a $200 catering charge, having grossly overestimated the amount of food needed for the banquet.

How could Gary not have learned from that experience? Even the behemoth game publisher Avalon Hill, which had enthusiastically promoted the first convention, dubbed the Malvern event "pretty much a flop"[2] in its in-house wargaming periodical, the *General*. Among other things, last year's event had taught Gary that most of his gaming peers were barely of driving age and couldn't be relied upon to show up, even if their various gaming clubs had promised to send representatives. Why would his event succeed when the previous one had failed?

After Speer resigned as IFW's president, the group's vice president, Scott Duncan, took the reins in an effort to retain its membership and resume the publication of its own wargaming newsletter periodical, the *Spartan*. Gary, as an IFW cofounder and officer, would step into the role of vice president and collaborate with Duncan during the transition. Gary was well suited to this position, as he was known as a leading wargamer, amateur game designer, and wargame periodical contributor in the Midwest. In fact, after he joined the predecessor group of the IFW, called the United States Continental Army Command, in September 1966, two of his columns appeared in the October issue of the *Spartan*. Numerous articles and contributions followed in various wargaming periodicals, including Avalon Hill's *General, Panzerfaust, Tactics & Variants, Canadian Wargamer*, and the IFW's *Spartan*. Consistent with the scale of the IFW and comparable wargaming clubs, these periodicals, sometimes known as "fanzines," were little more than fan club newsletters, but they did require significant writing and publishing effort, all undertaken on a volunteer basis.

These periodicals were not the extent of Gary's writing and gaming work at the time, however. He was also heavily involved in the development and refinement of assorted wargames. As such, he was an active member of the War Game Inventors Guild, which would frequently publish its concept games free of cost in its newsletters. He was also a regular poster in the Avalon Hill *General*'s free "Opponents Wanted" advertisement. In a 1966 advertisement Gary fittingly wrote, "Opponents wanted for face-to-face play. Any AH [Avalon Hill] Wargame, other type wargame or any form of chess (Shog[i] preferred). Will cooperate on game design."[3]

Fortunately, Gary never lost his focus on face-to-face games, nor his desire to "cooperate on game design." All in all, his fanatical involvement in the wargaming community during this time affectionately earned him the nickname "the Mad Lake Genevan."[4]

Gary was already emerging as a key player in the world of fan gaming, such as it was by the late 1960s. So who better to lead a gaming convention? Duncan, the current IFW president, had certainly felt he was the right choice, agreeing with Gary that locating a convention in Lake Geneva could make for a successful event. The Midwestern location would likely attract more gamers and IFW members, most of whom lived in the central states, and the costs and scale of the event could be better controlled than in the previous year.

Now it was up to Gary to deliver. He felt that the weight of the world was on his shoulders. And in many respects, the weight of many worlds, battlefields, levels, stages, and campaigns indeed rested squarely with him.

AFTER YET ANOTHER SLEEPLESS night, in large part due to his overly loud and excited dozen or so houseguests in town for the convention,

Gary rose early the next morning determined to make sure he had left no stone unturned.[5] The anxiety of the coming events weighed heavily, making usually simple tasks seem difficult. He quickly got dressed and ran a comb through his thinning dark brown hair, which was still oily from the pomade applied the previous day. He smoothed his mustache and applied his thick, black-rimmed glasses. He looked good—he looked professional. He was, after all, a professional—a senior-level insurance underwriter with the Fireman's Fund of Chicago. He was also one of the oldest members of the gaming community, not to mention one of the few able to grow a decent mustache.

Without further hesitation, he headed straight for the kitchen to have his morning coffee and cigarettes. As he lit the unfiltered Camel he realized that he had been smoking more than usual lately to help manage the stress. Though he usually had a healthy appetite, he had no desire to eat this morning. Even the brownies that sat on the counter, courtesy of the mother of Chicago gamer Bill Hoyer, seemed entirely unappealing. The nausea he felt from the stress and sleep deprivation was exacerbated by the coffee and cigarettes. These would do for breakfast this morning.

As he made for the front door, he carefully navigated through the maze of sleeping-bagged guests on the floor of the dining room and enclosed porch amidst a scattering of Fletcher Pratt miniature naval warships. In the 1940s, Pratt, a science fiction writer and close friend of pulp legend L. Sprague de Camp, had developed rules for this elementary miniatures combat game in which an attacker would estimate the distance of his unit from the enemy and then measure to see whether the estimate was correct, which determined whether the attack was a "hit."

It was still dark out when he left; the air was cool and moist. Fortunately the weather had cooled considerably from the previous day and would provide a far more comfortable atmosphere in the otherwise stuffy Lake Geneva Horticultural Hall.

Gary wished the one-block walk from his home to the hall was a bit longer so he could gather his thoughts. As he walked he noted the waning chirps of crickets surrendering to the twitter of waking birds. These sounds reminded him of his childhood, a simpler time. He longed again for the ease and adventure of being a kid, instead of the pressures of work and this blasted convention. But alas, the walk ended practically before it had begun.

At the hall, he stood on the front lawn and allowed himself a moment to take in the scene. It really was a striking structure. The half-timbered Tudor-style exterior was covered in emerald-colored ivy, probably as old as the building itself. Built in 1911, the hall had an aura that made it a perfect destination for a convention such as this.

A hall from another time for people of another time, he thought.

He dropped and trampled his cigarette on the front walkway and, without further reflection, entered the hall.

Every inch of the Great Hall was crammed with tables full of naval wargames and military miniatures. This made the modestly sized hall seem almost claustrophobic. However, the great wood crossbeams and iron lantern-style fixtures that hung from the vaulted ceiling gave the space a regal feel. As the coffee began to take effect, he realized that he'd better make haste, as the first game would be starting in just a couple of hours.

His spirits rose as he conceded that he was as prepared as he was going to be. It also helped that Gary's compatriots from his local gaming group and IFW, his co-organizers, began to show up. By the time the gamers had arrived at around nine thirty, the coffee was hot, the rolls were out, the tables were set, and Gary had begun to feel cautiously optimistic about this whole thing.

The next several hours were a blur. As soon as he was convinced that gamers were actually showing up, it didn't take long for him to take his organizer hat off and put his gaming hat on. Never had such an impressive group of gamers assembled in this manner, with an array of gaming alternatives to suit any taste. On one table would be World War I–era fighters figuratively buzzing targets, while on the next, massive warships were splashing about and shooting it out.

One display of particular interest to Gary featured a medieval castle and associated miniature soldiers used for a game called *The Siege of Bodenburg*. At the time, traditional board wargamers and miniatures battle players were still two distinct audiences. Wargame publishers, such as Avalon Hill, hadn't thought to use miniatures in its battle simulations, instead relying on hex maps and cardboard counters. *Bodenburg* seemed to have an appeal for diverse factions of gamers, and it sparked Gary's interest in miniatures gaming in the medieval setting, an interest that would inevitably lead to his greatest creation.

Not only the Great Hall, but seemingly every square inch of the facility—from the courtyard lawn to the patios and loggia—had been set up and used for gaming of any and all types. This event wasn't a flop at all. It was an undeniable success!

By day's end, ninety-six gamers attended the event, thirty-three from the IFW and sixty-three outside attendees who had purchased tickets. Not only did this unprecedented attendance make the financial ends meet, but it was a harbinger of growth for a gaming community that appreciated the convention's offerings, appropriate scale and convenient location. Beyond the gaming innovations, one of the event's highlights was Ray Johnson's lecture on Napoleonic wargaming—an area of special interest for Gary's creative design efforts. And Gary got to meet the creator of *Fight in the Skies*, sixteen-year-old Minneapolis native Mike Carr, who had agreed to referee the convention's tournament and subsequently talked his parents into a weekend getaway to Lake Geneva so he could attend. Gary and Carr would stay in touch beyond this event and find many opportunities to collaborate in the future.

At the event's close, the conventioneers had to be practically dragged from the hall, which now reeked of popcorn and hot dogs, the floor sticky with spilled soda. Gary, himself caught up in this spirit, allowed gaming to continue at his home for a select few people, who played well into the next morning. By the time his guests had left on Sunday, instead of reeling from a debacle, there was already a tentative plan in place for next year's event, Gen Con II.

A community was forming where none had been before. Disparate wargamers, *Diplomacy* players, miniatures enthusiasts, and game designers had begun to discover that there were others out there who were just like them. And with burgeoning clubs like the IFW, fanzines like *Panzerfaust* and *Spartan*; and now Gary's convention, there was suddenly a viable environment in place to nurture and expand this otherwise esoteric culture of gaming hobbyists.

+14

Fateful Encounter

THE FEEDBACK FROM Gen Con I had been overwhelmingly positive. In the weeks and months that followed, wargaming periodicals were abuzz with praise for the convention, while letters flooded Gary's mailbox expressing enthusiasm for the next event. Gary, though, didn't have time to revel in this minor victory, as he was busy filling the pages of gaming fanzines with bylines, columns, and new wargame variants. He had also dabbled in creating and retailing wargames under the label of Gystaff Enterprises, all while collaborating on a serialized piece of historical fiction called *Victorious German Arms*, an alternative and dystopian history of World War II in which Germany prevailed.

One year later, gamers returned to the Lake Geneva Horticultural Hall on a hot and sticky Saturday morning. Sunlight beamed through the windows, illuminating the dust particles that saturated the air in the musty Tudor-style hall. Every square inch of the hall was filled with gaming tables, displays, and booths, not to mention the more than one hundred gamers attending Gen Con II.

It was August 23, 1969, and Gary, once again the convention's main organizer, smiled contently as he worked his way through the chaos. A year ago he had sworn that he would never do this again, feeling defeated before Gen Con I had even started. Now, as he observed the turnout and enthusiasm of this gaming contingent, he knew it was the right decision to continue with the convention.

As he walked through the hall a table full of Napoleonic-era model naval vessels caught his eye. He had, after all, just published a variant of *Diplomacy* entitled *Napoleonic Diplomacy II*, both expanding this popular Games Research rules set and changing its setting. These models might yet serve some purpose for a Napoleonic-era game of a different type. He walked over for a closer look.[1]

"What have you got there?" asked Gary.

"Oh, these are models I've been working on. They're one-to-twelve-hundred-scale ship-of-the-line models," said the dark-haired, fresh-faced man sporting thick glasses and a patchy mustache. If not for the ten years between Gary and the younger man, one might think they were twins.

"Neat! What do you play?" asked Gary.

"We use the Fletcher Pratt naval rules. I play with my group in the Twin Cities. I'm Dave . . . Dave Arneson."

"Gary Gygax. Nice to meet you."

The natural wood hues of the Napoleonic-era ships seemed to perfectly complement the earth tones of Arneson's rugged flannel shirt, making the young man seem somehow an extension of the ships or vice versa.

"I love the concept of the *Great Age of Sail*, but I have some ideas to make it better—you know, make it more personal," said Dave.

Arneson had been thinking a lot about this concept of personalization lately, having recently played an interesting new game devised by a member of his Twin City gaming group, Dave Wesely. Wesely had created and refereed a scenario called *Braunstein*, where each player assumed an identity in a fictional town and sought certain objectives through diplomacy, guile, and other means. The game was relatively short-lived, however, as it lacked sufficient parameters and rule structure to deal with the infinite possibilities and range of actions that could be declared by its players. Though *Braunstein* ended practically before it had begun, the concept had impressed and intrigued this group of Twin City gamers.

"Really?" said Gary. "Let's talk . . ."

Over the following minutes the conversation covered everything from the deficiencies of the Fletcher Pratt naval combat rules and their shared introduction to wargaming with Avalon Hill's *Gettysburg* to Arneson's vast knowledge of weapon prices during the Napoleonic period—his area of specialization while majoring in history at the University of Minnesota. Gary felt he had met his match, and Arneson his.

Dave Arneson, of course, already knew about Gary, having been a reader of many periodicals to which Gary was a contributor, not to mention his involvement with Gen Con. Gary, for his part, also knew of Arneson as a mover and shaker of the Twin Cities gaming community. Neither man could fathom the importance of this encounter, but within a few short years they would be working together on the most important project of their respective careers.

+15

Tactical Studies, Anyone?

"CAREFUL, DON! WHAT, ARE you trying to kill me?" yelled Gary as the two men wrestled with the massive plywood frame. "OK, just a little further," he grunted. "And . . . there!"

Gary and Don slammed the huge, homemade wooden object onto sawhorses they had placed previously. Gary's ten-year-old son, Ernie, stood meekly in the corner to avoid being crushed. The structure clearly overwhelmed the poorly lit, cramped, unfinished basement.[1]

To the uninformed eye the piece might have appeared to be an uncovered box spring or perhaps an open casket for a giant. It was roughly six feet wide by ten feet long by twelve inches deep, and it rested somewhat precariously on three wooden saw horses spread evenly along its base.

"All right, phase one complete. Did you remember the sand?" asked Gary.

"Yes, Gary, for the twentieth time, I've got the sand—fresh from the treatment plant. It's in my truck," Don grumbled.

"Well, what are we waiting for? Let's go get it!"

Many hours later, after the two men and Ernie had worked well into the night, the table had begun to resemble a miniature desert terrain, complete with dunes, structures, roads, and vegetation. This was, in fact, exactly what is was supposed to be: A sophisticated gaming board that could be used and modified to re-create some of the most spectacular battles in history, with the use of miniature soldiers and structured gaming rules.

There was no doubt about it, the table was an impressive and imposing construction—so impressive, in fact, that Gary felt sure it would be

a draw for his gaming comrades. That was, after all, the point of building it in the first place. The local gaming crowd was so disorganized and
dispersed that it needed someone to take the reins and provide a base of
operation. Gary, having experience on a national level through his work
on Gen Con and with his editorial contributions to various gaming
periodicals, had decided it would make sense to serve in this capacity at
the local level. No one else in southern Wisconsin or northern Illinois
had a gaming "facility" of this magnitude or detail, and this was sure to
inspire creativity among his group, extending their reach and influence.

"All right, I think that's enough for tonight," said Gary as he brushed
the sand off his hands. "Don, make sure to close the door at the top of
the stairs when you leave. I don't want the cats coming down here and
pooping in it."

It was late 1969, and Gary was in the wake of another successful
gaming convention, Gen Con II. He had begun to recognize the potential reach of wargaming, and specifically how miniature figures could be
incorporated into this formerly fragmented market.

Within weeks of building his novel gaming table, Gary began to
drum up interest from other local gamers, who were now eager to parti-
cipate in gaming sessions on a more regular basis. The group included
his best friend, Don Kaye, and his son, Ernie, as well as another Lake
Geneva native, fourteen-year-old Rob Kuntz, who would prove instrumental to Gary's success in the coming years.

Equally encouraging was that Gary's gaming reputation, paired with
his new table, was attracting gaming advocates from northern Illinois
and the Chicago area, including Michael G. Reese, a native of Harvard,
Illinois, and a Northern Illinois University student; a Roosevelt
University professor of statistics, Leon L. Tucker; and Jeff Perren, a
Rockford, Illinois, native who was attending college in nearby Milton,
Wisconsin.

During this time it was a common protocol to name one's local
gaming group in order to provide a unique clan-type identity—much
like a fraternity chapter—and so that the group could be easily identi-
fied and recognized in the larger regional and national gaming circles.
True to form, this rag-tag group of gamers aged ten to thirty-one and

scattered throughout northern Illinois and southern Wisconsin, officially became the Lake Geneva Tactical Studies Association, or LGTSA, by early 1970.

Before long, the LGTSA was playing various miniature battle games weekly, usually on Saturday mornings, and with growing attendance. In fact, the group had drummed up enough regional notoriety that it managed to get the attention of the U.S. government who sent a pair of undercover Army intelligence agents, posing as a man-and-wife team of wargamers, to monitor the activities of the fledgling group. Because so little was known about wargaming and miniature combat groups, and it being a time of great social unrest, there was concern among various government agencies that such tabletop combat simulation was meant to train and plan for real-life insurgency. Mary Jo was both confused and anxious when this young, attractive "wife" seemed to be so interested in the basement gaming activities of this eclectic, if not nerdy, group of gamers. The LGTSA members, on the other hand, had struggled to stay focused between turns, distracted by her hot pants and unusually strong interest in their hobby. When the pretend couple felt satisfied that the gaming activities of the LGTSA were innocent and they were not a group of "bomb throwers,"[2] the man came clean and explained to Gary who they were and the nature of their assignment. He also asked if he could continue playing with the group.

More than anything else, the real draw of the LGTSA was Gary's unique gaming table and Jeff Perren's extensive collection of forty millimeter Elastolin medieval-style figurines, commonly used for the popular *Siege of Bodenburg*. Not satisfied with the selection of fantasy miniatures available at the time, Gary and Kaye had begun to craft their own fantasy miniature monsters, usually out of plastic dime-store dinosaurs. Accordingly, the group was progressing from being just gamers to designers and improvisers, quickly introducing their own concepts and house rules to their games.

Perren, despite his young age of twenty-two, was the LGTSA member most experienced with miniatures. He had already crafted a four-page set of medieval wargame rules, which the LGTSA had adopted and begun to use. Gary was very impressed by this set of rules but, true to his collaborative nature, immediately saw room for improvement. He had recognized a potential market for medieval-style wargames as early as February 1969, when he wrote in the *IFW Monthly*, "There is a great interest in wargames of ancient and medieval times but few games are published."[3] By April of that year, Gary had already released a concept game entitled *Arsouf*, a wargame set during a battle of the Third Crusade in which Richard the Lionheart defeated Saladin in an effort to conquer the Holy Land. This concept board game became a monthly contribution to the gaming periodical *Panzerfaust*. In Perren's homemade rules set, Gary found a combat system, though underdeveloped, that could have a more significant appeal. Almost immediately, the two went about refining and expanding this simple rules set.

Meanwhile, it had become plain to Gary that such a game would need marketing. He already knew that the key to building an audience was to promote it through publications targeted at a growing community of players. The LGTSA was a good place to start, but a more special-ized gaming group with its own periodical seemed necessary to ensure maximum exposure. For this, Gary teamed up with teenage LGTSA member Rob Kuntz to form a club with a hierarchy similar to a feudal kingdom, complete with a system for honors and awards based on levels of participation and achievement.

In Rob, Gary found a younger version of himself in many ways. The teenager, who lived just three blocks away at 334 Madison Street, was a bit of an outcast and freethinker, if not outright eccentric. Like Gary, he had an exceptional intellect, despite not being interested in school, and was acknowledged as a uniquely gifted gamer—later an adept game designer and Dungeon Master. Unlike Gary, Rob's young life had been plagued by personal tragedy. After losing his father in a fatal car acci-dent at age two, he had most recently dealt with his mother's nervous breakdown at thirteen, leaving him and his brothers in foster care, wards of the State of Wisconsin. Without parents or a stable home, Rob found in Gary not just a friend and mentor but a father figure.[4]

As before, the partnership of a thirtysomething man and a young teenager to organize a club seems almost comical by today's standards, but it was a necessary catalyst for innovation in the still disorganized gaming community of the time. In March 1970, Gary teamed with Kuntz to form a group called the IFW Militaria Medieval, later known as the Castle & Crusade Society (C&CS), which would seek to appeal not only to local gamers but also to a broader audience of medieval wargamers through its periodical, *Domesday Book*. Although Gary was the driving force behind C&CS, it was young Rob Kuntz who was appointed the group's first "king." Gary was no doubt amused by the concept of regional wargamers ages twenty to forty being subordinate to the whims of a fourteen-year-old king.

Starting as essentially an alternative name for the LGTSA, the C&CS saw its membership quickly grow to more than twenty-five members by July 1970, including a notable contingent of gamers from the Twin Cities, including Dave Arneson, who was assigned the title of baron. As the *Domesday Book* grew in regional popularity, dozens more joined the C&CS over the coming months. Gary now had a platform to promote and popularize miniatures-style medieval wargames, and in the July issue of *Domesday Book*, Jeff Perren and Gary released the sixteen-page result of their initial collaboration, uncreatively titled *LGTSA Medieval Miniature Rules*. Through Gary's influence, these rules would be republished in other, better-circulated gaming periodicals later in the year.

Of note, however, was that all of the publishing efforts of Gary and Perren were contributed "for the love of the game," or more explicitly, free-of-charge. Gary, though, would soon discover that this "hobby" might be far more of a career than he ever would have expected.

+16

Chainmail

GARY STOOD ON THE porch of his modest Center Street home for what seemed like hours. A jug of Gallo wine he had picked up on the way home sat at his feet. He couldn't bear to go and face what was inside. He thought back to when he was a boy and how nervous he had been to face his parents after the "brawl" of the Kenmore Pirates. This seemed but a happy memory compared to the real-world situation that faced him today. His life was so different now than it had been then, full of real responsibilities: a family, a home, a job . . .

This notion stopped him cold.

A job, he thought. *I guess that's one responsibility I don't have anymore.*

It was late October 1970 and Gary had just lost his job as an insurance underwriter at the Fireman's Fund of Chicago, a position he had held for the last eight and a half years. The cause of the layoff was termed a "change in management."[1] Of course, the underlying details of the layoff were far more revealing. Gary's fellow underwriter and rival, named Bruno, had been promoted to a management position, and his first move in his new role was to remove the competition, Gary. It surely hadn't helped Gary's cause that his gaming had occupied "good chunks of time supposedly being paid for by [his] employer"[2] and that his work typewriter at the Fireman's Fund was the same one used to produce *Domesday Book* numbers one through five, along with numerous other game-related publications and writings. This would suggest that his early mornings and late nights at the Fund were far less work-oriented than his employers evidently expected. Thus came the pink slip.

None of this mattered now. The issue at hand was how to tell his family that he had lost the means to provide for them. This was made infinitely more difficult by the fact that Mary Jo was eight and a half months pregnant with their fifth child, having added another daughter, Cindy Lee, in 1966. He was in for it, and he knew it.

Has this all been a mistake? he thought. *Should I have been sinking more time into that dismal job, even if it was killing me? Damn it, Gary! What are you gonna do now?*

He stood a while longer shivering on the crooked wooden porch while a range of possibilities raced through his head. He knew he had to go in—he knew he had to be strong.

What would Roland the Paladin do? he thought, yet he didn't move.

A moment passed.

What would Conan the Cimmerian do?

This thought successfully got him through the door. This hardship too would pass, and other doors would open.[3]

WITH THE EXCEPTION OF significant financial and familial pressures, Gary was in reasonably good spirits during the first months of unemployment, leaning harder on his hobbies. "During this temporary (forced) vacation I am working on a couple of board games for semi-commercial sales and trying to get some work in on miniatures rules,"[4] he would write in the *Wargamer's Newsletter*. By any definition, he was broke, to be sure, grossing only $882 in all of 1971, but he was doing more of what he loved.[5] However, unemployment compensation alone couldn't begin to keep up with the demands of providing for a wife and five children. In short, something was going to have to change.

As 1971 went on, Gary's physical appearance began to better match his situation, namely that of an unemployed, freethinking artist—"a hippie."[6] His long but thinning dark brown hair had grown to shoulder length, and he had let his beard grow full, as if to be a follower of Timothy Leary, the Pied Piper of psychedelic drugs. Around his neck was a string of wooden beads that he had picked up at the local leather shop. Gary visited the shop periodically, but not to buy leather goods—it was known as the local spot to purchase marijuana and other recreational substances.

Gary may have "turned on and tuned in," but he didn't drop out. He had been working hard, though no longer on insurance calculations—now he was working on game creation. It had been a period of hardship, but also one of unbridled creativity, and Gary had been in frequent correspondence with Don Lowry of Guidon Games. Lowry, a former Air Force officer and illustrator, lived in the southwestern Indiana city of Evansville and had recently started a mail-order hobby shop known as Lowrys Hobbies, as well as a boutique, semi-commercial gaming publisher called Guidon Games. Gary had known Lowry remotely for some time through their work with the IFW and from collaboration on a chess variant but had only met him for the first time at Gen Con III in August 1970. Now that Gary had some time on his hands, not to mention this connection, he saw an avenue to carry out some of his projects. Foremost among these was his ongoing collaboration with fellow LGTSA and C&CS member Jeff Perren on a set of rules for gaming with miniatures.

Before long, Gary had struck up an agreement with Lowry to edit Guidon Games' wargame line, which consisted of two board games and a miniatures rules booklet. Both board games were retrofits of some of Gary's earlier work with the IFW based on the exploits of Alexander the Great and another wargame about World War II. These games, however, now sported a more professional design, printing, and production, and were due for release in April 1971. Guidon Games would lead the release of these games with *Chainmail*, a modest set of miniatures battle rules derived from the Perren/Gygax work *LGTSA Medieval Miniature Rules*.

At over sixty pages, *Chainmail* was a much expanded and refined version of Gary and Perren's previous rules set. It provided for greater detail in all aspects of combat and it fundamentally changed some of the miniature pieces' function, from a multi-entity unit to an individual—a hero. In this respect, the game was cutting edge, as most war or miniatures games of the time recognized the pieces only as groups or battalions, but rarely individuals. This, paired with specific rules that provided the option of using a variety of different weapons and armor, made the game truly unique and gave it a level of individuality and personalization that had rarely been seen. It was a distinct detour in rule-setting for re-creating historical medieval battles. But it was the booklet's last section that got the attention of many of its earliest users.

The Fantasy Supplement, comprising the last fourteen pages of *Chainmail*, invited users to "refight the epic struggles related by J.R.R. Tolkien, Robert E. Howard, and other fantasy writers; or you can devise your own world."[7] The supplement provided a very loose framework to introduce magic and Tolkienesque creatures to the *Chainmail* rules structure. The *Chainmail* rules set, and its Fantasy Supplement in particular, would prove to be not only popular but also foundationally critical to the future development of *Dungeons & Dragons*.

Though Gary remained enamored of the medieval-type fantasy genre, it is notable that he actually disliked the writings of J.R.R. Tolkien, author of the overwhelmingly popular *The Hobbit* and the Lord of the Rings series. He would go on to say that Tolkien's work was "so dull. I mean, there was no action in it."[8] Instead of Tolkien's cultivated "high fantasy," Gary much preferred the imaginative but brutal swords-and-sorcery-type fantasy promulgated by writers like Robert E. Howard with his Conan the Cimmerian series, Fritz Leiber with his stories of Fafhrd and the Gray Mouser, and, most recently, Michael Moorcock's Elric saga.[9] Nonetheless, Gary was very familiar with Tolkien's characters and settings, and would have almost certainly conceded that Tolkien's recently re-released works were the main driver in the fantasy craze of the sixties and early seventies. Of course, Gary was to play his own important role in this genre before long.

Although much of Guidon's production money had gone into the two fully produced board games, it was ultimately *Chainmail* that led its success and put them on the map, selling over one hundred copies per month. This was a hefty sum for a wargaming company that wasn't one of the larger publishers, like Avalon Hill or Simulation Publications. Royalties from *Chainmail* and his other Guidon games, coupled with some steady work he had found cobbling shoes out of his basement, left Gary with a relatively stable financial situation for the time being.[10] Unfortunately for Gary, this stability had come at the expense of his beloved sand gaming table, which had to be relocated to Don Kaye's garage to make room for the cobbling equipment.

Not long after Guidon's March 1971 release of *Chainmail*, a few members of the C&CS, led by statistician Leon Tucker and Michael Reese, would collaborate to publish a wargame they had been working on for a number of years, called *Tractics*. Gary's contribution to the game included a combat system predicated on the use of a twenty-outcome random number generator, in this case a coffee can with twenty numbered poker chips inside. The group had felt that traditional six-sided dice and other common random number generators of the day were not sufficient to accurately represent realistic combat attack probabilities. With the coffee can approach, they could refine attack probabilities to 5 percent increments, which were better suited to simulate real-world combat outcomes, according to Tucker's extensive review of World War II combat statistics. Meanwhile, talk of icosahedral (twenty-sided) dice had been "rolling" around the wargaming community since the mid-1960s, but high costs and sourcing issues created challenges in obtaining them. Later, when Gary stumbled on a school supply catalog put out by California-based Creative Publications that featured various polyhedral dice, including the iconic twenty-sided die, he found a simpler, more efficient, and readily available solution to generate these twenty outcomes. Gary's simple combat system would prove foundational not only for the mechanics of *D&D* but also for the later d20 role-playing game system, much responsible for the post-2000 resurgence of table-top role-playing games. Even Gary later described the system somewhat ironically as the "one ring to rule them all"[11]— of course a reference to the Lord of the Rings series, which he so disliked.

With *Chainmail*, Gary, who had been dabbling in amateur game design for several years now, finally had a hit insofar as anything achieved "hit" status in the esoteric world of miniatures wargaming. Further, its modest price tag of two dollars per copy was certainly not about to make anyone rich, but it was a good start. More important,

Gary was proud of this rules set and pleased that he was able to publish a game that was relatively successful. He was now a professional. Given his significant involvement in the gaming community, there was certainly something to be said for this distinction—one that he would leverage into much bigger and better things in the coming years.

Level 4

DUNGEON MASTER: *You stand on the shores of Shadow Lake, which hasn't changed much since you were a boy. The water is dense and has the consistency of sludge. Surrounding the lake is thick forest, which your eyes cannot penetrate beyond a few feet. Beyond that, mountains rise high into the horizon in all directions, reminding you that you stand in a valley. Before you lies a small, unwelcoming cave—what do you do?*

PLAYER (SIR EGARY): *I enter the cave, keeping my eyes open for traps.*

DUNGEON MASTER: *There don't appear to be any traps, and as you enter the relatively small cave mouth, the cavern opens into a vast, dark chamber. You cannot see the ceiling of the cave, nor the walls, but there is a faint glow straight ahead and far off in the distance.*

PLAYER (SIR EGARY): *I draw my sword and carefully make my way toward the glow.*

DUNGEON MASTER: *As you travel you notice the ground is soft and muddy. You can hear various types of shellfish snapping and rustling in the mud. You realize that this cave had been flooded up until recently.*

PLAYER (SIR EGARY): *I pick up my pace and try to keep from sinking too deep into the mud. I also try to find more solid ground.*

DUNGEON MASTER: *[DM rolls a twenty-sided die] It's not long before you find a slippery stone causeway in the center of the cavern that leads directly to the glow. As you arrive at the source, you see a small chest sitting on a stone pedestal, radiating light from the inside. It does not appear to be trapped.*

PLAYER (SIR EGARY): *I carefully try to lift the lid.*

DUNGEON MASTER: *The chest is locked.*

PLAYER (SIR EGARY): *I try to pick the lock.*

DUNGEON MASTER: *You begin work on the lock, which is very unusual in design and appears to be in perfect condition.* [DM rolls a twenty-sided die] *Several minutes pass and . . . your lock pick breaks. However, you notice that the sword your father gave you begins to warm and glow. It seems to be imbued with magical properties.*

SIR EGARY: *I draw my father's sword and use the hilt to bash the lock.*

DUNGEON MASTER: *The lock breaks cleanly and easily, as if it were meant to. You open the chest to reveal a large golden key. A small, yellowed parchment inside the chest reads "The Key of Revelation."*

+17

Genesis

"I THINK WE CAN make something special out of that,"[1] Gary said to the young Dave Arneson as they walked out of Gary's Center Street home into the cool November evening of 1972.

It was after midnight, and the streets of Lake Geneva were quiet except for the gentle rustle of turning leaves. Arneson and his companion, Dave Megarry, a member of Arneson's Minneapolis-based gaming group, had a long drive back to the Twin Cities ahead of them, one that would certainly last well into the next morning. Gary's local gaming buddies, including Rob Kuntz and Don Kaye, on the other hand, had only a short walk of a few blocks before they could get some rest and quiet their busy minds.

Gary and this eclectic group had spent the last several hours playing a variation of his *Chainmail* game run by a group of Twin City gamers, headed and refereed by young Dave Arneson. But calling the game they had experienced just a variation of *Chainmail* would seem generous, as Gary had never seen or played anything quite like it. To be sure, the miniatures combat sequences played very much like his rules, as did the individual character types and classes. It seemed, however, that Arneson had taken Gary's loosely structured Fantasy Supplement to heart, not only setting this particular campaign in a make-believe world of swords and sorcery but also providing an element of gameplay that Gary had never seen used in quite this way. Arneson called this game *Blackmoor*.

AFTER GARY AND DAVE ARNESON had met in August 1969 at Gen Con II, they kept in touch by regular correspondence, and by December of that year Arneson had joined Gary's national gaming organization, the IFW. With Gary's recently published *Diplomacy* variant, entitled *Napoleonic Diplomacy II*, Arneson had also found the last pieces of the puzzle to launch his own *Napoleonic Simulation Campaign*, a game that he and his Twin Cities group had been developing since the previous year. Gary's *Napoleonic Diplomacy II* provided both the appropriate backdrop and the component rule structure that they had been missing. The Arneson-run *Napoleonic Simulation Campaign* notably combined two formerly disparate elements of wargaming: first, diplomatic strategy and negotiation, and second, an associated rules structure to fight battles using tabletop naval miniatures. Gary quickly realized how innovative this combined structure was, later writing, "They took the design, improved on it, and added miniature warfare to it. Thus, when hostile armies or fleets met play went to the table top, and a miniature battle was fought out."[2]

By mid-1970, Arneson's *Napoleonic Simulation Campaign* had grown in regional popularity, and dozens of local Twin Cities players, as well as gamers from throughout the Midwest, played the strategic component through the mail. Arneson, as the game's administrator and referee, quickly became fully immersed in the complex campaign, leaving time for little else.

During this time Gary had been working on an equally significant project of his own in *Chainmail*. Gary also took an active role as a player in Arneson's *Napoleonic Simulation Campaign*, as did many other members of Gary's local group, the LGTSA. Although preoccupied with these projects, Gary and Arneson finally found sufficient time to finish the rules set on which they had long collaborated, a naval miniatures game called *Don't Give Up the Ship*.

During the first stage of this collaboration, which lasted on and off from late 1969 through early 1971, it became evident that although Arneson had great ideas, he didn't seem to be able to put the pieces together. This is where Gary proved to be most valuable. Much of the interaction between the two was via letters because of the high cost of long-distance phone calls at the time. He also carefully analyzed Arneson's extensive but poorly kept notes, which were difficult to decipher. But Gary appreciated Arneson's significant creativity and imagination, and painstakingly worked through these issues, along with the help of *Fight in the Skies* creator and Twin Cities local Mike Carr, enabling the trio to produce something understandable and marketable in *Don't Give Up the Ship*.

If nothing else, both Gary and Arneson seemed to understand the benefit of working together. For Arneson's part, he found in Gary a complement who could not only help him organize his ideas but also offer him relatively strong gaming connections and resources. As for Gary, he saw in Arneson a young man who was full of great ideas and talent but lacked the seasoning or refinement to organize these ideas in a compelling and understandable way. The pairing proved to be an ideal blend of inductive and deductive creative skills.

Don't Give Up the Ship was finally released in June 1971 as a serialized piece in the *International Wargamer* fanzine, reaching more than four hundred gamers. This effort was, in large part, a battle supplement to Arneson's ongoing *Napoleon Simulation Campaign*, which Gary and many others in the region played with enthusiasm. Many hard copies were also printed and distributed at Gen Con IV in August that same year, where Arneson's Twin Cities contingent had reserved two tables to demonstrate the naval miniatures combat system. The system notably included mechanics similar to armor class and hit points—future mainstays of the *D&D* system. Because of its prevalence at Gen Con IV, *Don't Give Up the Ship* quickly got the notice of Don Lowry, owner of Guidon Games. With some coercion from Gary, his games editor, who had already delivered him a winner earlier in the year with *Chainmail*, Lowry agreed to illustrate, publish, and release the new game the following year.

This surpassed all that Gary and Dave had hoped for in their collaboration. Gary notched another successful publication on his belt, while Arneson finally got to see his name in print. While *Don't Give Up the Ship* didn't prove to be a huge commercial success, it did solidify a working relationship between the two that would lay the foundations for much bigger and better things, not the least of which was the activity that preoccupied them during the late hours in Gary's basement in November 1972—*Blackmoor*.

*   *   *

GARY, LIKE HIS *BLACKMOOR* gaming companions of the evening, didn't sleep much that night. Of course the boys from Minneapolis had a good excuse, as they spent the night driving, but the others simply couldn't sleep due to the adrenaline of the evening's adventures. Gary lay in bed recalling the night's events. He and his band of adventurers had, in the course of that evening, explored a dungeon, fought a troll, been chased from the dungeon by a fireball-wielding wizard, encountered a handful of Balrogs, and, to top it all off, skirmished with over a dozen ogres. It wasn't so much the fighting of these creatures that had his head spinning; to be sure, he had both encountered and conquered such creatures as part of his regular miniatures escapades in *Chainmail*. No, it wasn't the warfare that had his mind turning that night. It was the look and feel of the dank dungeon as they made their way through its dimly lit corridors; it was the plume of smoke that rose above the trees of the ogre camp as they approached. These visions had all been aptly described to them by the game's referee and creator, Dave Arneson. Furthermore, Gary's group was playing along, each adopting a persona with a certain set of skills, weapons, and armor. Each player spoke and acted as his character within the confines of the game, while the referee would describe not only the sights and sounds but also the effects of their actions.

In concept, this *Blackmoor* was not terribly different from Arneson's previous and ongoing brainchild *Napoleon Simulation Campaign*. In both there was a distinct component of diplomacy and negotiation, punctuated by playing out the various combat components on a table with miniatures. But never before had such a game been so immersive and flowing, with a single referee to set the game's parameters and keep the story going, while each player played his own part. It felt like a form of group storytelling, or a play with a director but no script. The game was spontaneous and improvisational, unleashing tremendous creativity, all within the confines of a generally preconceived plot line and, of course, a tight set of combat rules in *Chainmail*.

As the pale light of dawn began to enter Gary's bedroom, Gary knew the coming day would be exciting, but a challenge as well. Of course, the discomfort of sleep deprivation was a very familiar feeling for Gary. With five kids and an incomprehensively high level of creative production, usually achieved before dawn or after dusk, he rarely got more than a few hours of sleep per night. But this particular night of gaming and contemplation was worth it. He had discovered something special, something different—a concept that could change the way games were played. It certainly needed work and refinement, at least the way Arneson had presented the game the night before, but it could be published. Gary's sleepless night had not been in vain—many of the missing pieces had already fallen into place in his mind.

Now it was just a matter of muddling through another game-development exercise with Arneson, which included creating order out of the chaos that was typical of his creative process. But there was no doubt whatsoever that a new level of collaboration was at hand, one of a far more important scope than the last. The first step would be to look more closely at the rules Arneson had already composed. Then Gary would have a much better sense of what needed to be done.

+18

The Muse

THE EAGER KEY-SNAP OF Gary's small Royal typewriter could be heard throughout the Gygax household. The children had become accustomed to falling asleep to the rhythmic *clicks*, which usually continued well into the night and often the next morning. Tonight, however, the clicks stopped early—Gary was finished.

Only a few weeks had passed since Gary hosted the two Daves from the Twin Cities when they had played the exciting *Blackmoor* game. No sooner had Arneson returned home than Gary requested a set of the rules. Dave responded with "18 or so pages of hand-written 'rules.'"[1] Of course, and true to form for Arneson, they were neither organized nor comprehensible in many places.

Gary wondered whether these notes were the work of a madman—or, perhaps more appropriately, a mad genius. He certainly wouldn't have expected Arneson's extreme level of creativity to come with strong organizational or communication skills, let alone a knack for marketing. But Gary did not doubt that he brought to the process a combination of all those things, and he welcomed the challenge of putting these new pieces together.

Naturally, Gary also realized that it wasn't Arneson's creativity alone that had led to this innovative new system. In fact, it had been the ideas of *three* Twin City Daves that had made this work possible: Dave Arneson with *Blackmoor*, Dave Wesely with his *Braunstein* campaign, and Dave Megarry, who had inspired Arneson with his dungeon-themed board game, appropriately called *DUNGEON!*—a game also played with Gary's group during their November weekend visit to Lake Geneva.

Gary carefully rolled the last page out of his typewriter and placed it facedown in a stack of roughly fifty pages sitting adjacent. He turned the stack over, revealing a title page that read THE FANTASY GAME.

After Gary had received, deciphered, and compiled all of Arneson's notes, he attacked the new project on his small manual typewriter with considerable vigor, so as not to lose a minute of time or a scrap of information. "I write mainly because I have so much information inside I just have to . . . The main 'no-no' I have is not to ignore an urge to write. Ideas are ephemeral, slip away too quickly, so when the muse is there go like hell,"[2] he would later explain.

Gary had found a new sense of purpose as he went to work on the system. Remarkably, the fifty-page initial pass, which he had begun shortly after Arneson's November 1972 visit, had only taken a couple of weeks. Somehow Gary had known exactly what to do. These concepts had been lurking in his head in one form or another for so long that they seemed to jump from his head onto the page. It was as if every story his father had ever told him, every pulp novel he had ever read, and every childhood adventure he had ever undertaken were neatly contained in its pages. He borrowed many of the game's combat rules from his earlier *Chainmail*, but *The Fantasy Game* had an important added component—a cooperative, first-person narrative element that no other published game could offer. It was for Gary a process of the "recombining of existing elements to form a new compound heretofore unknown."[3]

Gary grabbed the cigarette that had been beckoning to him for the last hour and turned away from his precious stack of papers to light up. He sat quietly smoking in his dimly lit den for many minutes. He loved the feeling of completion.

"Well . . . I guess it's time to play."

+19

Bedtime!

"You open the chest to reveal that it's full of copper coins!" said Gary.

"Awesome," exclaimed Ernie. "Tenser takes the chest!"

"Ernie, first, you can just say 'I take the chest'; you don't have to say 'Tenser does this,' and 'Tenser does that.' And second, it's a huge chest full of copper coins—you can't carry it."

"But . . . but . . ." stammered Ernie.

Gary's thirteen-year-old son studied the note card in his hands as if it held some clue to solving his problem. Instead the card had little more than the pencil-written name *Tenser* at the top, followed by a number of attributes, such as *Strength*, with numerical values next to them, and an equipment list.[1]

"Fine," said Elise resolutely, joining the conversation. "I fill my bag with coins."

"Yeah, Tenser . . . I mean, me too," Ernie chimed in.

Ernie and his eleven-year-old sister, Elise, had been sitting on the couch in Gary's home office for the last few hours muddling their way through an imaginary dungeon of Gary's creation. Gary sat nearby at his desk, half hiding behind the drawn drawers of the adjacent filing cabinet. Ernie had created a wizard named Tenser, while Elise fashioned a cleric named Ahlissa, both referential to their real-life names.[2] Their conquests of the evening had been a giant centipede, a scorpion nest, and most recently, a band of kobolds—small doglike lizard-men. The newly opened chest of copper coins had been the well-deserved fruit of their labors.

"As you're loading your bags you hear a low, growling sound near the door. Then, out of the darkness emerges . . . Oh . . . Look at that. It's nine o'clock. Bedtime!"

"Dad!" protested Ernie and Elise.

"Sorry, kids, you know the rules. Don't worry. We'll do it again tomorrow," said Gary reassuringly.

As the children reluctantly headed to bed, Gary eagerly began to sketch a new map—a second level to the dungeon. He had used up all of his first-level dungeon material that evening and would need something new for tomorrow's session, especially if there were to be new recruits.

When the next evening came, Gary, Ernie, and Elise rushed through their dinner so as to not waste valuable gaming time. After all, there would continue to be a hard stop at 9:00 P.M., so the clock was ticking. This time Tenser and Ahlissa would journey to the dungeon's second level with the help of three new party members, Murlynd, Robilar, and Terik, created and played by locals Don Kaye, Rob Kuntz, and Terry Kuntz, respectively.[3]

Over the next few months, Gary ran his quickly growing Lake Geneva campaign, which he would call *Castle Greyhawk*, while Dave Arneson did the same with his *Blackmoor* setting in the Twin Cities—both campaigns part of a larger world they dubbed "The Great Kingdom." Running their respective campaigns simultaneously provided them the opportunity to compare notes on how well the game was working and allowed Gary to make revisions as he went. These communications, however, became less frequent as 1973 went on, in large part because they were not in agreement in many aspects of the game's direction. Gary knew that this type of working arrangement would stall the project, so he would keep communication alive but brief, adopt the ideas from Arneson that he liked and use his own vast creativity and experience for the rest. Arneson would later say, "It was very much a case of me providing various ideas and concepts but not having any say as to how they were used."[4] According to Gary, Arneson "complained bitterly that the game wasn't right"[5]—likely a reaction to Gary providing written structure around Arneson's hypercreative, shoot-from-the-hip design aesthetic. But alas, disjointed postal communications between the two, coupled with infrequent and still unaffordable long-distance phone calls, had served as natural barriers to the collaboration.

On a parallel track to Gary and Arneson's test campaigns, Gary had sent copies of his first draft to a number of his best wargaming comrades, asking them to give the system a go. Gary knew probably hundreds of gamers who would be pleased to test the system, but this was too important to let just any outsiders in until it was ready. Only a dozen or so of his best gaming friends would suffice. This effort was, of course, in addition to the "in-house" testing he conducted with his children and local gaming group.

Gary waited for feedback with great anticipation. He knew the game was good—he knew that it would work if he could just put the pieces together. It wasn't long before the feedback started to flood in. The positive response was overwhelming. Numerous phone calls and letters from his gamer buddies cited the strengths of the system while providing needed criticisms. Not surprisingly, he was already aware of many of its shortcomings, based on data he had gathered from his in-house testing.

Ernie, at thirteen, and Elise, at eleven, were at a perfect age to test the system. After all, they were close in age to one of his biggest potential demographics for the game. Gary also had other potential in-house testers lying in wait, namely eight-year-old Heidi, six-year-old Cindy, and two-year-old Luke. Gary loved that he could include his family in his work, as it combined the two things he was most passionate about. Though too young to be involved in the testing, it was Gary's youngest daughter Cindy, who when hearing all of the prototype names for the then unnamed *Fantasy Game*, famously said "Oh, Daddy, I like Dungeons and Dragons best!"[6]

Gary began his revision of the rules in the spring of 1973, which culminated in a second draft totaling roughly 150 pages. This draft he beta-tested with a somewhat broader audience of about thirty gamers; it received the same spectacularly positive response. At this point the prototype was essentially ready for publication, but by whom? Gary would quickly learn that publishing such a new and innovative game might be more challenging than he expected.

+20

Publishing: A Catch-22

"DON, THIS IS THE next big thing!" Gary exclaimed into the phone. "It will sell fifty thousand copies and put Guidon on the map! If you pass this up, you'll regret it forever!"

"I'm sorry, Gary. There's nothing I can do," came a voice over the receiver. "You know the state of gaming right now. Things aren't selling like they used to; even *Chainmail*'s sales have dried up. Gary, I love the concept, but this manuscript is long. The printing costs alone could shut me down."

It was the summer of 1973, and Gary had a nearly finished version of *Dungeons & Dragons*, a game that was going to turn the gaming world upside down. Now all he needed to do was find a publisher. With his reputation in the industry this shouldn't have been a difficult task.[1]

But in 1973, problems lurked around every corner. The economy was in free fall, due largely to high rates of inflation and spectacularly high oil costs. The unemployment rate was rising monthly, and the Vietnam War had taken a heavy economic and social toll on the country, as did the financial burden of keeping up in the Cold War with Russia. These factors affected every part of American consumerism, and the hobby gaming industry wasn't immune to the trend. Boutique gaming companies such as Guidon Games, owned by Don Lowry, were in poor financial shape and getting worse.

Lowry, in an effort to save his company, had recently relocated Guidon Games from Evansville, Indiana, to Maine. He had even invited Gary to come along as his full-time gaming editor, but the move was too drastic for Gary and his young family, and so he declined. Instead, the position went to a young game designer from southern Illinois named

Tom Wham. Unfortunately, any efficiencies or savings that Lowry had hoped to achieve through his move to Maine had failed. Although Gary continued to work closely with Lowry as editor of Guidon's gaming periodical *Panzerfaust*, it seemed that between the increased distance and the declining sales of their previous partnership, *Chainmail*, their collaborations were coming to an end.

After unsuccessfully pitching *D&D* to Guidon, Gary decided to call in a favor at gaming giant Avalon Hill. Avalon Hill was far and away the biggest and most respected name in wargaming at the time. Founded in 1954, this company had more or less created the wargaming industry with its successful initial release of *Tactics* and later *Gettysburg*. The company maintained its dominance through a steady release of games year after year and its widely read in-house gaming periodical, the *General*.

Despite Avalon Hill's high profile, Gary had a friend on the inside. His longtime gaming acquaintance Don Greenwood, who had been the editor of the gaming newsletter *Panzerfaust* for many years, had recently taken over as editor of the *General*. Gary was also well known to Avalon Hill's vice president, Tom Shaw, through his past contributions to the *General* and his involvement with Gen Con, for which Avalon Hill regularly served as lead sponsor. Furthermore, Gary knew that Avalon Hill was looking for new and innovative games. Shaw would even write that same year, "The wargame today is still much the same as it was in 1952 . . . It is my opinion that we have today far too many games on the market that are re-hashes of old formulas . . . I've seen nothing startlingly new in over a decade."[2]

The planets were perfectly aligned for Gary to pitch his revolutionary game to this legendary wargaming company, which, with its vast resources, could make *D&D* the blockbuster it was meant to be. Although all of the conditions seemed to be right, Gary's proposal to Avalon Hill met with an underwhelming response, proving the adage about the best laid plans of mice and men to be true for Gary.

He would later recall, "I mentioned *D&D* to Avalon Hill, but the reception was a trifle chilly . . . the 'establishment' was not about to jump into something as different and controversial as fantasy."[3] He also recalled that Avalon Hill even "laughed uproariously at the idea."[4]

The rejection of *D&D* by both Guidon Games and Avalon Hill was a humbling blow to Gary's dream of changing the gaming world. Where could he go from here? He didn't have the money or resources to publish and distribute a game on a large scale. He certainly couldn't do this alone.

Nonetheless, self-publishing was not an unfamiliar concept to Gary. As a fanatical contributor to several gaming periodicals as well as an on-and-off editor for some of them, Gary knew his way around printing and distribution, at least on a small scale. Further, he had developed, published, and sold a few rules sets through the fledgling mail-order company he had founded just a couple of years earlier, called Gystaff Enterprises. Though Gystaff hardly got off the ground and never made any money, it had served as a vehicle for Gary to test the waters of game development and production. Notably, it had produced a title called *Arbela*, which Gary later adapted to the board game *Alexander the Great*, published by Guidon Games. Further, Gary had found reasonable commercial success as a developer and editor for Guidon Games, *Chainmail* being the most notable example.

Even with his know-how, the fact remained that Gary had neither the funds nor the printing resources to accomplish a reasonable production of *D&D*—even his own mother had turned him down for a loan. But he also knew that he had to get this game published. Not only was it too good and too innovative to let it pass, but getting it to this point had also been extremely costly. Working with Arneson over the last year had often been like pulling teeth, not to mention the significant effort that had gone into drafting, revising, and play-testing the system. There had to be a way.

The solution, it turned out, was right under his nose. He would form a partnership. Not with Arneson, as their many disagreements during the development of *D&D* showed that this would never work, but with someone who had been with Gary since the beginning; someone who he trusted like a brother; someone who loved gaming and this game in particular. Of course, the answer had been there the whole time.

On Sunday, August 19th, 1973, Gary had just finished hosting another successful Gen Con event, Gen Con VI. The event had grown in prominence every year and this year was no exception, even in the face of economic recession. After touting his new game and trying to find a publishing angle everywhere he looked, he needn't have looked further than his best friend Don Kaye, who after the event was over, asked Gary, "Do you really think you can make a success of a game publishing company?"⁵

Of course, Gary had already floated the idea of partnership past him, so Don knew Gary's answer would be an emphatic "Yes!" Having known him almost his whole life, Don recognized that Gary never lacked for confidence, but he also understood Gary's unique level of creativity and drive. Lastly, and perhaps most important, Don knew *D&D* and how special it was, having participated in it since the second game-testing session. In fact, Don Kaye was so convinced, he would bet his life on it—a loan against his life insurance, that is—and Tactical Studies Rules (TSR) would be born.

+21

The Art of Making Art

THE LARGE BROWN BOX sat unopened on the dining room table, staring ominously back at Gary. A simple label on top read GRAPHIC PRINTING CO., LAKE GENEVA, WI.

Even getting it here was a much greater challenge than expected.

How the hell can paper weigh so much? Gary had thought as he trudged it up his snow-covered front stairs and into his dining room.

Now, the only challenge that remained was opening the box and exploring its contents. Gary shook visibly with excitement. Inside was the culmination of a long journey. A knight's quest to find the perfect game—and finally here it was.

Gary, now in his mid-thirties, fumbled around in a drawer, eventually coming up with a dull steak knife. With the vigor of a raccoon tearing open a garbage bag, he swiftly sawed away at the packing tape that held the box together. After freeing the top flaps, he carelessly dropped the knife on the table and flipped the box open. A chill ran down his spine as the contents were finally revealed. There it was—*Dungeons & Dragons: Rules for Fantastic Medieval Wargame Campaigns Playable with Paper and Pencil and Miniature Figures.*

Yes, the title was a mouthful. This had been the topic of debate between him and his collaborators for months. The challenge was how to concisely explain the game. It wasn't just a wargame, nor was it simply miniatures, playacting, or diplomacy. It had no precedent. He lifted a copy of the crudely designed box label and sighed as he admired it close up. The pen-drawn warrior, equipped with a hodgepodge of medieval armor, complete with cape, sword, and winged helmet, and mounted on a great rearing steed, seemed to smile back at his master.

This cover, however, was not a wholly original work, but was a redrawn copy of a panel from a favorite comic book of Gary's called *Strange Tales*.[1] Gary and his gaming comrades regularly copied or lifted illustrations directly from other sources for their semiprofessional games. With copyright laws not being nearly as stringent or vigorously exercised in 1974 as they would be in the future, there was little cause for concern.

Regardless of the source of the art, the printers had done well. This was a great relief, since he had been hounding them to expedite production of the booklets over the busy holiday season of 1973 to ensure delivery by early January 1974. Given the wait, egregious printing errors at this point would have been intolerable. Of course, there were some, as Gary would explain: "The printer assured us that the work would be corrected as it was typeset . . . The work was copied faithfully, so the errors were and are all there, just as they appeared in my original draft."[2]

Now there was work to be done. The sets still needed to be assembled, a task neither he nor his partners had been able to afford on the front end, and out of necessity, they had decided to bring the work in-house. This, of course, meant that he, his family, and his partners—Kaye and a third partner they had added to the mix, Brian Blume—would spend many hours in an assembly line, set up in Gary's dining room, populating each of the sturdy, faux-wood-grain boxes they had purchased at a discount with the three 5½-by-8½-inch booklets and stapled supplemental sheets that made up the original *Dungeons & Dragons* boxed set.

He returned the top page to the box, then rushed to the kitchen wall phone and dialed a number he knew by heart.

"Don, they're here. Come over, we have work to do."

GETTING TO THIS POINT had been no small task. These booklets represented months of trial and error, with no assurances that the system would work, let alone sell. But somehow Gary knew that they would. He was, after all, not a stranger to games and gaming. He knew gamers and what they were craving.

Compared to all that had come before, this game was different. In fact, it was a breakthrough that made it incomparable with other games, combining new dimensions of tactical strategy, miniatures combat, and diplomacy. It was the perfect game—a bet that he and his partner Don Kaye had made in October 1973 when they founded Tactical Studies Rules with $1,000 that came from a loan on Don's life insurance policy. In order to expedite the process and save costs, Gary had asked his uncle, attorney Hugh Burdick, to draw up the partnership agreement, which he did free of charge.

Gary, like Kaye, was not a man of means. Since losing his job at the Fireman's Fund, Gary had been in survival mode, "squeaking by"[3] on unemployment compensation, food stamps, shoe cobbling, and semi-professional game development. In short, Gary was poor.

Don and Gary were both all in, but their modest funds had still been insufficient to publish a game of the size and complexity of *Dungeons & Dragons*. Most amateur games and rules supplements of the time were simple pamphlets ranging from five to twenty pages and usually sold for just a couple of dollars or came free with one of the many circulating gaming periodicals. *D&D*, on the other hand, was to consist of the three detailed fifty-page booklets, along with various supplementary materials, all assembled in a high-quality box. In order to achieve any sort of meaningful production and release, they needed more money.

This had been clear to both Gary and Kaye upon founding TSR, so they had devised a plan to phase the process. TSR initially produced a more traditional gaming pamphlet that Gary had been collaborating on with Jeff Perren. Gary and Perren, of course, had previously collaborated successfully on *Chainmail*, and it was thought that the profits from a modest release would quickly provide the necessary funds to produce *D&D*. Unfortunately, this didn't occur. TSR's first product, *Cavaliers & Roundheads*, was released almost immediately after the company was founded in October 1973. It produced a mere trickle of money and was hardly a commercial success.

Even if *Cavaliers & Roundheads* gained traction, waiting for its sales to fund the production of *D&D* would take at least until 1975, or maybe forever. Furthermore, because early versions of *D&D* had been widely disseminated for playtesting, not to mention the fact that its two original campaigns continued to run under Gary in Lake Geneva and

Arneson in Minneapolis, there was always the worry that it was only a matter of time before someone else broke into the market with a similar concept. They instinctively knew that this game was too good and too important to let it wait. They needed to produce it immediately.

As fate would have it, Gary and Don had met a "friendly and amiable"[4] young gamer at Gen Con VI in August 1973 named Brian Blume, who had since become active with the LGTSA and Gary's ongoing *D&D* campaign. Blume, a toolmaker living in nearby Wauconda, Illinois, had tried to help the TSR partners market their *Cavaliers and Roundheads* game, and he was aware both of their desire to publish *D&D* and of their financial challenges. In November 1973 he approached Gary with a proposed investment of $2,000 to purchase "an equal, one-third partner-ship."[5] Although Gary had only met Blume a few months earlier, he had spent ample time with him over that time and thought he "seemed like a good chap."[6] In fact, it had already become commonplace for Brian to spend the night on Gary's couch when gaming sessions went late. More important, Blume wanted in and had cash. With his obvious enthusiasm for fantasy wargaming and *D&D*, he seemed to have all of the prerequi-sites for immediate partnership in TSR. Don, however, was not so quick to acquiesce and spent a week considering the offer. Kaye requested a meeting between the three and, "after questioning Brian at length,"[7] finally agreed to Brian's proposal.

In December 1973, just two months after TSR's launch, Brian Blume was officially brought in as a one-third partner. He would serve as vice president, with Kaye serving as president, leaving Gary as what he called "the oppressed and hard-working editor."[8] They now had the personnel and working capital to produce their gaming masterpiece, *Dungeons & Dragons*.

Gary's partnership with Don Kaye, his greatest friend, ultimately proved the perfect solution to ensure that *Dungeons & Dragons* would eventually hit the shelves. Adding a relative unknown in Brian Blume to the mix was a risk, but a necessary one if they were to accomplish their goal of changing the gaming world. But for Gary, hidden dangers still lurked in the shadows.

Level 5

DUNGEON MASTER: [DM rolls a twenty-sided die] *You swing your broadsword and hit the troll for* . . . [DM rolls an eight-sided die] *eight points of damage. The troll's arm comes clean off, and he crumples to the ground. The troll and his band are no more. There are bodies of trolls and orcs strewn all over the forest floor, not to mention the horde of stolen treasure they were transporting.*

PLAYER (SIR EGARY): *Where is Sir Kayedon?*

DUNGEON MASTER: *You don't see him anywhere—the last you saw him, he was chasing two trolls down into a ravine.*

PLAYER (SIR EGARY): *I run full speed to the ravine.*

DUNGEON MASTER: *You come upon the crest of the ravine and see three bodies lying motionless, covered in blood. Two are trolls, and one bears the crest of Sir Kayedon . . . Your companion, Sir Kayedon, is dead.*

✝22

Casualties of Wargaming

As THE LACQUERED WOODEN casket was lowered into the frozen ground, Gary could feel his hopes sinking with it. Inside was the lifeless body of Don Kaye, his lifelong friend, companion, and partner. How was he to go on? He had started this journey with Don; now was he to finish it without him?

Don's widow, Donna Kaye, was draped from head to toe in black and stood weeping with her two young children opposite the grave in a remote spot of Oak Hill Cemetery.

Those poor kids, Gary thought.

He remembered the wrenching experience of losing his own father after having neglected him for months. For Gary the wounds of guilt were still open.

Gary's relationship with Donna Kaye, on the other hand, had been a cool one and not terribly different from Mary Jo's relationship with many of his own gaming buddies. Donna certainly would be of no help as far as TSR was concerned. She had never fully approved of Don's passion for games and especially of his involvement in TSR. Her attitude had changed a bit when the sales of *Dungeon & Dragons* began to surge, but now that Don was dead TSR's direction was entirely uncertain.

The frigid February of 1975 passed slowly for Gary. Without Don around, so much of what they did now seemed unimportant. What good was all the treasure in the world when he had no one to share it with? Gary had his family, of course, but this was different. Don had been his companion from the beginning. They had conquered goblins and dragons in the tunnels of Oak Hill Sanatorium; they had battled wraiths in an abandoned house on Dodge Street; they had fought ogres in the woods of Lake Geneva. To die so young and with so much to live for was beyond tragic. After all, Don was only thirty-six years old when the sudden heart attack had taken his life. Even worse, it was later revealed that Don had been aware of his heart problem and had a corrective surgery scheduled just a few weeks later.[1]

Unknown to Gary, or anyone else at the time, Don's death would alter the trajectory of TSR and *Dungeons & Dragons* in ways that far exceeded the loss of his friendship and his direct managerial and creative input. Because Don Kaye was a one-third partner in the fledging company, it was his critical share that determined the balance of power at TSR and would eventually spell doom for Gary corporately and TSR creatively.

NOT LONG AFTER THE funeral, a large box showed up on Gary's doorstep that bore the label GRAPHIC PRINTING CO., LAKE GENEVA, WI. The box was now tattered, the label faded. Gary knew where it had come from. It had once contained the first printing of their gaming masterpiece. He thought of how different he felt now from when he had first opened this box over a year earlier.[2]

Gary sighed as he lifted the flaps—its contents had been carelessly assembled. As Gary had suspected, it contained many of Don Kaye's most important TSR and gaming materials, including the plastic dime-store brontosaurus-turned-dragon that Don had so lovingly crafted many years before. Gary had done a similar conversion that same evening with a stegosaurus.

Gary felt as though the wind had been knocked out of him. He struggled to choke back tears as he went through the contents, piece by piece. These were treasures to Gary, all of the tangible artifacts that remained of his best friend's creative legacy.

The package had been put together and delivered by Donna, as her way of saying that she wanted nothing to do with the business. Of course, from Gary's standpoint, this was just as well. As he would later tell it, "It would have been impossible to manage a business with her involved as a partner."[3] But where to go from here?

Naturally, Don's death and ownership share had already been a point of discussion between Gary and his remaining partner, Brian Blume. This conversation would have been all but moot, but for the staggering success of *Dungeons & Dragons* over recent months. Since the initial printing in January 1974, they had sold all one thousand of the original boxed sets and ordered a thousand more, also hand-assembled at the Gygax house and warehoused at the Kaye residence, often on the unlocked enclosed porch. At the time of Don's death, this second run was already half sold and a third run of two thousand copies was soon to be ordered.

This fact created two distinct challenges for Gary and Brian Blume. One was that Don's garage, porch, and basement had been serving as TSR's de facto warehouse, which would now have to return to Gary's modest Center Street house. Second, and most critical, Don's share was actually becoming worth something because of robust and growing sales.

Gary carefully returned each item to the box and brought it inside to his den. Without hesitation, he went to the kitchen and picked up the phone to dial a number that he knew better than any other.

"Donna, it's Gary. Let's talk . . ."

The conversation did not go as well as Gary had hoped.

Donna Kaye had briefly managed TSR's accounting, and it soon became clear that she would not be an easy or inexpensive sell. Worse, neither Gary nor Blume had the funds to comfortably buy out Kaye's one-third share. What occurred next provided Gary and TSR with an immediate solution but would have grave consequences for their future.

+23

A Makeshift Solution

"HEY, GARY, GOOD NEWS!" came a voice over the phone.

"Good morning, Brian. What is it?" replied Gary.

"I've solved our problem. I spoke to my dad this morning, and he's interested in helping us buy out Donna."

"OK?" countered Gary as he stalled for time.

Gary's heart raced as he began to see an elegant solution unfold; and yet there was something, a feeling in the pit of his stomach that made him uneasy.[1]

"Let me think about it, Brian."

"OK, Gary, but don't take too long. If we keep selling like we are, Donna's gonna want a million bucks for her share . . ."

Gary agonized over the proposal for several days. It was August of 1975, just a few months after Don Kaye's death, and Gary and Brian Blume had reorganized their business from a partnership to a corporation called TSR Hobbies, Inc., held jointly by the remaining two partners, with Gary owning 150 of its 250 shares.[2] TSR Hobbies, however, had no products or intellectual property, as *Dungeons & Dragons* was still owned by the three-way partnership of Tactical Studies Rules, consisting of Gary, Brian, and (since Don's death) Donna Kaye. Now, in order to continue selling *D&D* and their other gaming products under this new venture, it would be necessary for TSR Hobbies to buy out the assets of the partnership, requiring funds that neither Gary nor Brian had available.

While Gary considered the Blume proposal, he certainly kept in mind that Donna's one-third share of Tactical Studies Rules was getting more valuable every day, not to mention the fact that more production capital would be needed to meet *D&D*'s quickly growing demand. Further, this move would ensure that the company would stay in the hands of just two families, the Gygaxes and the Blumes. Gary had developed a strong personal and positive working relationship with Brian over the last year and a half while also becoming acquainted with Brian's father, Melvin, and his brothers, Kevin and Doug.

Melvin Blume was president of Wisconsin Tool & Stamping Co., where Brian had worked for a time. Gary considered him respectable and well intentioned. But the character of the Blumes was not Gary's main apprehension; it was the idea of giving up majority control of the company he had founded—*D&D* was his game, his baby.

After extensive deliberation, and without another viable option, Gary agreed that they should proceed with Melvin Blume's investment in TSR Hobbies, enabling the purchase of the Kaye interest in Tactical Studies Rules. Melvin Blume's investment of $20,000 was exchanged for two hundred shares in the new corporation, $100 per share. As an additional cash infusion, Brian purchased an additional 140 shares of his own with a loan from his father, which made him the largest individual shareholder, with 240 shares, 90 more than Gary and 40 more than his father.[3] This seemed a necessary course, as they were in the process of acquiring space in a modest two-story gray house on Williams Street to serve as their office space and ground-floor retail outlet. The retail space was to be called the Dungeon Hobby Shop.

For a time things went swimmingly. As Melvin Blume wasn't interested in the operations of the company, Brian and Gary managed it as if they were equal partners, Brian heading up the company's operations as vice president and Gary serving as the creative engine and president. Although Blume's primary focus was operations, he was not untalented as a designer and worked with Gary on several successful projects, including a miniatures game based on Edgar Rice Burroughs' John Carter series, called *Warriors of Mars*, in 1974, and in 1975 a Wild West role-playing game known as *Boot Hill*—an idea Don Kaye had helped conceptualize.

Meanwhile, sales of their flagship product, *D&D*, had exploded. They had sold roughly three thousand copies so far that year, with five thousand more planned for delivery to their new space on Williams Street.[4] This was not including the sales of dice (sourced from Creative Publications), which accompanied most sets at a not insignificant price of $1.75 per set.

TSR Hobbies had also begun to publish games from outside designers, such as *Empire of the Petal Throne* by a professor of Indian languages at the University of Minnesota named M. A. R. Barker. With many more internal TSR titles on the way, and the continuation of its in-house publication, aptly named the *Strategic Review*, things at TSR couldn't have been busier or better.

However, ominous signs began to surface. It didn't take long for the Blumes to start using their newly acquired majority control to influence company policy. Brian began bringing up the idea of letting family members work in some capacity in accounting or order fulfillment. To be sure, TSR needed help—lots of it—but Gary had other pressing needs in mind and preferred to procure essential staff before populating the start-up with friends and family on the payroll.

Among other things, the *Strategic Review* had become a serious challenge for Gary. Managing TSR had already gotten so cumbersome that he no longer had the time or energy to write and publish this important piece for the company, as he mentioned in issue 4: "The Fact of the matter is that we are not keeping up with the work that should be done."[5] Furthermore, he wondered whether the *Strategic Review*, which focused on traditional miniatures and wargaming as well as *D&D*, was the right vehicle for a gaming audience that was most interested in the fantasy and swords-and-sorcery elements of *D&D*. Nonetheless, he recognized how important it was to have such a periodical, to promote both the company and the gaming community at large. The precedent and need for such periodicals had been proven by virtually all successful gaming companies to date, most notably Avalon Hill and its *General*.

Fortunately, Gary had also been thinking strategically about the issue of staffing capacity for some time, and with the resounding success of *D&D* so far, there was both the need and funds to hire personnel. He had been in talks with one particular candidate for some time and made him an offer ahead of Gen Con VIII in August 1975. The offer was accepted, and the new employee was to begin in September—TSR's first outside hire.

+24

Kask Strength

IT WAS NOVEMBER OF 1975 when a fresh-faced journalism graduate named Tim Kask eagerly arrived at the small white house at 330 Center Street, then still serving as both Gary's home and TSR's interim headquarters. Kask, however, wasn't the ordinary deer-in-the-headlights college graduate. There was something hard and seasoned about him that made him different. Gary liked that. This was no doubt due to Kask's time in the armed forces—he had done a tour in Vietnam, leaving him a few years older than his graduating peers, but also a bit more savvy and rougher around the edges. He hit the ground running at TSR, having already worked on a couple of issues of the *Strategic Review*, but was still awaiting an assignment that he could sink his teeth into. Today he'd find it.

Kask, a graduate of Southern Illinois University, had relocated to take this job in order to write. He had, after all, been a journalism major and was excited to cut his teeth on challenging editorial assignments. Perhaps more important, Kask was an avid gamer. He had been playing Gary's *Chainmail* with a college group since the early seventies. In fact, his first contact with Gary had been a phone call in 1973, when Kask had called to get a rules clarification. He had subsequently met Gary in person at Gen Con VII in 1974 and, of course, again in 1975, where he had confirmed his acceptance of the employment offer.

Kask could hear heavy footsteps approaching the front door. Before he could adjust his collar, the door opened to reveal his new bosses, Gary Gygax and Brian Blume. Gary was carrying a large basket of papers.[1]

"Good morning, Mr. Gygax, Mr. Blume," said Kask, curiously eyeing the basket.

"Good morning, Tim, come on in. And, for the last time, it's Gary and Brian," answered Gary. "These . . . are for you," he said as he dropped the basket at Kask's feet.

"What are they?" replied Kask as he began to dig into its contents.

"These are Dave Arneson's notes for *Blackmoor*, the game we modeled *D&D* after. We've been trying to put together a *Blackmoor* supplement for the better part of a year, but Arneson is dragging his feet and we can't make heads or tails out of these," explained Gary.

As Tim began to dig deeper in what seemed a massive collection of chicken scratch and scribbles, he asked, "Are you guys serious?"

Gary and Brian shot knowing glances at each other, and then back to their young editor.

"Have fun!" Gary said with a devilish smile as he exited the room with Brian close on his heels.

And so Tim Kask, TSR's first outside employee, was given his first major assignment—to edit a box full of incomprehensible notes into a meaningful supplemental *D&D* book. Through his work on *Blackmoor*, as well as several issues the *Strategic Review*, Kask quickly proved his value to Gary and to TSR. *Blackmoor* would prove another vital component of *D&D*'s growth and was fundamental to TSR's business model in providing add-on material to reinforce its proprietary system. Gary had already tested this model earlier in the year by enlisting the help of former Castle & Crusade Society "king" and game design luminary Rob Kuntz to produce *D&D*'s first supplement, *Greyhawk*, based on the campaign they had jointly run during playtesting. The high $10 cost of the original system had been controversial in the gaming community, but the modest *Greyhawk* booklet, with its fifty-six pages, sold for a much more palatable $5. For that reason, *Greyhawk* and later *Blackmoor*, which required roughly one-third of the creative and printing effort involved in producing the original system, promised far greater profits than the original set.[2] These supplements were bought readily by a growing fan base eager to expand its resources for this addictive one-of-a-kind gaming system. Now, in Tim Kask, Gary had found an ally to which he could trust his next important project: a magazine called the *Dragon*.

The *Dragon* was to be TSR's next periodical, but it was to be grander in scope than other wargaming periodicals of the past. Most of these publications were essentially house organs for the company's games. The *Strategic Review* was in fact developed in this mold, but the *Dragon* was notably different. Its mission was to objectively and comprehensively cover fantasy gaming as a whole—more than a house organ by a gaming company ever had. Gary believed that the gaming industry was poised for growth and that a periodical focused not just on brand promotion but on the larger picture served as a better promotional tool than a narrow and biased company magazine. As such, it would steer away from negative reviews because, as Gary believed, "there are too many good games to talk about."[3]

As usual, Gary's instincts were correct. The *Dragon*, which debuted in June 1976, proved to be an exceptional success as both an in-house promotional piece and a legitimate specialty gaming magazine—one that had a circulation of over one hundred thousand at its height and would continue in one form or another into the twenty-first century, with more than four hundred issues to date. Concurrent with the *Dragon*, and with Kask as editor, TSR would also produce *Little Wars*, a successor to the *Strategic Review*, serving a more traditional wargaming and miniatures audience. Its title was an homage to the accepted inventor of modern wargaming, H. G. Wells, whose *Little Wars*, published in 1913, laid out the first known framework for miniatures combat. TSR's *Little Wars*, however, never achieved the success of the *Dragon* and folded after only thirteen issues, with its content becoming effectively enveloped (or, perhaps more appropriately, devoured) by the *Dragon*.

+25

Fun and More Games

GARY'S BLOOD BOILED AS he sat at his small writing desk reading the first issue of *Alarums & Excursions*, an amateur-oriented gaming fanzine of *D&D*. His eyes, already magnified by his Coke-bottle glasses, widened and then narrowed in disgust as he finished the brief periodical. Two statements, by two separate authors, had burned into his mind. The first, by a former IFW comrade, said "*D&D* is too important to leave to Gary Gygax. Gary has produced other games in the past. The problem has been that they are not interesting in their full form. They tend to be flawed by simple, bad solutions to complex problems."[1] As if this wasn't bad enough, the other, by a noted Los Angeles gamer and editorialist, piled on: "It seems obvious that the Game [*D&D*] has now outgrown its creators."[2]

"Bastards," he said to himself as he tossed the cheap newsletter on his desk.

He sat for a moment, still but tense. He felt like he should do something but didn't know what. As he reached again for the slanderous document, he noticed his typewriter sitting idly by.

Of course, he thought. *The pen is indeed mightier than the sword.*

By day's end, Gary had completed his response to these spiteful comments. But he had cooled down enough through the therapeutic process of written rebuttal that he decided to hold off a bit on sending it. He had learned that patience was a virtue and discretion often the better part of valor.

What had upset Gary most about these "reviews" were two things. First was the petty and almost envious appraisal of his design ability, as if these critics could create something as innovative as *D&D* or understand his creation better than he did. Second, they had stated the obvious about *D&D* outgrowing its creators. Of course it would! It was bound to, and was meant to. For these know-it-alls to sit there and cleverly point out what was elementary seemed particularly obnoxious. Not only was Gary intensely aware of this issue of obsolescence, but he had already made plans to keep up and stay ahead from a content standpoint.

The long-awaited second *D&D* supplement, *Blackmoor*, would be published by the end of 1975, providing a variety of new content for the growing system, including a dedicated module entitled *Temple of the Frog*—effectively *D&D*'s first published adventure module. Many more *D&D* and non-*D&D* projects were in the works, and TSR was on the verge of bringing in new creative staff.

By April 1976, TSR had effectively doubled its staff in six months, having brought in the full-time creative talents of Dave Arneson and his Twin Cities compatriots Dave Megarry and Mike Carr. Megarry had joined Arneson the night they unveiled the original *Blackmoor* concept to Gary and his Lake Geneva gaming group. He had since teamed with TSR in 1975 to publish a board game version of *D&D*, aptly named *DUNGEON!* Carr was the inventor of the ever popular *Fight in the Skies* wargame, a collaborator on *Don't Give Up the Ship*, and a visible presence in the gaming community. Local gamer and designer Rob Kuntz also joined the design staff, along with another Twin Cities transplant, staff artist Dave Sutherland. Though TSR's staff numbers were still relatively small, the creative talent now on board would prove to be greater than the sum of their parts, facilitating exponential growth in the company's creative output. This all came at a critical time, when demand for new *D&D* products was far exceeding TSR's capacity to supply them.

In spite of strong and ever-growing sales, TSR struggled with cash flow, making anything approaching a regular payroll with purely cash-compensation structures impossible. As such, many of the early TSR employees were compensated with a combination of pay, company stock, and generous royalty agreements on the games they designed. Not fore-seeing how these royalty structures might affect future profitability, some had royalty agreements that ran as high as 10 percent of net receipts on the games they designed, most notably for Gary's and Dave Arneson's work on *D&D*.

On April 24, 1976, TSR opened its long-anticipated hobby shop, the Dungeon, located at 723 Williams Street. Terry Kuntz, Rob's older brother, worked the counter and managed the store along with Gary's eldest son, Ernie. Terry had been hired as TSR's service manager in October 1975, just after Tim Kask, tasked with responding to rules questions and setting up the retail operation. The second floor of the former residential house, rezoned for commercial purposes, now served as TSR's creative and executive offices. The company had finally moved out of Gary's cramped basement, allowing his home to fully "return to its normal chaotic state."[3] This was no doubt a great relief to Gary, given that he still had five children ranging in age from five to sixteen in the house. By midyear, TSR had released its third *D&D* supplement, *Eldritch Wizardry*, not to mention the rerelease of a few earlier games designed by TSR staff, including Gary, Arneson, and Carr's previous collaboration, *Don't Give Up the Ship*, Carr's *Fight in the Skies*, and Gary's first board game design from years earlier, *Little Big Horn*.

Dungeons & Dragons was at this point growing uncontrollably, creating a new set of issues. If imitation is the best form of flattery, then *D&D* had been flattered by many burgeoning gaming ventures and amateur game designers. Games such as *Tunnels & Trolls* by Arizona game company Flying Buffalo, Inc., not to mention several unlicensed supplemental *D&D* companion pieces, were being sold by these small gaming operations for profit. Gary, having been previously involved at all levels of the gaming field, understood that while they were upstarts and rivals, he couldn't afford to alienate this eager and potentially lucrative audience. Yet, he also couldn't let them run wild with knock-offs of TSR-copyrighted materials or intellectual property. To strike this delicate balance, Gary decided on a two-pronged approach: First, TSR retained a lawyer to issue a few cease-and-desist letters, strategic-ally routed to the biggest offenders to stop them dead in their tracks. Next, Gary teamed up with third-party designers and publishers, who were sometimes the same as the original offenders, to license, develop, and distribute gaming supplements and accessories that supported TSR products. One such example was the Illinois-based Judges Guild, which consisted of two enthusiastic gamers and amateur game designers who would now make maps and gaming aids under the TSR license and, of course, pay royalties to TSR.

TSR had learned about licensing and cease-and-desist letters the hard way, being on the receiving end of such letters from the estate of Edgar Rice Burroughs, which halted TSR's unlicensed production of its 1974 miniatures game *Warriors of Mars*, and later from the Tolkien estate for its Middle Earth–themed wargames and its use of Tolkien references in *D&D*. But now it was TSR's turn to enforce such rights.

Ironically, it was these TSR-issued cease-and-desist letters that prompted these small imitators to develop a generic term for a *D&D*-type game, so they could still legally market their products. After TSR's threats of copyright infringement, *Tunnels & Trolls* maker Flying Buffalo removed all mentions of *Dungeons & Dragons* from its advertising, instead choosing to refer to *D&D* and other TSR games as "other fantasy role-playing games."[4] The first appearance of the term appears in a *Tunnels & Trolls* advertisement in the August 1, 1976, edition of the Metagaming Concepts catalog. Thus the term *role-playing game* was born.

Of course, the best outreach for *Dungeons & Dragons* was still gaming conventions. The game had naturally been a focus of Gen Con, but it was starting to become a featured event at several outside fantasy and science fiction conventions, including a dedicated *D&D* convention run by fans on the West Coast called DunDraCon. Following the model of Gen Con, Avalon Hill had since begun its own gaming convention, called Origins, based near its Baltimore headquarters. *D&D* had made a significant impact at the first Origins event in 1975, which included a few sold-out *D&D* gaming events. By the 1976 Origins event, *D&D* had become the "belle of the ball," much to the dismay of its host, Avalon Hill, who had turned Gary down on publishing *D&D* three years before.

By August 1976, TSR's Gen Con had become a leading gaming event, selling more than 1,300 tickets for its ninth event, Gen Con IX. It even featured some international figures, including Ian Livingston and Steve Jackson of the UK-based gaming company Games Workshop, which was TSR's UK distributor and soon to be the publisher of the successful *White Dwarf* gaming magazine. Celebrity guests also attended, including celebrated pulp fantasy author Fritz Leiber, who was promoting a board game called *Lankhmar* that he had co-developed with TSR. During his stay in Lake Geneva, Leiber became fast friends with Gary—and with Mary Jo, with whom he became longtime pen pals, affectionately referring to her as the "Pirate Queen" because of her sometimes less-than-ladylike language. Several other new TSR products graced the Horticultural Hall, spilling over to the nearby American Legion hall, as the event by this time had much outgrown this modest space. Other products included a new miniatures game by Gary called *Swords & Spells*, which was essentially a reworked version of *Chainmail*, and, most important, another *D&D* supplement, *Gods, Demi-Gods & Heroes*.

Developed by Rob Kuntz and part-time TSR designer Jim Ward, *Gods, Demi-Gods & Heroes* would prove a great commercial success, but would also be original *D&D*'s last supplement, as TSR had recently turned its attentions to developing an advanced form of its *Dungeons & Dragons* rules set. TSR also continued to produce other role-playing games, and in November 1976, Ward, who Gary had met only a couple of years earlier in the sci-fi/fantasy section of a local bookstore, would develop the first role-playing game geared toward TSR's growing science-fiction fan base. It was called *Metamorphosis Alpha: Fantastic Role-Playing Game of Science Fiction Adventures*.

ALL OF THIS ACTIVITY meant that every member of this ragtag group of early TSR designers and artists had become impossibly busy—everyone except for *D&D*'s co-creator, Dave Arneson.

Curiously, Arneson's name had been conspicuously absent from the credits of most of the company's new publications. Though the details are uncertain, it was likely that this inactivity, or a failure to produce usable material, led to the end of his employment at TSR after only ten months with the company. However, other accounts persist, including one in which Arneson was demoted to shipping clerk after refusing to accept a royalty reduction for *D&D*, thereby forcing his hand into resignation.[5] Whatever the case, the tenure of *D&D*'s co-creator at TSR was short-lived.

As for Gary, he was busier than ever on the creative side but still had found time to respond to his *Alarums & Excursions* critics who had antagonized him months earlier—the first of many such responses to disapproving members of the Amateur Press Association: "I too subscribe to the slogan '*D&D* is too important to leave to Gary Gygax.' Gosh and golly! Whoever said anything else. However, pal, best remember that it is far too good to leave to you or any other individual or little group either! It now belongs to the *thousands* of players enjoying it worldwide, most of whom will probably never hear of you or your opinions *unless* you get them into the *Strategic Review*."[6]

Ernest Gygax and Gary, c. 1939

Almina "Posey" Gygax and Gary, c. 1940

Gary, c. 1948

Gary's childhood home at 925 Dodge Street in Lake Geneva, Wisconsin

Mary Jo Powell, c. 1942

Mary Jo and Don Kaye *(back left)*, c. 1948

The Geneva Theater

Gary *(second row, center)* at age seventeen

Gary and Mary Jo's wedding,
September 14, 1958

Gary's house at 330 Center Street in
Lake Geneva, Wisconsin

Gary, Ernie, and Elise in Chicago, August 1963

John Rasch, Mary Jo, and Gary before Tom Keogh's funeral, April 17, 1963

The Riviera

Gary, c. 1965

Mary Jo at 330 Center Street, c. 1965. Gary's den/office is located through the closed arched doorway to her right.

Mary posing for a "glamour shot" in 1968. Such photos were to be carried in Gary's wallet "to keep his attention where it belonged when he worked in Chicago."

Gary's children, c. 1971: Ernie, Elise, Heidi *(back row)*, Cindy, and Luke *(front row)*. Before Gary was fired from Fireman's Fund Insurance, the Gygax children frequently waited for him at the Lake Geneva train station after work, and he was known to skip home with them.

Lake Geneva Horticultural Hall

Gary *(seated, with striped shirt)* planning his next move
during a miniatures wargame at Gen Con II, August 1969

Dave Arneson *(seated, with glasses)* playing a miniatures
wargame at Gen Con II, August 1969

Gary playing a wargame at a convention in Madison, Wisconsin, 1969

Gary playing a wargame with Mike Carr *(seated)* at a convention in Madison, Wisconsin, 1969

Don Kaye and Gary at Gen Con VI, August 1973. Gary and Kaye formed their partnership, Tactical Studies Rules, in the wake of this event.

Chainmail, 1971 (© Wizards of the Coast LLC)

Dungeons & Dragons box cover, 1974 (© Wizards of the Coast LLC)

Dungeons & Dragons Supplement I: Greyhawk, 1975 (© Wizards of the Coast LLC)

The Dragon #1, June 1976 (© Wizards of the Coast LLC)

A comic by TSR staff artist Dave Sutherland depicting the company's staff in mid-1976, ahead of their trip to Origins Game Fair. *(From left to right)* Mike Carr (as WWI aviator); Tim Kask (hat and pipe); Brian Blume (cowboy); Ernie Gygax (barbarian); Gary Gygax (on desk with whip); Terry Kuntz (Robin Hood); Dave Arneson ("Blackmoor U" T-shirt); Rob Kuntz (dragging a beholder); Neil Topolnicki (Napoleon)

Set of polyhedral dice used for *Dungeons & Dragons* from Creative Publications

Don Kaye's house

Gary at Gen Con IX, August 1976

Fritz Leiber, Gary, Professor M. A. R. Barker, Ian Livingstone, Rob Kuntz, and Steve Jackson *(foreground)* at Gen Con IX, August 1976

TSR's first dedicated headquarters, known as the Gray House. Later, it hosted the staff of *Dragon* magazine.

Gary and Mary Jo hosting a housewarming party at the first house they owned, located on Lake Geneva's Chapin Road, c. 1977

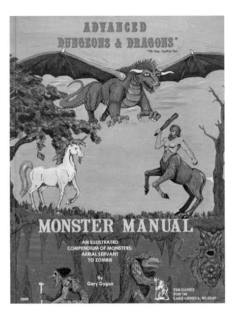

Advanced Dungeons & Dragons: Monster Manual, 1977 (© Wizards of the Coast LLC)

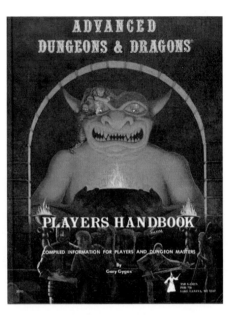

Advanced Dungeons & Dragons: Player's Handbook, 1978 (© Wizards of the Coast LLC)

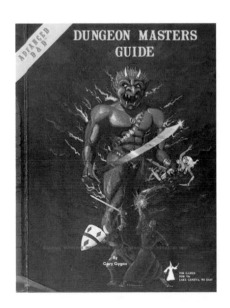

Advanced Dungeons & Dragons: Dungeon Master's Guide, 1979 (© Wizards of the Coast LLC)

TSR advertisement featuring Elise Gygax, c. 1978 (© Wizards of the Coast LLC)

The Dungeon Hobby Shop/TSR Hotel Clair, c. 1979

Tim Kask receiving an award from Elise Gygax for his work on *Dragon* magazine, c. 1978

One of Gary and Mary Jo's prized Arabian horses in front of their Clinton, Wisconsin, mansion, which was dubbed Dragonlands

A real estate brochure for Dragonlands, c. 1978

Ernie sunbathing at the pool at Gary's Beverly Hills mansion, c. 1984. Gary swam laps in the pool daily, which, coupled with a healthier diet, accounted for a much lower body weight during his time in California.

Interior of Gary's Beverly Hills mansion and Dungeons & Dragons Entertainment Corporation's headquarters, c. 1984

Gamers playing miniatures wargames on the sand gaming table in the converted barn on Gary's Beverly Hills estate, which was also TSR's west coast headquarters, c. 1984

Gary and his second wife, Gail, as featured in a 1985 *Milwaukee Journal* article

Stone Manor as it appeared in the 1960s through the 1980s.
Gary's apartment was on the second floor, left wing.

Tomb of Horrors, AD&D adventure
module, 1978 (© Wizards of the Coast LLC)

Dungeons & Dragons Basic Set (2nd
Revision), 1983 (© Wizards of the Coast LLC)

Advanced Dungeons & Dragons: Unearthed Arcana, c. 1985 (© Wizards
of the Coast LLC)

Patricia Pulling holds a photo of her son along with several books and games from "Dungeons and Dragons," which she blames for the suicide of her son, Irving.

SATURDAY OKLAHOMAN & TIMES March 23,1985

A newspaper story featuring Bothered About Dungeons & Dragons (BADD) founder, Patricia Pulling, 1985

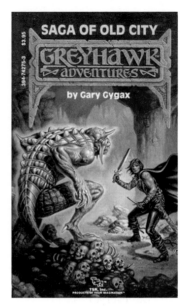

Saga of Old City, AD&D novel, 1985 (© Wizards of the Coast LLC)

Wizards of the Coast founder, Peter Adkison, *Magic: The Gathering* creator, Richard Garfield, and Gary at Gen Con 40, 2007

Figures 1, 2, 3, 5, 6, 8, 9, 10, 12, 13, 15, 16, 17, 18, 35, 42, 43, 44, 45, 46 and 47 courtesy of Ernie, Elise, Luke, Cindy, and Heidi Gygax, and Mary Jo Gygax-Walker; Figures 4, 7, and 19 courtesy of the Wisconsin Historical Society, Wisconsin Architecture and History Inventory: 925 DODGE ST, City of Lake Geneva, Walworth County, Wisconsin, Ref. 67106; 244 BROAD ST, City of Lake Geneva, Walworth County, Wisconsin, Ref. 66986; 330 BROAD ST, City of Lake Geneva, Walworth County, Wisconsin, Ref. 66990; Figures 20, 21, 22, and 23 courtesy of John Bobek; Figure 24 courtesy of Michael Cox (The Dragon's Trove) and Paul Stormberg (The Collector's Trove); Figures 25, 26, 27, 28, 36, 37, 38, 50, 51 and 54 courtesy of Paul Stormberg and with the permission of Wizards of the Coast; Figure 28 with the permission of Tim Kask; Figures 29 and 30 courtesy of Paul Stormberg; Figure 41 courtesy of Elise Gygax and Tim Kask; Figures 39 and 52 with the permission of Wizards of the Coast; Figures 32 and 33 courtesy of Ian Livingstone © Ian Livingstone 1976; Figure 40 courtesy of Tom Wham; Figure 48 with permission of the *Milwaukee Journal*; Figure 49 courtesy of Virgil Wuttke; Figure 53 photo courtesy of Paul Stormberg and with the permission of *The Oklahoman*; Figure 55 courtesy of Peter Adkison Copyright © Peter D. Adkison, 2007

+26

Gary's Other Job

"OH, C'MON, DAD! Can't I stay out just a little later?" whined Elise.

"No, Elise. Ten-thirty is it," replied Gary coolly.

"But everyone else gets to stay out till midnight at least!"

"Elise, you of all people should know that I don't care what everyone else does. Ten thirty is final!"

Gary and his eldest daughter, fifteen-year-old Elise, had been bickering at the dining room table for the last several minutes.[1] Gary was known to be a strict father who could drive the fear of God into his kids, and he certainly didn't have much patience for debate with his children. In fact, it was this inflexibility that caused seventeen-year-old Ernie, Gary's elder son, to move out of the house. Ernie had been dating a young woman of whom Gary did not approve. Gary had always told his son that "there are girls for fun and there are girls you marry,"[2] but Ernie's current interest must not have fallen into either of these categories as far as Gary was concerned.

Another point of dissension between Gary and his son was that Ernie had drifted away from his parents' faith, the Jehovah's Witnesses. In times past, Gary had made attempts to pull away from gaming in favor of devoting more time to his faith, but such efforts were always short-lived. And while not "devout" by Jehovah's Witness standards, Gary and Mary Jo had maintained this religious affiliation and expected their children to follow suit. In Gary's household "you were OK as long as you took the party line,"[3] and Ernie had not. Though Gary loved to play table games based on diplomacy and reason, when it came to managing his household he was far more autocratic than diplomatic. Mary Jo, on the other hand, still had her motherly instincts to reckon with, and after Ernie left the family home she frequently checked up on him in secret from a local pay phone.

Gary did have a soft spot for Elise, however, not only because she was his perpetual little girl, but also because she was so much like he had been at fifteen. In particular, she had inherited Gary's rebellious streak, and he knew better than anyone that this instinct needed a certain amount of supervision and structure.

Elise had indeed blossomed into a very fetching young woman, sharing in her mother's good looks and fiery red hair. Unsurprisingly, she had started attracting the attention of many young men around town, including crushes from several of Gary's gaming buddies. This night, however, she had been set up on a blind date by a friend, and the exciting evening would entail watching a local garage band perform, among other things. The would-be suitor was due to show up at six thirty, but now it appeared the evening would be embarrassingly short because of her ten-thirty curfew.

Just as Elise began another round of protests, a loud rumble was heard just outside. Gary and Elise went to the window to investigate the disturbance on the otherwise sleepy neighborhood street. A rusty Camaro had pulled up in front, rumbling loudly and occasionally back-firing, leaky muffler causing the loud ruckus.

"He's here!" squealed Elise as she blushed and ran to the bathroom to put the finishing touches on her face.

Gary watched as a scraggly, long-haired teenager exited the car and walked toward their front porch. It looked like he had been working on his car all day, as he was covered in grease.

He can't be much of a mechanic if his car still sounds like that, Gary thought.

Knock! Knock! Knock!

Elise burst out of the bathroom and rushed to the door to greet her date, Gary following close behind.

"Dad, not now!" she pleaded.

"What? I just want to meet him," retorted Gary.

As Elise opened the door, her carefully prepared smile slowly vanished. Gary could tell she was not enthralled with her visitor.

"Oh . . . hi!" said Elise with as much enthusiasm she could muster.

"Hey . . ." said the teen casually.

"Well . . . come on in!" she replied.

As the greasy teen sauntered into Gary's home, Gary began to size him up. *Yeah, I could take him,* he thought.

"Hey, nice to meet you! What's your name?" asked Gary.

"They call me 'the Doc,'"[4] the teen irreverently replied.

"Really? The Doc of what?"[5] inquired Gary.

"The Doc of Love,"[6] the teen confidently declared.

Gary stood motionless, smiling at the teen for several seconds.

". . . Well, it's nice to meet you, Doc!" he abruptly exclaimed. "Elise has been waiting for you."

There was a fair amount of irony in Gary's voice, but delivered in a way that only a family member or close friend might catch.

Elise cleared her throat, struggling for her next words. ". . . So, Dad, I've got to be in by nine thirty?"[7]

Gary smiled assuredly at his eldest daughter. He knew what he was supposed to say.

"Oh, no, honey . . . You can stay out as late as you want."[8]

At that Gary nodded at the young man, winked at his daughter and headed for the basement, leaving Elise in the foyer with her Saturday night dud.

Such antics were not uncommon for Gary. His tough-love yet light-hearted parenting style extended to all the Gygax children, not just Ernie and Elise. Heidi, for example, regularly suffered the humiliation of crossing paths with ex-boyfriends that Gary had previously recruited for his role-playing games, often when she was with a new boyfriend. Gary naturally provided similar torments for Cindy and Luke in later years.

✛ 27

It's Like Dungeons & Dragons,
but Advanced

GARY QUICKLY ROSE FROM his leather swivel office chair and lumbered down the long hallway to Brian Blume's office. This path represented a steep departure from their last office layout, where their offices had been separated only by thin bedroom walls in the converted residential office space on Williams Street, known as the Gray House.

"We're being sued," said Gary.

The bearded Blume looked up from a report he was reviewing. As usual, he was adorned in a Western-style shirt, boot-cut jeans with a large belt buckle, and of course cowboy boots. Although Blume was a Midwesterner, he had always fancied himself something of a cowboy.

"Sued by whom?" replied Blume casually.

"Arneson!" Gary exclaimed as he threw a court document on Brian's desk.

It was February 1979, and *Dungeons & Dragons* had become a legitimate gaming phenomenon, roughly doubling its sales every year since its inception. Since 1977, however, TSR had invested much of its time and resources into a new system of *Dungeons & Dragons*, known as *Advanced Dungeons & Dragons (AD&D)*, which now accounted for the majority of its sales. This new version of *D&D* bore little resemblance to the original system in its depth of gaming components and the quality of its books and supplements. The first of these *AD&D* materials was the hardcover *Monster Manual*, released in January 1978 to great success. This was followed in June 1978 by another high-quality rule book known as the *Player's Handbook*. A third product was already in development and slated for release in 1979, the *Dungeon Master's Guide*. The new books had been authored by Gary and edited by Mike Carr, who also contributed forewords to each. Arneson had neither worked on nor contributed to any of these prior to his departure, and because the new *AD&D* system had departed so greatly from the original *D&D* products, TSR had decided not to pay him royalties on these new rule books.

The document that Gary had presented to Brian was a summons naming TSR and Gary personally as defendants in a civil suit filed by Arneson in the Minneapolis Second Circuit Court. Arneson's legal claim alleged a breach of his 1975 royalty agreement as it applied to *Dungeons & Dragons*—in essence, it asserted that since he was entitled to his original royalty of 10 percent for *D&D*, it followed that he deserved the same for *AD&D*. Gary and Arneson had many disagreements in the past, to be sure, but Gary couldn't believe their relationship had degraded to this point.

"That ungrateful bastard!" shouted Gary as he stormed back down the hallway.

Of course, this lawsuit was the culmination of professional issues that had been growing between Gary and Dave Arneson for years. Even in their early collaborations, the two failed to see eye to eye on many fundamental gaming elements. Time had done nothing but escalate the already tense relationship between the two, reaching a boiling point with Arneson's brief employment at and subsequent departure from TSR.

On a personal level, however, Gary had once held Arneson in high esteem, and had even invited him along on a vacation to the family cabin a few years prior. In fact, if not for Dave's crush on Elise—a crush seemingly shared by everyone in the gaming community at the time—he would have been considered more or less family.

"He won't get a nickel," muttered Gary as he plodded down the stairwell.

Gary was incensed. Here, his former friend, who continued to collect generous royalties on the original *D&D* system per his agreement, had not even been a part of the creative effort and long hours that had gone into the new *Advanced Dungeons & Dragons* system. Yet now, with success at hand, he wanted a piece of the action.

The new *AD&D* system was a vast departure from the original *D&D* system, but was it so diametrically different from its forerunner that Arneson's legal rights to the underlying concept would be forfeit? Gary thought so, but court cases aren't so easily dismissed with a wave of the hand.

Since parting with TSR, Arneson had been making a modest income working with small gaming companies, including Heritage Models and Judges Guild, on a variety of *D&D*-like supplements. But while TSR's sales were booming, Arneson saw his royalties drying up, clearing just a little more than $5,000 per quarter from a company that was now grossing roughly $1 million.[1] A judge or jury, especially in Arneson's hometown, might be persuaded that Arneson deserved some relief.

ONCE GARY REACHED THE lobby, he exited the building in a flurry. He badly needed a smoke, and perhaps a pastry from Bittner's Bakery.

By this time, TSR had moved its headquarters and the Dungeon Hobby Shop into the once prestigious Hotel Clair, located in the heart of Lake Geneva's historic business district, on the corner of Main and Broad Streets. The Clair, affectionately known to TSR employees as "the Blatz"[2] because of the gaudy Blatz beer advertisement painted on the back of its brick exterior, was a relic from a different era, and though rundown, was still one of the most prominent buildings in town. The hotel's former lobby restaurant served as the storefront of the Dungeon, while the two upstairs floors housed the executive offices and design department. Most interesting to many of TSR's employees, however, was the building's basement. This former bowling alley was now reserved for employee gaming and hosted a replica of Gary's legendary sand-topped table, among other things. TSR employees and executives so frequently utilized this gaming haven that it was well accepted that at least 5 percent of the interoffice mail traffic was related to employees' ongoing games.[3] To be sure, this was a gaming company run *for* gamers *by* gamers.

As Gary walked through the quaint downtown, still fuming about the summons, he took notice of how rundown some parts of the town now looked. It reminded him of what seemed to be happening to the gaming community. Once an open forum for sharing new and innovative ideas, without the expectation of wealth or royalties, it had become an industry of closely guarded secrets, distrust, and back-biting. The rules had changed, and for Gary, you simply "couldn't change the rules in the middle of a game."[4]

Unfortunately for Gary this afternoon, neither cigarettes nor baked goods could fix his new problem. He grudgingly recognized that Arneson's case was at least moderately compelling, especially in a legal system that had little understanding of the nuances of role-playing game systems. This lack of understanding and disconnect with the legal arena would become especially apparent in years to come.

In truth, although *AD&D* products were superficially unrecognizable from their original *D&D* predecessors, the fundamental concept of the game was identical. Even though *AD&D* included more character classes, additional gaming mechanics, significantly upgraded artwork, richer campaign content, and higher-quality production, the game was still at its core a fantasy role-playing game, just like the original. Perhaps if TSR had not included the phrase "Dungeons & Dragons" in the title of *AD&D*, it would have been off the hook, but of course doing so would have denied the new system the name recognition of the *Dungeons & Dragons* brand the company had worked so hard to build. In this respect it had been a calculated decision and one that Gary, who had painstakingly written every word of the original and the majority of the content of *AD&D*—instead of just "providing various ideas and concepts,"[5] as Arneson had—was having trouble seeing the other side of.

AFTER MANY MONTHS OF deliberation among Gary, TSR, and the company's legal counsel, a decision was finally reached. Shortly thereafter Gary picked up the phone and dialed a number he knew by heart.

"Hello, Dave? It's Gary. Let's talk . . ."

Although Gary had decided that settling was the best course of action, it was not at all a simple matter, as reflected by the fact that Gary and Arneson didn't reach their compromise until March 1981, two years after Arneson had originally filed suit. The final agreement allowed Arneson a 2.5 percent royalty on all *Advanced Dungeons & Dragons* products, a result that amounted to a comfortable six-figure sum annually.

This wouldn't be the last legal skirmish between TSR and Arneson. Just three years after their *AD&D* settlement, TSR released a supplement called *Monster Manual II* and again refused to pay Arneson royalties on the new product. However, by this time, Gary was managing Dungeons & Dragons Entertainment Corp. on the West Coast and not directly involved with the operations of TSR, Inc. Unsurprisingly, Arneson sued and prevailed again, netting over $100,000 of royalties on the sale of that product in the first year alone.[6]

Level 6

DUNGEON MASTER: [DM rolls a twenty-sided die] *The brigand captain slashes you with his saber through an arm joint in your armor for . . .* [DM rolls an eight-sided die] *. . . six points of damage. You can feel the blood seeping down your arm. You're down to six hit points. What do you do?*

PLAYER (SIR EGARY): *I take my broadsword in both hands and, with all my might, thrust it into his chest.* [Player rolls a twenty-sided die. A 20 comes up.]

DUNGEON MASTER: *You hear a* crack *and then a* pop *as your sword plunges straight through his heart. The captain's body goes limp at the end of your sword and falls next to the bodies of his mates.*

PLAYER (SIR EGARY): *Phew! That was a close one! Where's my elven companion, the archer Elainorr?*

DUNGEON MASTER: *You notice her climbing the front mast ladder up to the crow's nest, but before you can reach out, you hear a ruckus behind you. You turn around to see another half a dozen pirates, armed with a combination of sabers and daggers, trying to flank you. What do you do?*

PLAYER (SIR EGARY): *Damn! Here we go again . . .*

+28

Trouble in Paradise

GARY FURROWED HIS BROW and rubbed his whiskered chin as he looked down at his desk. He couldn't make heads or tails of what was in front of him. He shot a puzzled look across the desk to his colleague and *Dragon* magazine editor, Tim Kask, who returned Gary's gaze with equal puzzlement.

The objects of study on the desk were a number of photographs of blank bulletin boards, each with a handful of thumbtacks seemingly randomly scattered about them. Meanwhile, stacks of *D&D* books, maps, atlases, and a globe were strewn about the office. The boards had belonged to a young Michigan State college student who had recently disappeared. Evidently the student often played *D&D* with his classmates, and detectives from East Lansing had brought the photos to Lake Geneva for Gary's analysis of the thumbtack positioning to see if there was a *D&D*-related code or map that might give a clue to the student's whereabouts. Gary and Kask had been cross-referencing their *D&D* materials, as well as Michigan maps, road atlases, and other geographic tools, in an effort to solve the puzzle. It was day three of the analysis.[1]

"You can go back to the Gray House, Tim," said Gary as he slapped his hands down on his desk. "There's nothing new here."

"You don't need to tell me twice," replied Kask with his usual gruffness. He hastily rose and left, in case Gary decided to change his mind.

A few minutes later, two suited men with East Lansing Police Department badges on their belts entered Gary's office.

"Sorry, boys, there's still nothin' here," said Gary.

"Are you sure?" replied the detective with the mustache. "We have strong reason to believe that these boards hold a clue and that this disappearance is somehow related to your game."

"How and according to who?" asked Gary pointedly.

"That's confidential," the other detective replied.

"Right, right, confidential—I remember," snapped Gary. He, Brian Blume, and Tim Kask had wasted the better part of three days now fooling around with these pictures, and he was out of patience with this fruitless exercise.

"Well, I'm sorry that we can't help you, and I certainly hope you find him," Gary said as he stood up, signaling that it was time for his guests to leave. "Good luck."

As the dejected detectives left TSR's Hotel Clair offices, Gary felt sure that this was the last he would hear about this strange but sad case.

A FEW DAYS LATER, Gary was sitting at the kitchen table reading his morning newspaper when his mouth dropped open. Very little took Gary by surprise these days, but what he had just read left him utterly stunned.

Gary's eyes darted back and forth on the page. He struggled to understand what he was reading. To be sure, he understood the individual words on the page, but when arranged in this particular way, their meaning seemed entirely preposterous to him. He returned to the beginning:

Tunnels Are Searched for Missing Student
By Nathaniel Sheppard Jr.
Special to the New York Times

EAST LANSING, Mich., Sept. 7—The authorities at Michigan State University and private investigators are combing an eight-mile maze of steam tunnels underneath the campus here in an effort to find a 16-year-old computer science student who disappeared Aug. 15.

The student's disappearance in summer school is shrouded in mystery, and school officials believe that he may . . . have become lost in the tunnels, which carry heat to campus buildings, while playing an elaborate version of a bizarre intellectual game called Dungeons and Dragons . . .

James Dallas Egbert [III], a sophomore, was last seen on campus Aug. 15 . . . He was reported missing a week later by a former roommate, and the search is now in its third week . . .

Captain [Ferman] Badgley said the authorities had received anonymous telephone calls from a woman who said Mr. Egbert and other students had been playing Dungeons and Dragons in the steam tunnels and that if the student was found he would be found dead.

Dungeons and Dragons is a game produced by T.R.S. Hobbies of Lake Geneva, Wis. The game is an apparent takeoff on the popular J.R.R. Tolkien trilogy, "Lord of the Rings," a fantasy that deals with the search for a magic ring and features an assortment of terrible creatures that menace the heroes and threaten the world . . .

Students at Michigan State University and elsewhere reportedly have greatly elaborated on the game, donning medieval costumes and using outdoor settings to stage the contest.[2]

"What the hell game are they talking about?" Gary said in disbelief. "If they were 'donning medieval costumes and using outdoor settings to stage the contest,' it sure as hell wasn't *D&D*!"

Gary couldn't decide what upset him more, the fate of this poor missing kid or how terribly *D&D* had been misrepresented in this widely distributed, high-profile *New York Times* article. Of course, Gary disliked the writings of Tolkien and didn't cherish seeing *D&D* represented as a "takeoff" on *Lord of the Rings*. To be sure, this was not the first time *D&D* had been associated with Tolkien, leading Gary to say, "The 'influences' from JRRT's work that I included in the game were mainly there to interest others in playing it, not what caused me to want to create it."[3] Suffice it to say, this Tolkien business was already a bone in Gary's throat. He also took considerable exception to *D&D* being called out as a "bizarre intellectual game," not to mention the fact that they got his company's name wrong, rendering it as "T.R.S. Hobbies."

"Real A-plus reporting!" he muttered to himself. Because Gary was already aware of the incident and its few known details, the representations in the *New York Times* seemed all the more preposterous.

No sooner had Gary taken in this morning's "news" than the phone rang.

What now? he thought as he labored up from his chair to answer.

He tried to avoid taking late-night and early-morning calls these days, as their volume had increased to unmanageable levels a few years back. Gamers from all over the country would call him for rules judgments, dungeon mastering tips, and sometimes jobs. While he enjoyed the banter, he no longer had the time to be so accommodating. As a result, his number had been unlisted since 1976. Today, however, somebody had the inside number, and he would make an exception and pick up the phone.

It was September 8, 1979, and *Dungeons & Dragons* had seen extraordinary success since its first release in 1974, with annual sales trending toward $2 million. In fact, almost everything would have been perfect but for what troubled Gary this morning: *Dungeons & Dragons* had just been unfairly attached to an unfortunate incident involving the disappearance of a young college student, and the story was now getting major media coverage. From a public relations perspective, the *Times'* description of the incident just added insult to injury for TSR, as it had already gotten unwelcome attention thanks to the ongoing litigation with Dave Arneson. Less pressing, but also troubling, was that Brian and his younger brother, Kevin, who had joined TSR's accounting department in November 1976 and since been brought into management, had begun to leverage their family's control of TSR, and Gary found them increasingly difficult to work with.

"Hello?" said Gary as he picked up the phone.

The voice on the other end belonged to an agitated Brian Blume.

Gary listened for a few moments, then calmly replied, "Yes, I saw it, Brian. It's utter nonsense."

Over the last few years, whenever Brian's stress level rose, Gary seemed to relax, and vice versa—a symptom of their increasingly antagonistic relationship.

"Don't worry about it. This will all blow over in a day or two," Gary said, and he hung up.

Unfortunately for Gary, the James Dallas Egbert III story didn't blow over. Instead, a national media frenzy would come to a boil in the days that followed. Articles similar to that in the *New York Times* appeared in every major U.S. newspaper, featuring headlines such as FANTASY CULT ANGLE PROBED IN SEARCH FOR COMPUTER WHIZ and STUDENT MAY HAVE LOST HIS LIFE TO INTELLECTUAL FANTASY GAME.[4] All over the country, self-pronounced experts came out of the woodwork with theories about the dangerous psychological effects of *D&D* on teens and how the game blurred the lines between fantasy and reality.

Even after Egbert was recovered alive and well in Louisiana by private detective William Dear just a few weeks later, stories about the dangers of *D&D* continued to gain traction. The media frenzy peaked in a 1980 novel by Rona Jaffe, which was turned into a 1981 TV movie called *Mazes and Monsters* starring a young Tom Hanks. *Mazes and Monsters* was a thinly veiled retelling of the Egbert incident based upon Dear's original, and later retracted and disproven, theory about *Dungeons & Dragons* and how the game confuses the real and imaginary among its players.

During Gary's many print and television interviews on the subject, he maintained that all of the speculation about *D&D*'s sinister effects on youth was complete and utter nonsense, calling such claims "as unscientific as you can get—it's nothing but a witch hunt." He later added that Jaffe was "a second-rate author for sure, and her M&M book was an evident potboiler . . . TSR did what was best—ignored the whole thing."[5]

The elements of the James Dallas Egbert III story represented a perfect storm of media sensationalism for TSR, debunked by a less sensational—indeed somber—reality. First, Egbert himself was a troubled young man who was very bright, but eccentric. His interests in computers, science fiction, and fantasy, combined with the fact that he was a five-foot-three-inch sixteen-year-old college freshman, couldn't have done much for his social life. Egbert was also under considerable pressure from his parents to succeed academically, as demonstrated by his already having skipped two grades. Lastly, Egbert was an emerging homosexual, living in a day when this trait was not widely accepted or tolerated. In short, Egbert was a social outcast and "geek" in the classical sense.

William Dear, on the other hand, was the missing ingredient in creating the media circus that ensued. Dear was a Texas-based private investigator hired by Egbert's parents after their son went missing. His methods were known to be unorthodox, while he also seemed fond of media attention. Dear had concocted a number of theories about what had become of James Dallas Egbert III, the most notable of which, and the one he leaked to the press, was his *Dungeons & Dragons* theory. After finding Egbert's *D&D* books in his room and speaking to his friends about the game, Dear surmised that this unusual game must be involved in the disappearance, or at least this was his most alluring theory. "In some instances when a person plays the game [*D&D*] you actually leave your body and go out of your mind,"[6] Dear explained.

Dear later detailed the case in a 1984 book entitled *The Dungeon Master: The Disappearance of James Dallas Egbert III*. Ironically, and contrary to his original theory, his book reveals the real circumstances around the Egbert case and how, once Dear found the young man in Louisiana a few weeks after his disappearance, the private investigator declined to go back to the press out of respect for Egbert's privacy. Yet the *D&D* part of the story was never expressly retracted on a large scale, and media speculation was left to grow unfettered and under false pretenses.

While *D&D*'s reputation declined, Dear found new prominence that he would later leverage into high-profile cases and book deals, some of which featured claims as sensational and outrageous as his original Egbert *D&D* theory. Besides *The Dungeon Master*, Dear would go on to publish *"Please . . . Don't Kill Me": The True Story of the Milo Murder*; the self-effacing *Private Detective: From the Files of the World's Greatest Private Eye*; and the especially absurd *O.J. Is Guilty but Not of Murder* and *O.J. Is Innocent and I Can Prove It: The Shocking Truth About the Murders of Nicole Simpson and Ron*

Goldman.[7] For an encore, there was Dear's involvement in Fox Television's 1995 *Alien Autopsy* broadcast.

In retrospect, the Egbert incident was but the first in a long chain of social controversies that stalked *D&D* over the coming years. The theories concocted by Dear and popularized by the media had opened the floodgates to a level of scrutiny and controversy around this unusual game that it could not seem to shake.

D&D, however, was not unique among table games in attracting controversy. In fact, new and experimental wargames had been drawing the ire of concerned parents since the beginning of organized wargaming with H. G. Wells' 1913 publication of *Little Wars*. Contemporary reviewers of Wells' seminal wargame held concern that "peace-loving parents will frown upon H. G. Wells for writing *Little Wars*,"[8] while another warned that the game might encourage children to entertain "war thoughts."[9]

Now, thanks to the imaginative William Dear and overzealous media, *D&D* was thought to be psychologically damaging to teens. Such sensationalism would continue to grow around the game; within a few short years, assertions would pop up that *D&D* was associated with suicidal tendencies among teens, not to mention the theory that it was used as a recruitment tool for devil worship. As Gary would explain it, "News media seeks the sensational in order to attract viewers, sell air-time ads, make money . . . The James Dallas Egbert III case was the turning point. Thanks to the publicity-seeking [detective] brought in, and the following ill-informed news media coverage—sensationalist to the extreme—there was a barrage of inaccurate stories and further biased charges of baseless sort. These in toto brought forth suicide, Satanism, and mind-control as supposed dangers of the game. Add to that the difficulty of the ignorant in understanding the RPG form, and what can one expect?"[10]

These later claims about suicide and devil worship were, in large part, the work of a grieving mother named Patricia Pulling, whose son, Irving, committed suicide in the summer of 1982. Searching for answers about his death, she discovered that Irving had played *Dungeons & Dragons*, and she believed the game was responsible. It turned out that

Irving had been playing the game for a couple of years, but she hadn't discovered this until after his death. Gary later suggested that this was a possible clue to the level of her parental involvement. She subsequently founded a group known as Bothered About Dungeons & Dragons (BADD), to which she committed significant time and resources. This organization, which picked up traction among religious fundamentalist and censorship groups, not to mention the media, also served as a vehicle for her book, imaginatively titled *The Devil's Web: Who Is Stalking Your Children for Satan?*

Nationwide, the efforts of sanctimonious critics and censors were gaining traction. Worried mothers were coming out of the woodwork, afflicted with *D&D* panic. One such mother even claimed that one of her son's *D&D* books screamed when she threw it in the fire.[11] Of course, when Gary heard of this, he only added proverbial fuel to the fire by offering $1 million to anyone who could pull a *D&D* product off the shelf and make it scream by burning it. Suffice it to say, he never had to pay. Nonetheless, these frightening claims by self-righteous monitors, along with a series of alarming comic strips by Jack Chick illustrating the insidious and allegedly satanic nature of *D&D*, left a bad taste in the mouth of concerned parents for years to come—a reputation the game has not entirely shaken to this day.

Before the panic waned, many other opportunistic and attention-seeking "experts," such as psychiatrist Dr. Thomas Radecki, also rode this wave of *D&D* fearmongering. Radecki, a founding member of the National Coalition on TV Violence, famously opined, "There is no doubt in my mind that the game Dungeons and Dragons is causing young men to kill themselves and others . . . Although I am sure that the people at TSR mean no harm, that is exactly what their games are causing."[12] Ironically, it appears that Radecki was the one with more uneviable faults, as his medical license was subsequently lost on two separate occasions, amid claims of sexual misconduct with patients.[13]

Despite the shaky credibility of his accusers, Gary still found himself beset with these attacks, needing to vociferously defend *D&D*, not only through the '80s but throughout his career. Of these he would later say, "In many ways I still resent the wretched yellow journalism that was clearly evident in (the media's) treatment of the game—*60 Minutes* in particular. I've never watched that show after Ed Bradley's interview with me because they rearranged my answers. When I sent some copies of letters from mothers of those two children who had committed suicide who said the game had nothing to do with it, they refused to do a retraction or even mention it on air. What bothered me is that I was getting death threats, telephone calls, and letters. I was a little nervous. I had a bodyguard for a while."[14]

Dungeons & Dragons would never find widespread media vindication from these outrageous claims even after they had been disproven on countless occasions, most notably in Michael Stackpole's 1989 article "Game Hysteria and the Truth," in which he shows that role-playing gamers are statistically less likely to commit suicide than nongamers. A second piece, Stackpole's 1990 "The Pulling Report," systematically undermines the credibility and research methods of *D&D*'s opponents, most notably Patricia Pulling. Given that board-gaming mainstays such as Parker Brothers and Avalon Hill had in years past gotten away with much bolder games of the occult, with their releases of *Ouija* and *Black Magic*, respectively, why was TSR and its geeky flagship game, *Dungeons & Dragons*, so vilified?[15] Whatever the reasons, TSR would be vindicated in its bottom line. In the year or so following the Egbert case, *D&D*'s sales had jumped from $2 million to over $8 million, more than double the company's projections. Within a few years, TSR's annual revenue would reach $30 million. True to the notion that "all press is good press," and in a bizarre twist of fate, *D&D* had benefited tremendously from the national uproar that surrounded the game. But it was also these controversies that would simultaneously make and break this unique game, providing it significant niche success, but forever holding it out of the mainstream.

+29

A Devastating Loss

"MAMA!"[1] EXCLAIMED GARY, SEEMINGLY out of nowhere, as he watched his mother's casket being lowered into the ground. Gary shielded his face with his hands as tears suddenly burst forth from his eyes, a phenomenon neither his wife nor his children had ever seen before.

It was the second time in five years that Gary found himself at Oak Hill Cemetery burying an important person in his life. The loss of Don Kaye had been hard, but life went on. This loss was different, though. This was his mother, the woman who had raised him and sustained him through hard times both as a child and as an adult. She had been a stabilizing force in his life, perhaps the only constant stabilizing force, now gone.

Gary was an orphan—he felt truly and completely alone.

The subsequent weeks and months passed slowly, and while Gary carried on business as usual at TSR, something had changed inside him. He had become removed and distant. He felt as though he was watching his life from the outside, as if his body was on autopilot. He began to think about the things he did. Were they important? Gary didn't know anymore. One thing that Gary did know for sure—and his mother's death had served as a poignant reminder—sooner or later, he was going to die.

In 1980 Gary had turned forty-one. By this time he had become quite well known through his involvement with *Dungeons & Dragons* and was now something of a favorite son in Lake Geneva. This was an irony because when he was a youth, teenager, and young man, the town had seemingly wanted nothing to do with him. Now he found himself serving on the board of a bank that used to refuse him loans and was frequently honored by town leaders at parties and civic events. Fame had brought with it many "friends" and "supporters" that Gary never knew he had.

Meanwhile, Gary's company, TSR, continued to flourish. Revenues were on pace to quadruple over the previous year, bolstered by the success of its *D&D* and *AD&D* lines, and supported with new, strong-performing products like 1978's *Gamma World: Science Fantasy Role-Playing Game* and 1980's *Top Secret*, the industry's first espionage-themed RPG. These successes were due in no small part to TSR's 1979 exclusive distribution agreement with publishing behemoth Random House—a partnership orchestrated by Gary and initiated by Random House Vice President Mildred Marmur.

Marmur, like Gary when playtesting and naming his fantasy game, knew when to listen to her children. It was her twelve-year-old son Nathaniel who had become enthralled with *D&D* and recommended that his mother look into the game on Random House's behalf. On September 4, 1979, just days before the James Dallas Egbert III story broke on a national scale, the Random House executive had Gary on the phone inquiring about TSR's interest in publishing with the renowned press. Of course, TSR was its own publisher, so there was little interest there, but when Marmur mentioned a distribution deal, Gary's interest was piqued. Even at this time, TSR was still largely working catalog and hobby store channels and did not have a particularly wide or formalized distribution network. A week later, Gary and TSR vice president Will Niebling were on a plane to New York to finalize the deal. When they left, *Dungeons & Dragons* had access to the commercial reach of the nation's largest publisher.[2]

The timing of the deal proved serendipitous for both TSR and Random House, as it occurred in the wake of the Egbert incident and the media frenzy that followed. Now the same mysterious and controversial game that was making headlines all over the country could be picked up at any bookstore. With these events, TSR quickly became a national leader in the game publishing industry.

Nowadays Gary was always "on"—he felt he had to be. He was, after all, the president of a big and growing company, and he had to play the part. Even with all of this responsibility, Gary continued to crank out bestselling material of his own, including *AD&D* adventure modules like *Tomb of Horrors* in 1978, *The Village of Hommlet* in 1979, and the wildly successful *The Keep on the Borderlands* in 1980. Most recently, Gary completed an extensive campaign world book based on his original in-house campaign entitled *The World of Greyhawk Fantasy World Setting.*

Between his position and his continuing level of production, Gary got a lot of attention. In fact, according to some employees, "everyone treated him like he was a god."[3] As such, even Gary would forget who he was from time to time, and it was here that his mother had been most valuable, with her ability to bring him back to earth. Almina "Posey" Burdick Gygax Gatlin, much advanced in age, once divorced and twice widowed, had become a regular visitor at her son's fourteen-room mansion and twenty-three-acre horse farm, located at 7201 E. Starkwood Road in Clinton, Wisconsin, that Gary had nicknamed "Dragonlands." The grand colonial mansion featured a large pool overlooking a barn where Gary and Mary Jo kept and bred Arabian horses—a hobby they originally undertook as a tax shelter.[4]

Gary and Mary Jo had bought the property in July 1979 for the bargain price of $325,000 when the previous owners encountered marital difficulties. Ironically, this property had been on the couple's radar since 1977, when Mary Jo hung a real estate brochure for the home on the kitchen bulletin board and told the family, "We will live here in a couple of years."[5] It was their dream home.

When Gary moved into Dragonlands, he finally felt as though he had made it—like royalty. But when Posey visited, she held Gary's ego in check. It was during such a visit to the mansion that she experienced chest pains, which got progressively worse through the day. By the time Gary and Mary Jo got her into the car and were heading to the hospital, however, it was too late. Gary's mother suffered what would prove to be her fatal heart attack while in the car on the way to the emergency room. This episode left Gary and Mary Jo traumatized. At the hospital, Posey was immediately put on life support, remaining on it for a few days. On October 20, 1980—the sixteenth birthday of Gary's second daughter and Posey's favorite grandchild, Heidi—she was taken off life support and passed away.

Adding another layer of instability to their lives, Gary and Mary Jo had recently dissociated themselves from the Jehovah's Witnesses. Gary's "controversial" game was met with disapproval from their local congregation, as were his smoking and drinking, and they had decided to part ways.

So much of Gary's support network that had sustained him all these years was now gone. Who were his friends—his real friends? Whom could he count on? Many of his earliest friends and supporters like Dave Megarry, the Kuntz brothers and most recently, Tim Kask had since parted ways with TSR. Even Gary's manual Royal typewriter—his "faithful old clickbox"[6]—that had gotten him through his earliest versions of *Chainmail* and *D&D* had ceased to function in March of that year. Gary was off balance and alone.

Through all of this turmoil, Gary had started to change. He had begun saying to his family and friends, "I'm going to die soon—I'm going to experience everything."[7] And Gary's demeanor had indeed changed. Oddly enough, it had lightened. His personality became almost unrecognizable to those who knew him best, a change that would have been welcome except for the melancholy for which this behavior was so clearly compensating.

One thing was for certain: Gary's life was a far cry from "cushy Camelot,"[8] as it had been described in a *People* magazine article earlier in the year. In fact, the closest thing to "cushy" for Gary now was his regular booth at the Lake Geneva Playboy Club, where his visits became increasingly frequent. Meanwhile, as his royalty checks reached several hundred thousand dollars per year, his tastes grew more extravagant, and his already erratic temperament became even more so. His highs were very high, and his lows were intolerable.

Of course, Gary wasn't the only executive at TSR with an uneven temperament. In fact, according to some TSR employees, the Blume brothers made Gary's abrasive moments seem mild by comparison. These issues of temperament, ego, and the inability among TSR's ownership to peacefully coexist would have significant consequences for both Gary and the Blume brothers in the future.

+30

The Dictator

"I don't care what Gary said. I own controlling interest in this company and it will be done the way I say!"[1] a voice bellowed from down the hall, spoken deliberately loud enough for all to hear.

The voice was that of Brian Blume, who was reacting to an instruction Gary had delivered earlier that day. Gary was, after all, still the president and CEO of the company, but without a controlling interest, he was little more than a figurehead. Unfortunately, by 1982 raucous displays such as this had become commonplace among all of TSR's leadership. "Philosophically we [TSR's leadership] run in different directions,"[2] Brian had said in a recent interview, with a certain amount of understatement.

Brian's brother, Kevin, for his part, had recently stopped playing *D&D* and was now interested in "playing a much larger game called business. That's why we're intuitively good businessmen—because games are a great way to learn,"[3] he would say in the same *Inc.* magazine article. This "game" evidently included firing a dozen employees in April 1981 for having a bad attitude, in what was known to employees as "the Great Purge."[4]

In Gary's mind, the Blume brothers, perhaps emboldened by their newfound power and wealth, seldom missed an opportunity to remind him, or anyone else for that matter, who was in charge. According to Gary, this included a proposed policy where "Kevin [Blume] was going to use his 'medical training' to examine employees for drug use and fire them if he found they were using . . . When one of their relatives was discharged for lack of capacity, though, she was allowed plenty of time before having to leave."[5] Later it was discovered that TSR was "paying for her college tuition."[6] According to employees, Kevin Blume's "medical training" amounted to being a military medic.

Gary had become callused and found ways to deflect the growing authoritarianism of the Blumes, but these defense mechanisms had left him brooding and inaccessible. He often exhibited a disconnected and indifferent demeanor, punctuated by intense fits of anger. His experience with and under the Blumes for the last several years had taken its toll and left the otherwise jovial and childlike man broken, bitter, and occasionally ruthless.

Gary could hear what he thought was the anxious scamper of staffers' feet rushing up and down the hallway, eager to fulfill the demands of of his partner and now adversary down the hall. His blood began to boil, but then he remembered there was recourse.

Maybe today is the day, he thought. Gary drew a blank piece of letterhead from his overflowing desk and quickly scrolled it into his typewriter. He hurriedly lit a cigarette, as to not disrupt his momentum. He was moving with purpose. The hum of his IBM Selectric typewriter seemed to beckon him, as it had done so many times in the past. He knew this sound. It was the sound of creation—the sound of action.

The *snap* of the keys was slow and sporadic at first but soon grew in frequency and fluidity. A smile had started to replace the frown on Gary's face. Before long he was nearing the end of his composition. After a few more snaps of the typewriter, which he delivered playfully like a pianist completing a recital, Gary rolled out the page. He leaned back in his office chair, and read.

To: TSR Hobbies, Inc. Board of Directors
CC: All Employees
From: E. Gary Gygax
Re: Resignation of Duties

To Whomever it May Concern:
This letter serves as notice that I, Ernest Gary Gygax, am formally resigning from my position as President and CEO of TSR Hobbies, Inc., effective immediately.[7]

The letter continued with a listing of the causes for this decision—his personal version of Martin Luther's Ninety-five Theses. It was formal, to be sure, but it also included some subtle digs to let the Blumes and everyone else know that he was done being pushed around.[8] Gary hastily grabbed a thumbtack from his desk and rose to post the letter on the hallway bulletin board. Just then Gary was interrupted by his creative assistant, Frank Mentzer, who was holding a bright red booklet featuring an illustration of a warrior battling a fearsome red dragon.

"Hey, Gary, you wanna take a look at this? It's a proof for the new basic set. I'd say it turned out pretty well . . ." He handed the booklet to Gary, then left.

Mentzer had joined TSR two years earlier and had quickly earned Gary's trust, not by routinely agreeing with him, as there were already too many yes-men around for Gary's taste, but instead by pointing out his errors. This had been the case during the development of Gary's adventure module, *Keep on the Borderlands*, which featured many clerics and holy men, but no chapel to justify their presence and employ. Shortly after his arrival at TSR in January 1980, Mentzer was quick to point out this omission, and he instantly earned Gary's respect. Soon thereafter, Mentzer further distinguished himself by winning Best Overall Dungeon Master at TSR's first DM Invitational. Following this honor, Gary asked him to found and administer the Role Playing Game Association (RPGA), a trade group started by TSR to encourage the spread of role playing in the gaming community. With these successes, Mentzer quickly became Gary's right-hand man.

The booklet that Mentzer had handed to Gary was the soon-to-be released *Dungeons & Dragons Basic Rules Set 1*, a revised-and-expanded version of previous basic sets released in 1977 and 1981, respectively. It had indeed turned out well, featuring a much-needed revision to the rules by Mentzer, not to mention its vibrant colors and top-notch illustrations by Larry Elmore and Jeff Easley. In fact, Gary had personally inspired the cover during an unscheduled visit by Elmore, who had become frustrated with the numerous secondhand comments he had received about how to revise it, none of which had contained any direct explanation as to what really needed to happen. Once Gary leaned forward and put up his hands like claws, explaining that the dragon needed to be "jumping out at you,"[9] Elmore knew exactly what to do.

As he flipped the pages of the newest version of TSR's flagship product, Gary suddenly remembered why he couldn't post the letter—why he couldn't leave. He loved creating games. He loved *D&D*, and he couldn't just leave it behind, no matter what indignities the Blumes put him through.[10]

Damn it! Foiled again! Gary thought as he grabbed the unposted resignation letter and tore it up.

This was not the first time he had considered resigning . . . and it probably wouldn't be the last.

+31

Parting Ways

"More champagne, ma'am?" asked the flight attendant.

"Yes, please," quietly replied Mary Jo.

"And for you, sir?"

"Absolutely," bellowed Gary. "This is the life, huh, Mary?" he said as he raised the glass to his lips.

"I guess so," she softly replied.

As the engines of the 747, en route to London, hummed ominously in the background, Gary, Mary Jo, Luke, Cindy, and a couple of Cindy's friends sat comfortably in the aircraft's forward section—in first class.[1] It was always first class these days, but this wasn't necessarily "the life."

Tensions between Gary and Mary Jo had continued to rise of late, and talk of divorce had entered the discussion on numerous occasions. In fact, Gary had threatened to cancel the kids' trip to London without assurances from Mary Jo that they would stay together.

"So, like I was saying, now is the time, Mary Jo. We need to go while we have momentum. *D&D* is ready to explode, and we've finally got interest from Hollywood. We'll just sell the horses and the farm and go!"

"But what about my mother? What about Ernie and Elise?" retorted Mary Jo.

By now, Gary was agitated. He pulled his seat upright and turned to his wife.

"They can come too! Mary . . . with the Blumes running TSR, you know I can't stay in Lake Geneva. I know we've had our problems in the past, but things will be different there—you'll see."

Gary realized with some irony that he was now fighting to save a marriage that had become far from civil. In fact, anyone close to the

Gygaxes knew that there were many "knock-down, drag-out"[2] skir-
mishes between the two. It was also known that there had been affairs
on Gary's part, but the two had struggled through and persisted in their
love for each other.

"I'm sorry, Gary. I'm not moving with you. Not this time." said Mary
Jo coolly.

She didn't look at him, but instead looked down and swirled her
glass of champagne.

"What do you mean?" asked Gary. "You're not divorcing me? You're
not divorcing me!"[3]

Mary Jo quickly raised her glass of champagne and drank it down in
one gulp. She shut her eyes tight and breathed heavily for a moment.

"I'm sorry, Gary," sighed Mary. "It's over."[4]

To Gary, the already cramped first-class compartment seemed to
shrink, and he felt as though the air had just been sucked out of the
cabin. He thought to respond, but he knew Mary Jo too well. He could
see in her face that this was not a ploy. She was serious, and she wasn't
going to change her mind.

The "energetic,"[5] if not tumultuous, relationship had been one of
conflict over the years. But it also had been one of tight partnership,
shared tribulations, and even intense passion, as evidenced by their five
children. Now the energy was gone. Too much had changed. For too
many years they had been ships passing in the night. They were different people now, each set on a course that did not include the other.

It was March 1983, and Gary had been spending much of his time in
Hollywood laying the groundwork for a soon-to-be formed subsidiary
of TSR called Dungeons & Dragons Entertainment Corp.[6] Though
Gary was eager to expand TSR's presence into other forms of media,
he hadn't undertaken this enterprise entirely by choice. Gary had essentially been forced out of his day-to-day management and creative role at
TSR and directed by its board to manage this new Hollywood venture.
This had been orchestrated by the Blume brothers, who now used their
majority stake in the company to exercise absolute authority.[7] To this
end, the mission of the startup Dungeons & Dragons Entertainment
Corp. was to introduce and promote the *Dungeons & Dragons* brand

into new media, while ensuring that Gary and the Blume brothers wouldn't have to share an office location.

Gary leaned back in his seat. His heart was racing, and his throat felt choked. Fearing that his emotions might get the best of him, he quickly rose and headed to the small lavatory at the rear of the cabin.

If not for the dead seriousness of the moment, the sight of the tipsy, rotund man fumbling along the aisle and forcing himself through the narrow lavatory doorway was almost comical. By this time Gary's uneven temperament was perfectly matched by his appearance, which featured a bushy graying beard and long, but balding, salt-and-pepper hair. He had the frazzled look of an absentminded college professor—someone too caught up in his own affairs to care what others thought.

Gary quickly slammed the door and rested with his arms extended around the miniature sink, his head hanging down.

"Damn it!" he shouted as he cupped one hand under the water and operated the sink with the other.

Gary removed his glasses and splashed the cool water on his face. It didn't seem to have any effect. He looked up at himself in the mirror as he rubbed his hand down his face.

What's next? he thought.

For the next several hours Gary seethed in his seat next to his wife without speaking a word. It was the worst flight he had ever taken. To think that just hours earlier they had departed Dragonlands with so much excitement and optimism about their trip. Now divorce loomed on the horizon.

Gary felt broken and angry—he couldn't think straight. His life had spiraled out of control. First the death of his mother, then the loss of creative control over TSR, and now the end of more than two decades of marriage.

The pressures of an early marriage and several children paired with his demanding schedule at TSR had worn on both spouses considerably. Mary Jo had taken to heavy drinking, while Gary's growing cocaine use aggravated his already eccentric temperament. The couple's behaviors had set them on a collision course for which they had finally made contact.

"Flight attendants, prepare for landing," the loudspeaker blared.

Maybe we never had a chance, he thought. "If you believe in Chinese astrology, it was a foregone conclusion. She's a buffalo and I'm a tiger. The two don't mix,"[8] he would later explain.

It's over, Gary told himself as the plane touched the ground. *Move on . . . Maybe Hollywood will be a fresh start.*

+32

There's No Business Like Show Business

"WE WOULD LIKE TO acquire you, joint venture with you, or engage in just about any co-venture you name,"[1] said the short, bespectacled man behind the large desk. His oversized glasses were almost as big and thick as Gary's.

Gary couldn't believe what he was hearing and, for once was at a lack for words.

"I was knocked back on my mental heels, but I think I kept a poker face,"[2] he would later say about the event.

The year was 1984 and the man behind the oversized mahogany desk was Sid Sheinberg, president of Universal Studios. Sheinberg was a giant in the movie industry, having been behind blockbuster films such as *Jaws* and more recently *E.T.* He had also been integral in the emergence of directing legend Steven Spielberg, among others. The movie posters around his lavish office served as trophies of his accomplishments. For the last hour, Gary had met with the studio head discussing the prospect of a *Dungeons & Dragons* movie. Now it looked like it might become a reality.

Gary would not have gotten the meeting if Sheinberg had not already been familiar with *D&D*, and the game's brief inclusion in *E.T.* was proof of just that. It was certainly the game the "kids" were playing these days, and both Spielberg and Sheinberg knew it. By now, TSR's annual sales pushed $30 million and *D&D* products could be found on the shelves of every major bookstore, hobby shop, and toy store.

As a matter of context, TSR's revenue of $30 million, even in 1984 dollars, isn't astronomical, but still quite impressive considering that many of its products were developed and marketed to a self-limiting audience: that is, prospective Dungeon Masters, not players. While a module or sourcebook might be purchased by a single Dungeon Master, the materials were regularly used to facilitate gaming groups of four to twenty individuals. The pricey *Dungeon Master's Guide* even includes this caution in its introduction: "Discourage players from reading this book, and certainly don't let players consult it during the game."[3] For better or worse, this may have been an inherent flaw in TSR's business model. The company also suffered from the rampant unlicensed photocopying of TSR products—the reason behind the hard-to-duplicate and exotic aqua, magenta, and chartreuse colors of *AD&D* adventure modules, and their light blue Xerox-proof adventure maps. Thus, TSR's $30 million represented a popularity and prominence far greater than the numbers would suggest.

Of course, *Dungeons & Dragons* was still not without its controversy, as both Gary and Sheinberg were well aware. Indeed, claims that the game was harmful to young people were now frequent and widespread. But both men also understood the axiom that all press was good press. The media frenzies and other sensationalist claims had done nothing but spark a surge in sales and interest in *Dungeons & Dragons* that it never could have achieved through conventional marketing. *D&D* was now ready for the next level: the big screen.

As Gary gathered himself, he had the strong impulse to shake hands with Mr. Sheinberg and make a deal. But only a moment later he was struck by a troubling thought—the Blume brothers. His stomach suddenly got queasy as he realized that a deal with Sheinberg and Universal was not a decision he could make alone. According to Gary, "the reality of the Blumes came to cloud the rosy vistas I had glimpsed."[4]

"Thank you for the offer, Mr. Sheinberg," he finally said. "I assure you that we are very interested, but I am only a minority partner at TSR and will need to discuss it with my board of directors at our next meeting."

"Suit yourself," said Sheinberg. "We'll talk then."

As Gary's car pulled out of the grand studio gates, he began to get caught up in the energy and excitement of this town that had made and destroyed so many dreams. He could see the clouds parting for him and his creation. He had finally found an avenue to make *D&D* fully mainstream.

To this end, Gary had already developed a script with local cartoon writer Flint Dille, with whom he and his son Ernie had worked with recently on a series of choose-your-own-adventure game books entitled *Sagard the Barbarian*. Dille, like seemingly everyone in Hollywood, had an interesting story of his own. His grandfather, John F. Dille, had been the head of the National Newspaper Syndicate and had published the original *Buck Rogers* comic strip—his family still owned the rights. Flint had recently worked on a CBS cartoon called *Mr. T*, based on the actor of the same name. Between the work of Gary and Dille, not to mention a discarded script that TSR had commissioned the year prior from James Goldman, famed screenwriter of *A Lion in Winter*, Gary already had over $1 million invested in the movie project—a movie, Gary had promised *Dragon* readers, that would rival *Star Wars* and *Raiders of the Lost Ark* in quality.

Gary was certain the day looked more sparkling and pristine than it had before. Everything seemed a bit more vibrant, inasmuch as anything looks vibrant from the backseat of a tinted-windowed Cadillac Seville. This movie thing was going to work.

"This is our next stop," said Gary as he handed an address to his fair-haired driver and bodyguard, Jim Johnson—a transplant from Lake Geneva.

So far, Gary's time in Hollywood had been well spent. He had already managed to get a cartoon version of *Dungeons & Dragons* produced by CBS, which starred the voice of Don Most (who had played Ralph Malph on *Happy Days*), and the show led its Saturday-morning time slot. This and other successes with the *Dungeons & Dragons* game and cartoon, such as a lucrative licensing agreements with toymakers Mattel, LJN, and Larami, had afforded Gary luxuries such as his rental of a six-acre Beverly Hills estate once owned by fabled producer/director

King Vidor, complete with a bar, pool table, hot tub, and peach tree. From the patio of King Vidor's mansion one could see all the way to Catalina Island and hear the occasional howl of a coyote. After only a year, Gary had fully assimilated into the Hollywood lifestyle, enjoying the ambience of the culture.

Of course, this lifestyle also had its hazards, which for Gary included an appetite for young women and a growing taste for cocaine and other recreational drugs. For lack of a better term, Gary was living the "high life." It was not uncommon for him to be seen in one of the "power booths"[5] at the celebrated Beverly Hills Hotel in company with one or more twentysomething Hollywood starlets. He was also known to host extravagant parties at his estate, including an especially memorable event hosting contestants of the Miss Beverly Hills International Beauty Pageant. More frequently, though, the estate was populated by the team of writers working on the CBS cartoon, who would come by the mansion to game or work. It had become clear that Gary's last few years of terrific success, after many years of poverty, had created and nurtured his appetites for a larger-than-life reality. This, coupled with the instability caused by the death of his mother and the end of his marriage of more than twenty years, rendered him off balance and volatile at times, but also oddly fun and carefree. Only the six-by-twelve-foot sand gaming table he'd set up in the property's converted barn and the occasional visit from TSR's entertainment attorney and Gary's old buddy Mike Magida served as reminders of Gary's humble gaming beginnings.

Gary's two sons, twenty-four-year-old Ernie and thirteen-year-old Luke, had also come to live with him and share in the luxury. Ernie worked on the *Dungeons & Dragons* cartoon and other TSR projects, while Luke was kept busy with high school, gaming, and sports. Nonetheless, with a panoramic view from the mansion and Hollywood beauty queens hanging around the premises, it was hard for the young men not to get caught up in the fantasy that was now their reality. For boys who had grown up with few toys, worn hand-me-down clothes, and never got to pick out what they wanted from the grocery store, this lifestyle was almost too good to be true.[6] In fact, Gary had even recently investigated getting Mr. T to make an appearance at Luke's birthday party, but he thought the $5,000 price tag was unreasonable, and the idea was scrapped. In short, it wasn't clear whether Gary served as more of a friend or a father to his sons during this time. What was clear was that Gary's inner child was alive, well, and flourishing.

Just hours after leaving the meeting with Sheinberg, Gary took another meeting, and for a second time that day he left in disbelief. This meeting had been with legendary actor and director Orson Welles, star of the iconic films *Citizen Kane* and *The Third Man*. Welles had just agreed to join the *D&D* movie project in a main supporting role, as the "villainous mage."[7] Gary had been a fan of Welles' work since he was a boy, and he was astounded to think that the acclaimed actor was going to be a part of his *D&D* movie project. When discussing the project years later, Gary made sure to point out that "I find no greatness through association."[8] Of course, Gary didn't need greatness through association—the future would judge his own accomplishments.

"Barney's Beanery," Gary said to his driver as he entered the back of the dark blue Cadillac.

This would certainly be an occasion to celebrate. He had not been this excited since *D&D* had first taken off. This movie deal was going to be the next big thing for the franchise. But as the car rounded the corner of Santa Monica Boulevard near the western end of Route 66, the troubling thought of the Blumes returned.

Even they will be able to see the opportunity here, won't they? he thought.

His stomach again grew sick, and he was no longer in the mood to eat, let alone celebrate.

Despite Gary's concerns about the Blume brothers and their support of the project, Gary pushed forward with the plan over the coming weeks. He managed to get his script in front of another prominent producer and director, John Boorman, who had films such as *Deliverance* and, more recently, *Excalibur* to his credit. Boorman was interested in producing and directing the film. The only remaining step was to present the current package to Sheinberg, who had already agreed in principle to working on such a project. In fact, all the stars were perfectly aligned for Gary—that is, until he got a disturbing phone call from New York.

✝33

The Coup

"IN SUMMARY, GENTLEMEN, I demand the resignation of Kevin Blume as CEO due to his clear mismanagement of TSR," Gary calmly stated to a group of five men seated around a conference table at TSR's Lake Geneva headquarters.

Kevin Blume could do nothing but glare at Gary, who had dismantled his record of leadership over the last half hour.[1]

It was December 1984, and the call Gary had gotten from New York just two weeks prior had been from a friend and associate who had informed him that "Kevin Blume was shopping TSR on the city streets,"[2] asking a rumored $6 million for the company.[3] This made Gary's blood boil. Not only did it undermine the company's reputation, but Kevin hadn't even done Gary the courtesy of vetting a sale proposal with TSR's founder and one-third owner.

With the movie deal hanging in the air, as well as a possible spin-off of the CBS cartoon, Gary hastily left California to investigate the allegation of a sale and the financial state of the company. Much to his dismay, Gary discovered that TSR's bottom line was far worse off than he had feared. Though the company was grossing $30 million in sales, it was only marginally profitable. TSR had also managed to accumulate $1.5 million in debt. The financial difficulties were all the more surprising because they had occurred in the face of some ostensibly spectacular successes under the Blumes' watch. These included the successful release of a new role-playing game called *Marvel Super Heroes*, based on characters from the popular Marvel Comics universe, and a 1984 series of bestselling *D&D* modules and novels based on a new campaign setting developed by Tracy Hickman and Margaret Weis called *Dragonlance*.

With these recent successes, Gary could only believe that the financial troubles were the result of numerous missteps by the Blume brothers, which according to Gary included the overprinting of various *D&D* books, leaving millions of unsold copies in inventory; spending more than $1 million on office furniture, much of which was sitting unused, "sufficient for hundreds of employees that did not exist"; overstaffing of the company, which was carrying "300 plus employees, while operations needed less than 200"; and purchasing or leasing "over 70 automobiles."[4] This, not to mention the company's financing the recovery of the *Lucius Newberry*, a 115-foot-long, seven-hundred-passenger excursion boat that had sunk to the bottom of Geneva Lake in 1891, a costly project that netted TSR a rusty ship's boiler;[5] a rumored down payment on a helicopter; and, last but not least, the acquisition of a craft company called Greenfield Needlewomen, allegedly operated as a pet project by Kevin's wife. These expenditures were all in stark contrast to the effusive praise heaped on the company in the 1982 *Inc.* magazine article ironically titled "Tsr Hobbies Mixes Fact and Fantasy," which claimed that TSR was a "well-run operation" and "spends money only with the greatest of reluctance and makes a mission of finding ways to boost its operating margins."[6]

Gary summarized his disturbing findings in a lengthy paper that he had prepared over the previous week. As he finished presenting all of this to the board, the room fell silent for several moments.

Abruptly breaking the tense silence, Brian asked, "And how do you propose we could run the company without Kevin?"

"The same way it did prior to Kevin's elevation to senior management,[7] by you and me," responded Gary with a smirk.

"I cannot run the company anymore!" Brian shouted, slamming his fist on the conference table.

To this, Gary shrugged and said calmly, "Very well. In that case, I will run it alone because Kevin has proven himself totally incompetent."[8] Gary was on top of his game—cool and collected. He had resigned himself to the fact that he would be quickly dismissed from TSR, so he felt at complete liberty to express to the board his view of the dismal state of the company as a result of its Blume-dominated management.

Though the majority of the company was still owned by the Blumes, the structure of the company had changed, which explained this collection of six board members instead of three. In 1982 the Blumes had joined TSR with a trade organization called the American Management Association (AMA). As part of their involvement in the AMA, the Blumes contracted an operational assessment, which included "endless meetings"[9] and workshops for all of the senior-level personnel, held at "expensive"[10] resort facilities. According to Gary, "I attended one only, and my judgment was that the whole of the program was farcical, nothing but waste. As I was vocal in my opinion, it is likely that that solidified the Blumes in their commitment to the AMA."[11]

Based on recommendations from the AMA, and later pressures from TSR's creditors, the Blumes decided to expand TSR's board of directors from three to six members. The three new members would be outside directors, members of the AMA, and accomplished in their various fields, which included law, human resources, and medical equipment. Much to Gary's disappointment, none of the three had any sort of experience in gaming or the hobby industry, nor any serious knowledge or understanding of the creative culture Gary had created at TSR. Early on, these new "outside" directors were openly opposed to Gary and his leadership, as was Gary to them, not so affectionately referring to them as "Moe, Shemp, and Larry."[12] Once this six-member board was fully in place, Gary's initiatives were all dead on arrival, "likely to be voted down by a five to one margin."[13] Gary's control of the company had diminished to a new low.

As Gary studied the faces of this unfriendly board of directors, he realized it was now or never.

What would Conan do? he thought, and with a deep breath he began. "So gentlemen, I move that we vote to remove Mr. Kevin Blume as CEO. All in favor?"

Gary was certain that his would be the only hand in the air, but to his amazement, his was only one of four hands that rose. The outside directors, the "three stooges,"[14] had agreed with him!

Apparently Gary's evidence had been too overwhelming to ignore, even by recruits of the Blume brothers. Ironically, these board members had been brought on in an effort to foil Gary, and now they had given him a majority. The final vote was four to one, as Brian had abstained and Kevin naturally voted for his own retention. Much the same way that Conan might have slain a serpent with his broadsword, Gary had slain Kevin Blume with rhetoric. One thing Gary had not accomplished, however, was regaining control of the company.

Although the new board members had enabled Kevin Blume's removal from TSR, they still didn't like Gary and insisted that outside management help was required. This decision was likely due in part to the financial strain that Gary had subjected the company to as a result of his opulent Hollywood lifestyle and expensive movie development project. As such, the board brought in a member of the AMA as a pro tempore president and initiated an outside audit to determine a valuation of TSR's assets. The board members were convinced that the only chance to preserve TSR was to begin selling the company's assets or auction the company outright. This fire sale was to begin with Gary's beloved *Dragon* magazine, a move that he vehemently opposed.

Ironically, Gary had brought the Blumes an offer from a wealthy Beverly Hills investment firm, the Forman Group, only months earlier in an effort to regain creative control over the company. According to Gary, the deal would have bought out the Blume brothers at $7,500 per share, totaling over $5 million for Brian and $1.5 million for Kevin. Most important to Gary, though, was that he would remain in charge of TSR creatively. As Gary told it, the Blumes had made no response to the offer at the time, but now that Kevin had been ousted from TSR's leadership and Brian had no desire to manage the day-to-day operations, they were both interested in selling their interests.

Vying for control was one thing, but Gary didn't believe that selling the company or any of its assets was the right choice. TSR was Gary's baby, and he was going to do whatever it took to save it. He began by approaching the Forman Group to see if it was still interested. Fortunately it was, and the firm quickly provided TSR a letter of intent regarding the purchase. As the point person with the buyer, Gary was afforded some protection from an otherwise hostile board—just the security he needed to hatch the other half of his plan. Of course, Gary's preference was not to sell anything at all, but to regain control by whatever means necessary. To further this, he attempted to get a modest bank loan to finish production on a couple of important projects that were sure to get TSR back in the black. Then came a brutal surprise: TSR's financial situation had become so precarious that Gary's request for a meager $50,000 was denied. In an attempt to generate more cash for the company, Gary directed his staff to drop all other projects and expedite production of TSR's next *Advanced Dungeons & Dragons* book, slated to be, more or less, a compilation of supplemental *AD&D* rules mined from the last few years of *Dragon* magazine. With the support of the new president, Gary deferred all salary and royalties for himself and convinced his officers to accept 50 percent of their usual compensation. Now, even without the loan, he believed there might be just enough time and resources to get this product to market.

Meanwhile, an external audit discovered disturbing effects of the company's "mismanagement"[15] over the last few years. The company was in financial shambles, and, unsurprisingly, the buyer's offer began to drop with each new auditor's footnote. Just when it seemed that the board would acquiesce to the buyer group and allow TSR to be purchased for pennies on the dollar, Gary announced at the March 18, 1985, board meeting that he had exercised a seven-hundred-share stock option he had held since incorporating TSR Hobbies in 1975.[16] Together with the shares of his family and trusted friends, his maneuver provided him with enough shares to achieve just over 50 percent of the voting power. Brian Blume held a similar option that he chose not to exercise immediately; evidently he had become disillusioned with the company and didn't want to involve himself any deeper.[17]

With these events, and for the first time since Don Kaye's death, Gary Gygax had complete control over TSR, and he wasted no time in flexing his muscle. Upon exercising his option, he called a board meeting at which he declared himself president and CEO (again) and fired the pro tempore president, who, in Gary's estimation, had begun to make unreasonable salary and stock demands. Next, he informed TSR's now virtually powerless board that he was declining the offer on the table from the Forman Group, insisting that TSR could be saved using its existing resources.

Gary was now back in control, but his company still faced severe financial difficulties. His staff was down to ninety-five employees, reduced from a high-water mark of nearly four hundred worldwide in 1983, and many of those who were still with the company were working for reduced or deferred salaries. Gary and his team were in a race against the clock to produce new, revenue-generating material to satisfy their creditors and keep TSR in business. This included reaching out to *D&D* co-creator Dave Arneson and commissioning a series of *Blackmoor* adventure modules—a sort of homecoming for the campaign and the man.

As the spring of 1985 went on, TSR's financial footing grew more precarious as sales continued to weaken for their leading products, the *Dungeons & Dragons* basic set and its *Advanced Dungeons & Dragons* line—no doubt a symptom of TSR's failure to release new products coupled with ever-growing RPG competition from companies like Chaosium, Game Designers' Workshop, and West End Games. But right when Gary and TSR's fate appeared to be sealed, a new hardcover *AD&D* supplement called *Unearthed Arcana* hit the shelves in June of 1985, and to Gary's relief, attained spectacular success.

Because TSR had not released a significant *AD&D* supplement in two years, *Unearthed Arcana* benefited from significant pent-up demand for new *AD&D* products. Selling ninety thousand copies in its first month, *Unearthed Arcana* provided the needed cash not only to save the company from immediate insolvency but also to fund production of a number of other successful works that were already in development, such as a samurai-style *AD&D* supplement called *Oriental Adventures*.

At this point, Gary, who was never known to celebrate his victories nor mourn his defeats silently, implied that he would soon call a shareholders meeting at which changes in the composition of the board would be discussed, essentially giving his board members their notice. Gary later revealed, "That was an error, certainly, but I was so full of indignation at how the stooges had facilitated the near-ruin of the company I could not restrain my better judgment."[18]

Gary's "better judgment" would be questionable at best as he moved forward with TSR, and his next moves would prove fatal to his involvement with the company he founded.

+34

Trojan Horse

"MOVING FORWARD, I'D LIKE to see all TSR employees gain share ownership when the corporate crises are past, in recognition of their loyalty," said Gary.

Lorraine Williams, TSR's relatively new general manager and vice president, glared at Gary for several moments.[1] She seemed entirely unimpressed with Gary and uninterested in the mountains of gaming memorabilia that adorned his office. These were Gary's trophies—the fruits of his labor. A poster-sized version of the original *AD&D Player's Handbook* cover illustration hung on his wall; a whole library of *D&D* and other gaming books, many of which Gary had written, sat on his shelves; dice of every color and shape were strewn about the office, as were miniatures of every imaginable sort. He was certain that she had never given these things a second glance.

Without any further hesitation, Lorraine turned to Gary's assistant, Gail Carpenter, and said, "Over my dead body!"[2]

Both Gary and Gail were left speechless as she rose from her chair and walked out of Gary's office.

Who is this person? he thought as he exchanged a puzzled glance with Gail.

Lorraine Dille Williams had been brought into TSR by Gary in April 1985 to help manage the company's operations after he took control of the board. His intention was to bring in someone who was business-minded to focus on operations, while Gary managed the creative side. Gary had met Ms. Williams during his time in Los Angeles and considered her trustworthy, in large part because she was the sister of Flint Dille, Gary's close friend and movie script collaborator. When

Gary had spoken to Flint about TSR's recent financial trouble, Flint recommended his sister as a potential investor. This seemed a natural fit, as the Dille family came from a creative background.

When Gary first met Williams, she declined to invest at that time, but instead suggested that she be given a management role, in which she could help turn the company around and be in a better position to understand a future investment in the company. Gary accepted this arrangement, with some deferred-compensation investment stipulations written into her contract, and named her vice president and general manager, while he attended to creative matters. This seemed to work well for a short time, but Gary quickly became apprehensive when he concluded that Lorraine, whom some employees described as "intimidating," liked neither games nor gamers. He claimed that he discovered this when he overheard her imply that she "held gamers in contempt" and "that they were socially beneath her."[3] This troubled Gary, not only because he was a gamer through and through, but because gamers were TSR's audience and business. How could this company be run effectively under someone who didn't understand gaming and liked neither the products nor the target audience? From Williams' perspective, their relationship soured when she was trying to stabilize TSR's finances shortly after her arrival and Gary threw a "temper tantrum"[4] when she informed him that the house TSR owned on the Isle of Man, in the United Kingdom, had to be sold. On another occasion, Williams recalls that "Gary went ballistic"[5] when she informed him that the bank wouldn't advance any more money to fund his expensive Hollywood projects and operation.

Since Gary had resumed control of TSR in March 1985, he and the Blumes had been involved in negotiations regarding a severance package and the tender of their shares per the shareholder agreement. With a combined holding of 990 shares against Gary's 1,371, the Blumes still held a large and important stake in the company.[6] Gary's first attempt to acquire the Blumes' shares through TSR in April 1985 failed, as the company didn't have enough liquid cash to buy the shares outright, nor could it get a loan to purchase Brian's shares, now valued at roughly $500,000. When the Blumes were notified, they voiced their resistance to executing a severance agreement, stemming from their anxieties about having no corporate control in a company where they had such a large holding.

During a recess in the April 1985 board meeting, a private meeting occurred between Gary and the Blumes. What transpired in that meeting is still contested. According to the Blumes, Gary offered to purchase their holdings personally—a claim given credence by follow-up communication by the Blumes, their subsequent acceptance of a severance package in May of 1985 and a second intent-to-sell letter issued to TSR on October 8, 1985. Gary's version was that he agreed to help them find a buying group for the shares but that "no offer or promise was ever made"[7] regarding a personal offer from him.

Whatever the case, negotiation with the Blumes proved challenging for Gary at this point, as they had been openly hostile with one another for some time. Gary often wondered how these relationships had come to this. Brian was not a bad guy, and in fact he was talented, witty, and generally well liked around the office. Before TSR, Brian used to regularly sleep on the couch of the Gygax household and frequently had dinner with the family. Now they were adversaries. Nonetheless, Gary and the Blumes had history, and he felt certain they would eventually be able to work something out as the year went on. Gary also believed he had strong bargaining leverage over the Blumes as a sort of sole offerer, given the apparent protections offered in the shareholder agreement. He clearly wasn't prepared for what followed.

On Tuesday, October 22, 1985, Gary left his office en route to TSR's boardroom for what he assumed would be a contentious but relatively innocuous after-hours board meeting to discuss the company's royalty and copyright policies. Over the previous weeks, Gary had argued with board members that employees should retain such royalties and copyrights to their works instead of assigning them to TSR. Generous royalty agreements for TSR designers had been a thorn in the company's side since the very beginning. Gary and the Blumes had begun to realize how costly these agreements were to TSR as early as

1976, when they began to tighten their policies around royalties and negotiate reductions. But the company still suffered under these agreements, which paid Gary alone more than $2 million in his biggest year. Still, these policies were a complicated issue in that TSR's existing copyright and royalty structure served as a key tool to recruit, retain, and recognize its top design talent.

What Gary didn't expect to find when he arrived in the boardroom that evening were the disenfranchised Brian and Kevin Blume at the table. The meeting went on per the agenda, but Gary was nervous about the presence of the Blumes and finally asked the board secretary whether any stakes in TSR had changed relative to his own. He discovered that Lorraine Williams had exercised her option for fifty shares and, more significantly, that Brian Blume had exercised his option for seven hundred shares.[8] At this, Gary instantly knew that he was no longer the majority shareholder. Even worse, he quickly discovered on whose behalf Brian Blume's option had been exercised and who was the unnamed subject of the Blumes' October 8 intent-to-sell letter: Lorraine Williams.

Despite having had reservations about Williams and her alleged contempt for gamers and gaming, Gary had made her employment at TSR a high priority when he brought her on just six months ago, and he had brought her into his confidence. Gary was stunned. To learn that she had been in secret negotiations to purchase all of the Blumes' shares—a fact known ahead of time by all the other board members present—was for Gary the ultimate act of betrayal. Of course, Gary was short on friends in TSR's boardroom those days, as he had already warned the outside directors of an upcoming reorganization. The meeting concluded with Williams voted in as Gary's replacement as president and CEO.

In the coming days, after the shock had worn off, Gary sought legal counsel and made a last-ditch effort to purchase Brian's shares, even to the point of writing Brian Blume an unsolicited check on November 5, 1985, for $113,750 as a down payment for 650 of his shares.[9] Interestingly, this down payment for only a portion of Brian's shares may explain why Gary hadn't bought the Blume shares earlier and further draws into question whether he would have made them a personal offer at their April meeting—Gary didn't appear to have the money. An opulent lifestyle combined with a costly divorce and decreasing royalties had likely left Gary with minimal liquid funds and questionable overall assets to personally arrange the buyout.

Regardless of Gary's true financial situation, by the time he made this last-ditch attempt to acquire Brian Blume's shares, Brian couldn't have sold them to Gary even if he had wanted to. His TSR interests resided in escrow as a result of his October 8 agreement with Lorraine Williams.[10] Gary and his lawyers were adamant that the deal between the Blumes and Williams violated the shareholder agreement, and the matter went to court in 1986. But alas, for Gary the combination of the intent-to-sell documents issued by the Blumes and the uncertain nature of the private meeting between Gary and the Blumes at which Gary had allegedly offered to buy their shares convinced the local judge that the Blumes had satisfied their obligations under the agreement, and he allowed the Blume-Williams deal to proceed.

Ironically it was one of Gary's former adversaries who presided over the legal proceeding. The judge was a Lake Geneva local a few years Gary's senior and had once, according to Gary, "strong-armed"[11] him out of a BB pistol when he was a boy. Now it seemed to Gary that he had strong-armed him out of his company. Throughout the rest of his career Gary maintained that the judge's decision was baseless and that it was opinions like this that cost him reelection in his next term.[12] Whatever the case, it was too late—the damage was done.

So in late 1985, Williams, in an odd twist of fate, convinced Brian Blume to exercise his option, and she subsequently purchased all TSR shares held by Brian and Kevin Blume for the modest sum of $350 per share, more than $7,000 less per share than the original offer that Gary claimed he had brought them a year and a half earlier.

Gary again found himself on the outside looking in. Even worse, now that Lorraine Williams had control of TSR, she no longer hesitated to make it clear that she neither liked nor respected Gary. As he would explain, "From what I can make of it, it seems there was much personal enmity involved in the matter. I dared to contest Lor[r]aine Williams['s] right to control the company, and she disagreed with all that I wished to do with TSR."[13]

According to TSR employees, this feud was indeed personal. Gary had allegedly disrespected Williams publicly at a Gen Con event, pointing out her lack of knowledge and involvement in *Dungeons & Dragons*. This was supposedly a significant motivating factor in her approaching the Blumes and eventually gaining control of the company. According to Williams, her motives were simple: "I may not have understood it one hundred percent, but I understood intellectually that it was the right product for the right time."[14] She also apparently felt entitled to purchase the Blume shares without Gary's knowledge, so as to prevent him from carrying out his desire to "just try to screw it up, and to once again try to thwart the ability of the Blumes to sell their stock and to get out and to go about their lives."[15]

After his costly legal defeat, Gary sold his stock holdings (and his legal right to appeal) to Williams for $700 per share, earning him just under $1 million. By October 1986, he had publicly resigned from all his TSR positions.

For Gary, losing TSR had been like "losing a child."[16] But, perhaps greener pastures still waited around the bend.

Level 7

DUNGEON MASTER: *You have been wandering through the desert for what seems like days. Nothing but sand runs off into the horizon for as far as you can see. The hot desert sun is beating down on you, making your armor unbearably hot. Your party is dehydrated and their pace is starting to drag.*

PLAYER (SIR EGARY): *I pull out the map and try to get my bearings. Am I still headed south?*

DUNGEON MASTER: *As far as you can tell, you are still on course and you should be close to the spot indicated on the map.*

PLAYER (SIR EGARY): Onward, men! It's not far.

DUNGEON MASTER: *You push on for another hour or so with no sign of anyone or anything.* [DM checks Egary's constitution modifier and rolls a twenty-sided die] *Heat exhaustion has begun to set in among you and your men, and it's become very difficult to push forward. Just as you feel that you might faint, you see in the far distance a shimmering light.*

PLAYER (SIR EGARY): *Yes, finally! C'mon, men! We found it! We've rediscovered the Key of Revelation! With all of my remaining strength, I run full speed ahead.*

DUNGEON MASTER: *The light grows brighter and more pronounced as you make your way toward it. By now your muscles are burning and you badly need a drink. Then, all of a sudden, as you grow nearer, the light starts to fade.*

PLAYER (SIR EGARY): *No! I try to increase my pace.*

DUNGEON MASTER: *Now the shimmering light is growing dimmer and dimmer, until you arrive. The light is gone. There's nothing here—it was nothing but a mirage.*

+35

New Beginnings

THE SPACIOUS, ULTRAMODERN boardroom was uncomfortably still, with the exception of the nervous clicking of a retractable pen and the impatient ticking of a wall clock. The view from the corner room was impressive, providing a panoramic view of massive skyscrapers and the busy Chicago streets below. The gathering, however, was well removed from the hustle and bustle of the downtown streets, and the stillness seemed to heighten the tension in the room.[1]

"Don't worry, I'm sure they're coming," said Forrest Baker, a well-dressed accountant sitting at the table, along with a pair of assistants who remained mute.

"Well, it wouldn't be the first time one of these things didn't work out," said Gary, preparing himself for yet another round of professional disappointment.

Almost a year had passed since that fateful day in October 1985 when Gary had lost both his company, TSR, and the game that fueled its success, *Dungeons & Dragons*. It had been another several months before the shock and bitter disappointment wore off and he was in a good enough psychological state to "get back on the wagon," creatively speaking.

Other major changes in his life had occurred at this time, some good, some bad. Gary continued to be mired in a long and difficult divorce proceeding with Mary Jo. The failure of his marriage was due in no small part to the struggles that had unfolded over his last few years at TSR, a work environment exacerbated by his volatile relationship with the Blume brothers. Professionally, Gary was often known to be a brooding figure with a quick and "fiery temper that he could unleash in a nanosecond."[2] He had the temperament of a creative visionary, one who had been foiled at every turn professionally and artistically. But Gary was also capable of being outgoing and charismatic, and possessed a reputation for "making time for anyone," especially those who "acknowledged his creativity."[3]

On the positive side, he finally found himself with the time and resources to embark on other creative endeavors that he had wanted to continue for so long, namely, writing fantasy fiction—a passion he had pursued in early editions of the *Dragon* under the pen name Garrison Ernst. Now Gary had sought to continue and complete his Gord the Rogue fantasy novels, an intellectual property that he had been allowed to keep as part of his buyout agreement with TSR. The first two books in the series, the bestselling *Saga of Old City* and *Artifact of Evil*, had been released by TSR prior to his departure. Set in his original *D&D* campaign world of Greyhawk, the Gord the Rogue books largely fulfilled Gary's aspiration to write stories similar to the pulp fiction of Robert E. Howard, Jack Vance, Fritz Leiber, and L. Sprague de Camp that had inspired him so much as a young man. Until now, Gary had been unable to continue the series, having been pulled in so many directions by both professional and familial responsibilities.

In exploring outlets for his Gord the Rogue series, Gary had recently discussed a partnership with a wargaming acquaintance named Forrest Baker, who had learned of his separation from TSR and called on Gary to see if he was interested in starting a new company. Baker had worked for an accounting firm that had consulted TSR during its financial troubles in 1984 and 1985. Gary, with his modest but not insignificant TSR settlement funds, agreed to help finance the new company, but contingent on Baker's ability to raise the remaining capital—a sum between $1 million and $2 million. At this point in his career, Gary had no interest in the management and administration of another gaming company and instead wanted to focus entirely on creative work. If the company was to go forward, Baker would be responsible for the banking, legal, accounting, and primary fund-raising elements of the operation.

On the personal side, Gary was again a new father. Born to his former TSR assistant and now girlfriend, Gail Carpenter, Gary was the proud father of a baby boy the couple named Alex—his third son and sixth child overall. Gary, keenly aware that he had made mistakes as a father and husband in the past, was determined not to make them again. Being childlike himself, he loved having a young one around the house again, believing children to be the "greatest thing in the world."[4] Of course, Gary was also a realist and knew what good fatherhood would demand, especially at his age. In this way, he grew a new appreciation for how his middle-aged father must have felt when he was born.

In the Chicago conference room, many minutes passed with still no sign of the investors that Gary's host had promised. Gary noticed that Baker had begun to perspire and seemed agitated. He was now nervously dialing numbers he had on a notepad, but had yet to reach anyone. Just as Gary's hopes for the project were nearly gone, Forrest Baker finally reached a voice on the other end.

Baker listened and nodded for several moments. Finally he spoke. "Mmm-hmmm . . . Yes . . . I see. No, no problem! It could happen to anyone. Just a moment, let me put you on speaker," replied Forrest as he pressed the phone's speaker button.

"Yes, so, as I was saying, it is with our sincere apologies that we missed you today, but the deal is still on," said a confident voice on the other end.

At this the tension evaporated, and the group in the room breathed a collective sigh of relief. The absent investors *had* followed through.

With this initial investment in hand, Gary partnered with Baker in a new company called New Infinities Productions, Inc. Baker was to serve as CEO and Gary would hold the position of chairman of the board, while also leading the company's creative efforts. At this, Gary immersed himself in generating RPG concepts and continuing with his Gord the Rogue novels. He was thrilled to be working again in an entirely creative capacity.

Within a few months, Gary had made tremendous progress on his fantasy novels and had conceptualized a new role-playing game that he wanted to produce immediately. To speed the process, he had teamed up with his former TSR creative advisor, Frank Mentzer, and *Dragon* editor Kim Mohan to develop the new RPG material—a move that provoked Lorraine Williams and ensured the subsequent dismissal of Ernie and Heidi Gygax, who had retained their positions at TSR even after Gary's departure. Williams followed with a 1987 lawsuit against New Infinities based on its release of an adventure module by Frank Mentzer that he had worked on while employed at TSR. Mentzer had allegedly been granted TSR's permission after the company declined to publish it, but such permission had not been not made in writing. Hence the legal action.[5]

In spite of the troubles brought on by poaching some of TSR's best design talent, Gary could now be assured that his new company's gaming products were in good hands, allowing him to focus on his novels. However, it was also becoming clear that, although New Infinities had succeeded in attracting initial investors, a larger pool of capital would be required to produce and launch the new gaming systems.

In the midst of this, Forrest Baker informed the board that he was leaving New Infinities, apparently in part due to his inability to raise sufficient funds to produce gaming materials on a large scale. At this, Gary was incensed, believing Baker had left the startup company in a precarious financial and operational situation.

In the middle of a promising bid to regain a foothold in new projects, Gary again found himself overcommitted financially and forced to wrestle with corporate management issues instead of the creative work that he wanted to pursue. Fortunately, Gary had enlisted an expert creative staff to work on the new gaming products while the latest financial challenges were sorted out, but he knew that dedicated and experienced managerial talent would need to be introduced if this venture was to survive.

Seeking help to stabilize the fledgling company, Gary turned to friend, game designer, and former managing director of TSR UK, Don Turnbull, in February 1987. Turnbull was a well-respected member of the gaming community and had been instrumental in popularizing role-playing games in the United Kingdom through his contributions to the gaming periodical *White Dwarf*, along with his work with the respected English gaming enterprise Games Workshop, now a force on the fantasy miniatures market with its *Warhammer Fantasy Battle* series. While heading up TSR UK, a TSR subsidiary founded after an expired distribution agreement and failed merger with Games Workshop, he served as editor of its bestselling products, including the 1981 *Advanced Dungeons & Dragons Fiend Folio*, and published its in-house gaming magazine, *Imagine*—an early vehicle for the writings of Neil Gaiman, among others.

After bringing in Turnbull, Gary returned to his Gord the Rogue novels, working feverishly to keep the lights on at his new venture. His novels included *City of Hawks*, *Night Arrant*, and the bestselling *Sea of Death* in 1987, followed by *Come Endless Darkness* and *Dance with Demons* in 1988. Unfortunately, it seemed that no matter how many copies he sold, it still could not compensate for the company's underperforming gaming line, which included an innovative but underdeveloped science fiction role-playing game system entitled *Cyborg Commando*, conceptualized by Gary and written by Frank Mentzer and Kim Mohan, and a series of generic RPG modules called *Gary Gygax Presents Fantasy Master*. Even with all of this, Gary still found time to write a few projects on the side, including Putnam/Perigee's 1987 book *Role-Playing Mastery*—in which Gary evidently felt pressured into including several warnings about separating the real from the imaginary, almost ten years after the resolution of the Egbert incident—and its 1989 sequel *Master of the Game*.[6]

However, even between Gary's exhaustive efforts and Turnbull's managerial know-how, they were unable to turn New Infinities around. The needed blend of investor funding and reliable management was never achieved. With the situation exacerbated by the ongoing lawsuit with TSR, the company was forced into bankruptcy in 1989. Sadly, Gary had used his "last available funds"[7] to pay vendors and maintain the operation in hopes that the sales of new gaming products would return the company to financial health, similar to what he had been able to do a few years earlier at TSR with *Unearthed Arcana*. Unfortunately for Gary, this hadn't happened.

Though New Infinities proved to be short-lived and very costly for Gary financially, it did produce a number of notable fiction and gaming titles between 1987 and 1989. These titles did not prove to be profitable to Gary personally, though, and he again found himself without the resources or motivation to start another gaming operation. Fortunately, he did still have something valuable to offer—himself. By this time Gary's name and talent in the gaming industry preceded him and it was only a matter of time before a new opportunity would arise.

+36

Dangerous Journeys

"I'M SORRY, MR. GYGAX, but NEC will be pulling out," said a voice over the phone.

"No, you don't understand. We've changed the name—we're in the clear. TSR's lawsuit is completely baseless . . ." Gary insisted.

"Mr. Gygax, NEC cannot be attached to a lawsuit of this type. We are very sorry," said the voice, followed by an abrupt *click* and dial tone.

"No, wait!" bellowed Gary. "Hello? Hello . . . ? Damn it!" he shouted, slamming down the phone.

The voice on the other end had belonged to an executive from the NEC Corporation, whose TurboGrafx-16 Entertainment SuperSystem had pioneered arcade-quality 16-bit graphic technology for home gaming consoles, selling more than ten million units worldwide. Gary had been working with NEC and electronics leader JVC over the last several months on a video-game version of a new role-playing game called *Mythus*, derived from an innovative and complex system he had created called *Dangerous Dimensions*. Comparatively, *Dangerous Dimensions* was a role-playing game system, like *Dungeons & Dragons*, while *Mythus* was akin to a campaign or setting, like *D&D*'s *Greyhawk* or later *Oriental Adventures*, *Dragonlance*, and *Ravenloft*. A phone call virtually identical to that of NEC occurred with JVC in the following days.[1]

It was late 1992, three years since New Infinities had folded. Gary had found new inspiration in a new role-playing system he was working on with a talented game designer named Mike McCulley. It was by far the most extensive rules system he had ever undertaken, a "veritable encyclopedia of rules."[2] By this time, the role-playing game industry had gravitated toward increasingly complex gaming systems, known in the industry as "rules-heavy" systems. The rules-heavy system of *Dangerous Dimensions* was developed to be adaptable to several different campaign genres, but it was initially focused on the horror and fantasy settings.

Although New Infinities had not been financially successful, it had managed to produce a few well-received products, and Gary's reputation in the industry as a designer was as strong as ever. It wasn't long before *Dangerous Dimensions* drew interest from both NEC and JVC, who wanted to license the rights for a video-game version, while the successful Illinois-based Games Designers' Workshop (GDW), one of TSR's largest competitors, sought to produce the paper version of the game. Unsurprisingly, the strongest interest in Gary's new system from these potential partners was geared toward the fantasy setting, though he had hoped to initially produce the system in the horror genre under the title *Unhallowed*. Responding to NEC and JVC's priorities, he teamed with freelance writer and game designer Dave Newton to produce the fantasy version of the game, entitled *Mythus*. Gary and Newton had worked feverishly over several months on the *Dangerous Dimensions: Mythus* setting to meet the demands of these exciting new opportunities.

Gary finished a prototype of the new system just in time for the Game Manufacturers Association (GAMA) trade show in Las Vegas in March 1992. Unfortunately, while the game drew strong interest from an eager gaming audience, it also attracted the attention of TSR and Gary's nemesis, Lorraine Dille Williams. It certainly hadn't escaped the notice of Williams and her staff that with *Dangerous Dimensions* Gary had created a competing fantasy role-playing game—abbreviated *DD*, no less. This name was too close for Williams' liking, and TSR wasted no time in threatening legal action and, subsequently, filing an injunction to halt production of the game due to name and product confusion. While Gary claimed the name was based on JVC's preferences, there can be little doubt that he knew it would be a deliberate shot across TSR's bow. But he also surely didn't expect it to prompt a lawsuit.

Gary was living under various conditions from his original buyout agreement with TSR and, fearing that this all-too-similar name might not hold up in court, he quickly contacted NEC, JVC, and GDW to approve a name change, to which they all agreed. From that point on, Gary and his partners believed they were in the clear and moved forward with the development of the game, now called *Dangerous Journeys*.

Meanwhile, publishing giant Penguin, under its Roc imprint, signed on to publish a series of novels based on the *Mythus* setting—now a common strategy to pair novels with role-playing games, *Dragonlance* being the most notable example. Gary would write a trilogy of such *Dangerous Journeys* novels between 1992 and 1993 entitled *The Anubis Murders*, *The Samarkand Solution*, and *Death in Delhi*.

In spite of the name change, and much to Gary's grief, TSR still moved forward with legal action, seeking an injunction against the newly retitled *Dangerous Journeys*, this time claiming the game was a derivative of the *D&D* and *AD&D* product. Although the injunction failed, TSR persisted in copyright litigation against Gary, his partners, and the producer of the paper version of the game, GDW. The large and powerful companies NEC and JVC were conspicuously absent from the lawsuit, leaving Gary and his partners with little recourse to combat the eight-hundred-pound gorilla that TSR had become.

Gary couldn't believe it. He was convinced that TSR's legal action was, first and foremost, a result of Williams' vindictiveness and not a legitimate copyright concern on the part of TSR. After all, it wasn't the first time that Williams had sued Gary since his departure from TSR, though now for an entirely different cause. Why hadn't New Infinities been sued over this issue when it was producing the same type of fantasy material? But, now that he had developed a game that achieved some real traction in the market, Gary believed that Williams was leveraging her vast resources against him, knowing full well that he wouldn't be able to meet the financial demands of a costly lawsuit.[3] TSR was evidently afraid of him and intent on putting him out of business.

As to the merits of the case, Gary would illustrate its precarious nature in this way: "Imagine someone not familiar with either chess or checkers. So the publisher of the checkers game goes to court claiming chess infringes on checkers. Your Honor, look at the similarities: the board is exactly the same, the game is played by two opponents, each side has pieces called men and there are kings in play. Moves alternate and are varied and, as in checkers, chess pieces can promote to be more powerful. To top that off there are captures, and one side eliminates the other to win! That was the sort of thing we were facing."[4]

Unfortunately for Gary and his team, TSR's suit and its intended chilling effect worked to perfection. Once NEC and JVC learned of the litigation, they promptly pulled out of the project, not wanting to be involved in a complex copyright lawsuit that would hold up their projects, not to mention the fact that they had many other options in the realm of fantasy RPGs to choose from. To Gary this was "devastating,"[5] as he had again been cut off at the knees by the powers he created in Williams and TSR. Because TSR's lawsuit had shaky legal merit, Gary believed that had NEC or JVC gotten involved in the matter, TSR would have had no choice but to drop the case. TSR may have been a "big fish" in the world of RPGs but wouldn't have dreamed of playing a litigation version of Russian roulette with these two multibillion-dollar electronics companies. Nonetheless, the two companies did drop out of the deal, leaving Gary and his team vulnerable and making the outcome all the more painful.

After many months spent in the pretrial discovery phase, Gary and his partner's financial resources were spent. They couldn't continue with the costly legal proceedings and knew something must be done. Sensing that TSR might itself be feeling the financial pressures of litigation, Gary picked up the phone and dialed an office number he knew by heart because it had once been his.

"Lorraine? It's Gary . . . Let's talk . . ."

Though the conversation proved to be frigid at best, Gary and Williams eventually agreed to settle.[6]

On March 18, 1994, Gary found himself in the same boardroom at TSR headquarters where he had been ousted several years earlier. The room hadn't changed much except for the defiant glare of Lorraine Williams, who now held a seat at the end of the table. It was Gary's former seat.[7]

Fortunately for both Gary and Williams, the lawyers did most of the talking while they played the part of silent observers. After all, neither had anything nice to say about the other, and the tension in the room was thick enough as it was.

Although TSR was still far and away the largest producer of role-playing games, the company was secretly concerned, having lost an estimated half of its gaming audience due to TSR's transition to *Dungeons & Dragons 2nd Edition* in 1989, according to Gary's inside sources.[8] Led by David "Zeb" Cook, *2nd Edition* represented a huge and costly revision to the game's mechanics, revising and reorganizing many sections while dramatically expanding others. Of paramount interest to Gary, though, and yet another point of conflict between he and Lorraine Williams, was that it had been rumored that one of TSR's primary reasons for the revision was to change enough of Gary's copyrighted material to deny him ongoing royalties. According to Gary, "to save 2.5 percent they wrecked the company."[9]

As with the transition from *D&D* to *AD&D*, the fundamental concept of the game had not changed and much of its content was likely well served by further development and revision, but many felt that the game's grittiness had been removed in an effort to "make Dungeons & Dragons 'mom friendly.' Demons and devils were renamed . . . the assassin class was removed, and the game focused on playing heroic, noble characters."[10] As a result of these changes, paired with a robust and ever-growing list of competitive games, *2nd Edition* found only a lukewarm reception among a stubborn gaming contingent that knew what it liked and had many options to choose from. TSR was evidently so desperate that it was now willing to essentially buy out and scrap the products of certain competitors, Gary's *Dangerous Journeys* being just such a product. According to Gary, "TSR paid us a very large sum and they got all the rights to the *DJ* system and *Mythus*."[11]

It wasn't a win for Gary, but it certainly wasn't a total loss either. Gary had invested a great deal of time, effort, and money in the complex gaming system, to be sure, but unlike his experience with New Infinities, this time he wasn't leaving empty-handed. Even better, it was at least mildly gratifying to know that these funds had come from the coffers of his antagonist Lorraine Williams. Perhaps it was Gary who had gotten the last laugh with her. On the way out of the boardroom Gary recalled suggesting "that the next time I wrote a new RPG they [TSR] just offer me $1 million for the rights to it, thus saving at least that much money."[12]

Unfortunately for TSR, the company's troubles would only get worse, as it made misstep after misstep. After only a few short years, the company was $30 million in debt and entering bankruptcy when it was acquired by *Magic: The Gathering* maker Wizards of the Coast.

For GDW, *Dangerous Journeys* proved to be its last major release; the company closed just a couple of years later. In spite of the settlement from TSR that reimbursed it for its production costs, GDW, like other game companies, relied heavily on the sales of new gaming products, and with waning *Traveller* sales and its major investment in a *Dangerous Journeys* game that never hit the market, the company was left without a viable means to generate future revenue.

As Gary left TSR's headquarters for what would be the last time, he realized that this dangerous journey had truly come to an end.

Level 8

DUNGEON MASTER: *You are escorted into the great hall, flanked by six fully armored knights. The smell of smoked meats and perfumes waft about the room as you enter. The vaulted timbered ceiling is black with soot, the room dimly lit by candle chandeliers that hang every few feet. You pass a collection of tables where members of the court are feasting. There's a beautiful blonde dancing on one of the tables to the music of a bard playing a mandolin. You are being led to the far end of the hall, where you can see a podium and throne. On it sits the king.*

PLAYER (SIR EGARY): *I ask one of my knight escorts, "Can one of you tell me what's going on here?"*

DUNGEON MASTER: *No response.*

PLAYER (SIR EGARY): *Hey, I want to know why you brought me here!*

DUNGEON MASTER: *Nothing. They just keep prodding you forward. As you approach the throne, you can see that the king has not aged well. His skin looks leathery under his long gray hair and beard.*

PLAYER (SIR EGARY): *Your Highness, it has been a long time . . .*

DUNGEON MASTER: *"Sir Egary," the king says majestically. "Do you know why I have summoned you here?"*

PLAYER (SIR EGARY): *I believe so, Your Highness. But you must know that the Key of Revelation was lost a long time ago and I never rediscovered it. I'm sorry, but I cannot complete your quest . . . I have failed.*

DUNGEON MASTER: *The king frowns at you for several moments, but then a smile begins to creep onto his face. He begins to laugh.*

PLAYER (SIR EGARY): *Forgive me, Your Highness, but what is so funny?*

DUNGEON MASTER: *The king stops laughing and gets very serious. "Sir Egary . . . you accomplished your quest many years ago. I didn't bring you here to punish you; I brought you here to reward you! Your days of gallant quests are over, my friend. You shall join me, now and forevermore, in my court as Lord Egary—Master of Shadow Lake!"*

+37

Justified

A YOUNG RED-HAIRED man sat unconscious, tied to a chair in what appeared to be a control room. The dark, narrow room was lit only by flashing console lights, computer screens, and gauges. As the man came to, suddenly out of the shadows emerged four dark shapes.

"Who are you people?"[1] asked the frightened young man.

"I'm Al Gore, and these are my Vice Presidential Action Rangers, a group of top nerds whose sole duty is to prevent disruptions to the space-time continuum . . ." replied the stoic vice president. "Meet the Action Rangers," he continued. "You already know Stephen Hawking. Also with us are Nichelle Nichols, AKA Commander Uhura . . . To my left you'll recognize Gary Gygax, inventor of *Dungeons & Dragons*."[2]

"Greetings!" Gary said, then rolled a pair of dice on a table and eagerly awaited the results. "It's a pleasure to meet you!"[3] he finished enthusiastically.

Of course, Gary didn't quite look himself today. In fact, none of the Action Rangers did. They looked yellow, round, and crude. More to the point, they looked animated.

The Action Rangers were not live representations, but cartoon characters on the hit animated Fox television series *Futurama*. The voices of the four characters, however, were not actors, but those of the four real-life people they represented. Developed by *The Simpsons* creator Matt Groening, *Futurama*, now in its second season, attracted more than six million weekly viewers.

Several hours had passed in the fictional universe, and the Vice Presidential Action Rangers found themselves floating in what appeared to be a white abyss. The space-time continuum had been destroyed.

"Anyone want to play *Dungeons & Dragons* for the next quadrillion years?"[4] asked a jolly-sounding Gary as he gestured to his *AD&D Monster Manual*.

The group enthusiastically agreed, while Vice President Gore exclaimed, "I'm a tenth-level vice president!"[5]

By 2000, Gary Gygax and his game *Dungeons & Dragons* had certainly come a long way since the James Dallas Egbert III incident or the days of Bothered About Dungeons & Dragons. In the 1980s no politician or elected official, let alone the vice president of the United States, would have dared to touch such a controversial game as *Dungeons & Dragons*. Now the current vice president, Al Gore, was boasting that he was a "tenth-level vice president," all for the sake of comedy on a popular cartoon series. In a strangely poetic twist of fate, Gore's wife, Tipper Gore, had been one of the leading censorship advocates of the '80s who had spoken against *D&D*, linking it to satanism and the occult in her 1987 book, *Raising PG Kids in an X-Rated Society*. Accordingly, she was an ally of figures such as Dr. Thomas Radecki and BADD founder Patricia Pulling, two of the most outspoken opponents of *D&D* during the height of its controversies. What could this all mean? Had *D&D* finally entered the mainstream and found popular approval?

The world had surely changed, and Gary had changed along with it. Now a distinguished silver-haired man with beard and ponytail, he was a legend who had finally begun to look the part. He had become more diplomatic in some respects, but in some cases also more set in his ways, especially his politics. Once a staunch Republican and conservative, he was now an outspoken libertarian. And even though he was now linked with Al Gore, at least in a fictional capacity, he was still careful to point out to a fellow gamer that, "as a Libertarian, I'll have to concur with your assessment of Al Gore, somewhat lower than 10th level."[6]

Despite his age and many setbacks over the last few years, his child-like humor had returned to him, describing himself as "'mature,' shall we say, even though I haven't g[r]own up."[7] He again spoke with a twinkle in his eye and could rattle off a conversation entirely in puns, if so motivated. While not wealthy, Gary had also gained some semblance of financial stability. This was in no small part due to the purchase of

Gary's residual rights to many of his TSR and post-TSR works by the company's new owner, Seattle-based Wizards of the Coast, garnering Gary a six-figure sum.[8]

Gary's appearance on the popular Fox television show was a high-water mark in many ways. Twenty-five years after Gary had sold his first hand-assembled *Dungeons & Dragons* box set, the game had indeed found its place in popular culture. No longer perceived as dangerous and subversive (though some continued to contend otherwise), the game now firmly held a prominent place in the world—a mainstay among the geeks. This was not bad company given that these geeks were beginning to take over as computer programmers, engineers, technology experts, writers, economists, software designers, film directors, and CEOs. They were everywhere, and they were in charge.

Also significant was Gary's presence among the Action Rangers. All of them geeks or geek icons in one way or another, but even a cursory look would reveal much more about each of them. Here was Al Gore, the sitting vice president of the United States, standing with Stephen Hawking, considered by many the greatest mind on the planet, and our own Gary Gygax, the humble inventor of *Dungeons & Dragons*, the world's first role-playing game. Could it be that *D&D* had made a greater impact than was first believed?

Whatever the case, Gary was not one to rest on his laurels. Since *Dangerous Journeys* had been bought out in 1994, Gary had taken a break from paper RPG games and had directed his energies toward computer role-playing games (CRPGs). Although his experiences with NEC and JVC had been disappointing, he was convinced that CRPGs were the future of mainstream fantasy RPGs and the like.

Between 1994 and 1996, Gary worked on a number of CRPG concepts, a couple of which were purchased but never developed. Interestingly, Gary had seen this potential in CRPGs since the late 1970s, and early issues of *Dragon* magazine had even featured an ongoing column about computer technology called The Modern Eye, but TSR had not been positioned technically or financially to invest in such a radical industry at the time. Now, the technology had caught up with the concept, and Gary had the capacity and desire to pursue it with full force.

By 1996, Gary had developed one of his many CRPG concepts into a traditional tabletop role-playing game system and had begun testing it with his local gaming group. Gary, who had recently designed by far his most complex system to date in *Dangerous Journeys*, had decided to go back to the basics, favoring simplicity rather than complicated gaming mechanics. Meanwhile, Gary's old company, TSR, had begun to suffer from severe financial difficulties, resulting in a reduced output of *D&D* materials. Seeing this as an opportunity, Chris Clark, founder of Inner City Games and a designer whom Gary had worked with on and off since the '80s, subsequently approached Gary about partnering on some generic adventure modules to fill the void left by TSR's diminishing output. The result of this collaboration was the 1998 *A Challenge of Arms* and the 1999 *The Ritual of the Golden Eyes* adventure modules, both published by Inner City Games.

Riding this wave of new fantasy role-playing material, and on the heels of TSR's near bankruptcy and acquisition by Wizards of the Coast, it was Gary's turn to approach Clark about developing his former CRPG system, since converted to tabletop, which he had been running for his local group since 1996. After an unsuccessful attempt by Gary to line up investors to fund the project, Clark recommended they form a partnership to publish it themselves. Gary agreed, and they began working together as Hekaforge Productions.

Developed and published by the fledgling partnership, the new game was called *Lejendary Adventures*. Gary considered this "rules-light" system to be his "best work."[9] Although the Hekaforge venture had a limited production and marketing budget of only $14,000, Gary was convinced that *Lejendary Adventures* was the game and system that gamers had been craving.[10] The system's core trilogy of books was released between 1999 and 2000, including *The Lejendary Rules for All Players*, *Lejend Master's Lore*, and the *Beasts of Lejend*—a tried-and-true three-book model pioneered with his original *AD&D* books.[11] But Gary no longer approached full-out game development and marketing lightly and wondered whether he had the endurance required to face this challenging and often disappointing process again.

To be sure, Gary's outlook on work and recreation had changed over the years. He had in many ways matured and settled down, in as much as Gary ever settled down. He was a grandfather many times over now, and his days of illicit drugs and Hollywood starlets were well behind him. He had been given the gift of a second chance at both marriage and fatherhood, and he was determined to not repeat the mistakes of his past. Writing with a certain amount of understatement, Gary observed, "I should have spen[t] a bit more time with family matters tha[n] I did."[12]

With *Lejendary Adventures* and other projects, Gary still had his work, but unlike in the past, he had set limits on his workdays. Though still quite rigorous, his schedule was roughly 6:00 a.m. to 6:00 p.m. daily, seven days per week—a noted reduction from past binges of work that sometimes consumed up to twenty-four hours straight. Gary, like the genius Thomas Edison, could get by on just a few hours of sleep per night, and this new approach allowed most evenings to be "strictly family time."[13] Nonetheless, he had committed significant time and resources to the *Lejendary Adventures* project and had high expectations for its success.

With the game rested Gary's hopes and dreams for another hit—another *D&D*. But would lighting strike twice?

+38

Silver and Gold

GARY TOUCHED THE CRYSTAL brandy snifter to his lips and took a sip. The rich, warm Armagnac took over his mouth and throat, leaving a beautiful finish of oak and roasted nuts. It didn't burn—it was just smooth, velvety, and warm. Gary had never had anything like it.

"How is it, Papa G?" interrupted his son Alex.

Gary smiled and looked around the generous porch of the grand yellow Victorian home he now occupied on Lake Geneva's Madison Street. Surrounding him were his six children and six grandchildren as well as Gail, his wife for fifteen years now. The seventy-five-year-old Armagnac had been a gift from François Marcela-Froideval, a former TSR employee, comic book author, and key figure in introducing the French to role-playing games. The bottle had come from François' father's cave, and Gary had been saving it for seventeen years.

"Seems better to drink it than save it for my wake, eh?"[1] said Gary before taking another sip.

A Romeo y Julieta cigar sat burning in the ashtray in front of him, wafting up sweet Cuban tobacco smoke—the same his father used to smoke. The cigar, paired with the Armagnac, proved to be the perfect finish to the delectable quail dinner and lemon meringue pie dessert. It was a perfect end to a perfect day.

It was July 27, 2003—Gary's sixty-fifth birthday. It was a rare occasion, as all of Gary's six children and six grandchildren were present to celebrate with him. In fact, according to Gary, it was the "first time that'll ever have happened."[2]

Maybe it was the Armagnac or maybe it was the company, but Gary was glowing. He was so proud. Ernie, Elise, Heidi, Cindy, Luke, and

Alex were all so special in their own ways, as were their respective offspring. Every one of his children touched his heart in a way that was unique, and he saw different parts of himself in each.

Although his girls had all played *Dungeons & Dragons* when they were young, none of them had continued to play. Of course, Elise had played since the beginning, but even she had drifted from the game due to the natural inclinations toward boys, work, and life. Heidi and Cindy, however, had lost their interest when Luke, who had been appointed DM by his two older sisters, finally "took charge"[3] of the game. Prior to that, the girls would "'suggest' the monsters encountered and then dictate the sort of treasure they found after slaying them."[4]

Gary chuckled as the memory crossed his mind. It seemed like only yesterday, but alas, here they were, all grown up and with children of their own, no less.

Gary's boys, on the other hand, had followed in his footsteps and continued to game as their respective schedules allowed. In fact, just a year earlier, Ernie and Luke had even collaborated on a major adventure module called *The Lost City of Gaxmoor*, published by Troll Lord Games, which Gary had playtested with his sons in groups that ranged from twelve to twenty-four gamers. This effort had been on top of Ernie and Luke's busy work schedules, Ernie at Abbott Laboratories and Luke as an officer in the United States Army who served in the first Gulf War.

As for Gary's work, his latest project, *Lejendary Adventures*, had not achieved the popularity that he had hoped. Since the game was released in 1999, sales had fallen well short of expectations. Nonetheless, the system had recently gotten the notice of a more prominent games publisher, Arkansas-based Troll Lord Games. Gary was now working with that company on a number of other projects, including a series of customizable RPG "world-builder" books, appropriately called the *Gygaxian Fantasy World Series*. As an added benefit of this collaboration, Gary had developed a close friendship with two of the company's owners and designers, brothers Stephen and Davis Chenault.

Other projects Gary undertook with "the trolls,"[5] as he called them, was a re-creation of his original *D&D* Greyhawk dungeon, called *Castle Zagyg*—a play on his last name. This began as a collaboration with his old friend and associate Rob Kuntz, but after the two split because of creative differences, it was completed with Gary's bright young game designer protégé, Jeff Talanian. Nonetheless, Gary loved his *Lejendary Adventures* game most and continued to run a weekly Thursday night game with his local gaming group, which included his son Alex.

This, however, was not the full extent of Gary's ritual gaming, even while he continued to work twelve-hour days. It was assumed that because Gary had invented role-playing games, those were all he played, but Gary was and always had been a lover of all game types. He indulged in non-RPG games on Monday afternoons with his local gaming group, which included his son Ernie, Guidon Games and TSR veteran Tom Wham, local gamers Dennis Harsh and Russ Ingram, and occasionally his grandson Mike Gygax. Wham had the most impressive collection of board games and, as an obsessive train enthusiast, would often steer the group toward *Rail Baron*, *Railroad Tycoon*, or *Ticket to Ride Europe*, but other games certainly got their fair share of play, including *Settlers of Catan*, *San Juan*, *Big Business*, and Gary's favorite, *Operation Overlord*. This was not to ignore his enduring passion for chess, a game that he would play with anyone who was willing. "Gary loved chess. He played chess. He wrote chess. He designed chess. He lived chess,"[6] remarked Gary's friend and *D&D* historian Paul Stormberg.

On Fridays Gary would lunch with Gail. This was their special time to connect over whatever experimental dish or restaurant they were trying that day. Sushi was often the choice, but occasionally they would sojourn to nearby New Glarus, a charming Wisconsin village where Gary connected with his Swiss roots through generous portions of traditional Swiss fare and beer. Gary now understood the importance of dedicating time to these simple yet hugely important activities. In fact, he had sagely recommended to a newlywed gamer that he "pay more attention to her than to gaming. If she doesn't like RPGing, keep your own down to the 'one night a week ou[t] with the boys' level."[7] This was indeed a far cry from the Gary Gygax who once played six or seven marathon sessions per week despite significant work and family commitments.

Gary smiled as he took another puff of his cigar. Family chatter and laughter drifted in the background, and through the thick haze of Cuban cigar smoke, Gary could see everything so clearly. This was what it was all about—this was his reward.

Gary was a changed man. After many years of turmoil, both professional and familial, he had finally achieved balance. But for Gary, the scales had a tendency to tip unexpectedly.

+39

King of the Nerds

GARY SIGHED AS HE peered out of the frost-covered window of his drafty home office. Snow covered every inch of the ground, and he could hear the howl of frozen wind swirling outside, causing the aged Victorian to creak. Gary used to love Lake Geneva winters, but not anymore.

The room was dark except for the light of Gary's computer monitor, which illuminated his face and hands. A badly worn computer keyboard sat before him, its letters barely visible anymore due to heavy use. This was at least a bit problematic, as Gary always had been a clumsy and fat-fingered keyboardist—a self-described "Columbus Method typist . . . discover and land!"[1]

Gary yawned while lifting his glasses and rubbing his eyes. It had only been an hour or so, but he was feeling spent.

"I think that's it for today," he said aloud to himself.

Not long ago Gary had been able to spend twelve straight hours at the keyboard, writing vigorously, but this was not the case anymore. Now Gary was lucky if he could get an hour or two at the computer, most of which was spent answering e-mails or message threads.

It was December 2005, and Gary was tired. The last couple of years had taken their toll. Strokes in April and May 2004 had almost killed him, and the physical traumas paired with the doctor-required medication had severely limited his ability to work. Worse still, 2004 was capped by the passing of Gary's oldest friend and best man, Dave Dimery.

Dimery, a fellow Kenmore Pirate, had stayed in close touch even after Gary moved to Lake Geneva. In fact, Dave had been present during some of Gary's most formative moments, including his first poltergeist incident and the day that they sat in the bleachers rooting for their beloved Cubs as they played the Brooklyn Dodgers on May 18, 1947—Jackie Robinson's first game at Wrigley Field. Over thirty years later, Gary hired Dimery to run TSR's advertising department. The much beloved animated TSR spokesperson, Morley the Wizard, was one of Dimery's creations, among others.

So far, 2005 had not proved much better. Gary lost another of his longtime friends and co-workers when renowned TSR artist and designer Dave Sutherland died in June. Sutherland had been best known for designing the cover art for two of *AD&D*'s most successful products ever, the original *Monster Manual* and *Dungeon Master's Guide*. Memorial gatherings arranged by Gary's dear friend and former TSR employee Harold Johnson, held at Lake Geneva's Cactus Club, seemed to happen more and more, leaving Gary wondering who might be absent the next time around. Gary had lost so many people over the years—surely more than his fair share. Worst of all, though, Gary had discovered earlier that very day that *he* was likely to be next.

Gary rose from his desk and lumbered as quietly as he could into the kitchen. Gail had fallen asleep on the couch, and Alex was out and about, probably working one of his two jobs or spending time with his girlfriend. Gary opened the refrigerator to reveal a six-pack of Samuel Adams and a carton of buttermilk.[2] Gary grabbed both and brought them to the table.

Since his health problems surfaced the year prior, red wine had been his nightly custom—just two glasses per day, though, and not the whole bottle that he had once selectively heard his doctor recommend. This moderation was in addition to switching from his Camel cigarettes to moderately "healthier" cigars. Yes, Gary had become a real health nut, but this night buttermilk and Sam Adams won out.

Gary sat at the table and poured himself a glass of the buttermilk, which prior to his health issues had been his preferred drink at the end of a long workday.

What the hell difference does it make now? he thought as he took a swig.

The news Gary had received earlier that day had been a diagnosis of an abdominal aortic aneurysm, a ballooning of the largest artery leading into the heart. Gary's case was reasonably advanced. If the artery continued expanding, it would rupture and he would almost certainly die.

Gary finished the buttermilk with his second gulp and wasted no time cracking the Sam Adams on the table.

"What the hell do doctors know anyway?" Gary grumbled.

Surgery was an option, but his recent experience with his strokes and subsequent medications had done nothing but shown him that the cure was often worse than the affliction. Gary simply didn't trust doctors, save Dr. Kathryn Chenault, the wife of his dear friend and Troll Lord Games CEO Steve Chenault, both of whom he held in the highest regard.[3] In fact, Gary's general distrust of doctors was so deep that Gail and his eldest daughter, Elise, had recently rented a car and driven him all the way to Arkansas to see his only trusted medical advisor, Dr. Chenault. Of course, it hadn't been lost on Gary that this "medical" trip was also a great opportunity to get in some quality working and gaming with the trolls.

Well, Gary, he thought as he raised the beer bottle to his lips, *at least we now know how it's gonna go.*

Lejendary Adventures had not sold as he had hoped, despite its relationship with Troll Lord Games who released a new source book earlier in the year called *Lejendary Adventures Essentials Rulebook.* Meanwhile, his health had gone from bad to worse, but he was managing. Things were not perfect, but he didn't expect them to be. Sixty-seven years of a hard-knock life and what had now become daily Bible readings had taught him at least that much. By now, Gary had grown accustomed to a pattern of his significant efforts leaving him with little or nothing to show for it, whether it be the fish he caught off the Riviera, his painting of the Back 40, or the loss of his games, his companies, and his millions. But Gary was not one to complain, and he knew he had a lot to be grateful for.

Besides closer relationships with his family and friends and creative work that was still fulfilling, Gary had found a new level of fellowship with gamers worldwide. The advent of the Internet had allowed him to connect with gamers across the globe, sharing in online chats and message boards, where Gary frequently participated under the screen name Colonel Pladoh—a reference to his favorite character from *Clue* coupled with a self-effacing, humorous comparison between himself and the philosopher Plato.[4] Via the Web, thousands began to express their gratitude to Gary for his creation, or just to share in usual gaming banter, which Gary enjoyed immensely. With this, Gary had finally begun to realize the impact of what he had done, and he was humbled by it. The world had indeed changed.

Thanks to the computer age, smartphones, and *Harry Potter*, it was finally cool to be a geek, and this made Gary about as cool as they come. In fact, he had become nothing short of a legend. In 2002 *GameSpot* magazine had Gary tied with J.R.R. Tolkien for eighteenth place on the list of the "30 Most Influential People in Gaming," which was probably the first time Gary didn't mind being mentioned with Tolkien in the same sentence. More recently, Gary had been ranked thirty-seventh on *SFX* magazine's "50 Greatest SF [Science Fiction] Pioneers" list. Perhaps most appropriate, and what Gary was most proud of, *Sync* magazine had recently named Gary as number one on its list of the "50 Biggest Nerds of All Time."

Gary had really made it. He was the King of the Nerds.

+40

The End of the Road

"AND THE NEW YORK GIANTS have defeated the New England Patriots to become the 2008 Super Bowl Champions . . ." the television blared in the sitting room of Gary's Madison Street home.

Gary's longtime friend and co-worker, Frank Mentzer, sat quietly on the couch. At a glance, one might have mistaken Mentzer for Gary's twin, as he was heavyset and featured the same long silver ponytail and beard. In fact, this seemed to be the prototype look of many of Gary's old gaming buddies, often referred to as "the old guard" or "grognards,"[1] a French term for "old soldier." But on this particular winter evening, Gary looked quite a bit more worn and gray than his comrade.[2]

Although the events depicted on the television were exciting, it had been a very quiet evening for Gary. Most years he could raise great enthusiasm for the Super Bowl; he was a huge football fan. For Gary the fall season was dominated by watching his beloved Chicago Bears, often while brandishing his fuzzy Bears faux-helmet hat.[3] These seasons, however, had ended in disappointment for many years now. The Bears hadn't been champions since their legendary 1985 season, and Gary knew how they felt. He also hadn't won much since his expulsion from TSR in 1985, at least not on the business side of life.

Now he was too sick to socialize much, let alone take delight in a sporting event that had little bearing on his remaining life. Time was short and he knew it.

"Well, I better get back, Gary. I've got a long drive ahead of me," said Frank as he put on his coat. Mentzer now lived several hours north of Lake Geneva in the fishing and resort town of Minocqua, Wisconsin, where he owned and operated a commercial bakery with his wife.

"Thanks for coming, Frank—it was good to see you. And thanks also for the pie crust cookies. Keep 'em coming," replied Gary weakly from the couch.

As Frank exited the front door of Gary's spacious home, a gust of cold air blew in and met Gary's face, making his hair stand on end.

"Whew!" muttered Gary. "At least I can still feel something."

To be sure, Gary didn't feel much these days, and what he could feel he didn't like. He hurt everywhere. His body was shutting down and had been for many years. He was dying.

He sat quietly on his couch in reflection for several minutes. Tears began to well in his eyes. He had come to the realization that his visit with Frank that evening might have been the last time he would see his friend. How many others would he need to see before the end?

Gary was never one to gush emotionally or otherwise with his friends or family, but he also knew how important it was to make sure they knew they were loved. Gary had never quite forgiven himself for neglecting his father prior to his death, and he wasn't going to make the same mistake twice. Gary was now on the other side of the equation and understood better than ever how important these connections were. So Gary had taken to writing e-mails or making phone calls to all of his children, making sure they knew how much he loved them. These had already occurred ahead of scheduled surgeries aimed at correcting his condition, but Gary always canceled those procedures at the last minute. Although he knew his aortic aneurysm was a ticking time bomb, for him the fatigue and risk of complications outweighed the possibility of the surgery's success—his only chance to live.

Gary, though, hadn't taken his mortality lightly. He had gotten a number of medical opinions on his condition, but the prognoses were never consistent—a fact that undermined his confidence in the medical field.[4] Gary understood probabilities, and with the chances of a successful surgery ranging between 50 and 90 percent, depending on who he was consulting with, this was a game of chance he was not eager to play. All this had done little but convince him that if he went into surgery, he would die on the operating table—a fate he was determined to avoid.

Work, however, still occupied a place in his life. Gary had been designing games for over forty years now, and expressing his feelings to his loved ones was not the only thing he needed to do. A month earlier Gary had passed along a fairly comprehensive game design and publishing "to-do" list to his Troll Lord Games publisher, Steve Chenault. Steve had been confused by how extensive the list was, but Gary knew what he was doing. He needed to create, and there was still much to be done, dead or alive.

As far as his health went, however, Gary had no regrets. "Seeing as I've been smoking Camel straights for 50 years and love it, and drinking for damned near as long, I reckon that, or something else, is bound to kill me . . . Meantime, I want to have fun and enjoy life the way I like it," he would explain.[5] With these habits, along with his periods of illicit drug use, Gary had come to know and respect the rules of life, as he did with his games—his time was almost at hand.

When family and friends would stop by these days they always wanted to remind him of all the great things he had done, but Gary didn't need the testimonials. He had done what he had done, nothing more and nothing less. He wasn't overly impressed with himself; he had simply "come up with the idea for making 'Let's Pretend' into a game and publishing it."[6] Gary contended that "Let's Pretend" had been around for "a lot of centuries,"[7] and that he could really only claim authorship of the first formal RPG.

Whatever the case, Gary had been important. This self-described "risk-taking, Camel-straight-smoking, nonconformist who loved gaming but wasn't averse to hanging out in a biker bar"[8] had accomplished great things—remarkable things. He had invented an entire industry that had, in many ways, sparked a revolution of creativity and imagination.

A BLEAK AND BLUSTERY Lake Geneva winter month had now passed since the Super Bowl. Gary's condition had declined, and he had been spending more of his time at home. This, however, hadn't stopped him from answering fans in message boards on his regular cyber hangouts, including EN World, Troll Lord Games, the Lejendary Adventures website, and Fans for Christ.

More important, Gary had tied up all of his loose ends with family, friends, and work. He had even made peace with God. "All I am is another fellow human that has at last, after many wrong paths and failed attempts, found Jesus Christ,"[9] he wrote in January of that year, signing the e-mail with his favorite Bible verse, Matthew 5:16. This would no doubt be a great surprise to the critics who had for many years accused him of both promoting and practicing Satan worship. All in all, Gary was prepared.

On Tuesday, March 4, 2008, a dark-robed figure entered Gary's bedroom. Gary was immediately startled and could do nothing but pull the covers up to his face. The figure stood motionless at the foot of Gary's bed for several moments, its face shrouded in darkness.

Gary tried to shout for help, but the sheer terror of the moment prevented his vocal chords from producing anything more than a whisper.

The form slowly raised its arm and unfurled a bony finger toward the corner of the room, illuminating a chess board that hadn't been there previously.

"Wanna play?" said a raspy voice that chilled Gary to the bone.

Gary studied the figure in disbelief and then glanced at the stately chess set. It really was a nice set. Gary cleared his throat and sat up against the bed's headboard.

"Well . . ." said Gary, matter-of-factly, "I never could say no to a good game of chess."

Gary was outmatched that day, just as he knew he would be, and the game was lost.

The legendary Gary Gygax had passed away. But his newest adventure had just begun . . .

Level 9

DUNGEON MASTER: *It is dawn and a heavy fog begins to lift from murky Shadow Lake. Enclosed by mountains on all sides, the enormous Shadow Lake extends into an otherwise barren landscape full of dead trees and plants. A small cave reveals itself through the fog on the opposite shore of the lake.*

A nearby procession of humans, elves, orcs, and dwarves, as far as the eye can see, approaches over the tiny pass into the valley. Heading the procession is a group of six armor-clad knights carrying an ornate silver-and-blue coffin. As they come into focus, the coffin reveals a crest, the crest of Lord Egary. They have returned to deliver the body back to the lake where the Key of Revelation was found and lost. As they approached the shore of the lake, the seemingly never-ending procession begins to funnel in.

People of all classes, races, and alignments begin to fill the shores around Shadow Lake, solemnly paying their final respects to the man who had done so much for them. Without hesitation, the knights enter the water carrying the casket as high on their shoulders as they can manage. When they have ventured as far as they can go, they release the box, which peacefully floats away toward the breaking sun. Lord Egary has passed, but his legacy lives on.

+41

The Legacy

ON MARCH 5, 2008, comedian Stephen Colbert departed from his usual closing remarks on his popular comedic TV news show to pay tribute to Gary Gygax. A day earlier, the *Dungeons & Dragons* creator and role-playing legend Ernest Gary Gygax had died of an aortic aneurysm. An uncharacteristically sincere moment for Colbert, he began, "Before we go, nation, I have some sad news. Yesterday, Gary Gygax, creator of Dungeons and Dragons, passed away at age sixty-nine. Gary, you will be missed . . . How much will you be missed?" he asked with a twinkle in his eye. Colbert, who could never resist the opportunity to create a laugh, revealed a twenty-sided die and rolled it on his desk. "Twenty," he said. "May your prismatic spray always bypass your target's Reflex saving throw."[1]

The Emmy Award-winning Colbert, the self-proclaimed "second most popular fake newsman" and a known gamer, was not the only one who took notice of the life and passing of Mr. Gygax. Every major newspaper, magazine, and broadcast-news source quickly churned out stories on Gygax's passing and extolling his achievements. A giant twenty-sided die was erected in Killan Court at MIT in honor of the man, while the popular animated Fox Television series *Futurama* aired a brief tribute. Hadn't Gary Gygax simply invented a game, and an esoteric one at that? It was hardly a footnote in the increasingly fast and complex information age that we live in. What was all of the fuss about?

The reason for all of the fuss, among those who understood his work, was simple: Gary Gygax and his seminal game creation, *Dungeons & Dragons*, had influenced and transformed the world in extraordinary ways. Yet much of his contribution would also go largely unrecognized by the general public. Although it is debatable whether *D&D* ever became a thoroughly mainstream activity, as a 1983 *New York Times* article had speculated, referring to it as "the great game of the 1980s," *D&D* and its RPG derivatives are beloved by a relatively small but dedicated group of individuals, affectionately known as geeks. Although the term *geek* is not exclusive to role-playing gamers, the activities of this particular audience have often been viewed as the most archetypal form of geekiness. Labels aside, what is notable is that the activities of this RPG audience were highly correlated with interests in other activities such as early computers, digital technologies, visual effects and the performing arts. In this way, these geeks, though relatively small in number, became, in many instances, the leaders and masters of this era. With the advent of the digital age, geeks worldwide found opportunity and recognition never previously available to their predecessors.

Icons and innovators such as George R. R. Martin, Mike Myers, Richard Garriott, Vin Diesel, Tim Duncan, Anderson Cooper, David X. Cohen, John Carmack, Tim Harford, Moby, and the late Robin Williams, to name just a few, were all avid role-playing gamers in their younger years. The list of those who included *D&D* as a regular activity while growing up is both extensive and impressive. But did *D&D* inspire these individuals to greatness? Some certainly believe it did.

Celebrated *New York Times* bestselling author Sam Lipsyte, writer of *The Ask* and *Home Land*, attributes his desire to become a writer to *Dungeons & Dragons*: "I think that I became a writer because I couldn't be a DM. I think that I wanted that control over a world. So I turned to fiction. When you're writing, you're both the Dungeon Master and one of the players at the same time. It's kind of creating problems for yourself to solve. You're creating dungeons and worlds for yourself to explore, and not die in."[2] Junot Díaz, Pulitzer Prize–winning author of *The Brief Wondrous Life of Oscar Wao*, had a similar experience with the game, calling it "a sort of storytelling apprenticeship."[3] This is not to ignore dozens of other award-winning writers who credit at least some of their success to the game, including Pulitzer Prize–winning playwright David Lindsay-Abaire and *New York Times* bestselling author Colson Whitehead.

Regarding *D&D*'s influence on technology, Adam Rogers, senior editor of *Wired* magazine, contends, "Mr. Gygax's game allowed geeks to venture out of our dungeons, blinking against the light, just in time to create the present age of electronic miracles."[4] And so they did. It wasn't the jocks or the prom kings and queens who created the social and business infrastructure of the twenty-first century. It was the geeks and the nerds who spent their Friday nights playing with their computers and Saturday nights playing a little *D&D* with their friends. In this way, *D&D* filled an important social gap for those less inclined to mingle.

Providing camaraderie through *D&D* and its role-playing offspring might, in fact, be Gary Gygax's greatest legacy. "It founded a means for socially awkward people to socialize,"[5] said early TSR employee and *Dragon* editor Tim Kask. What greater gift can a man give than the gift of friendship? To many, socializing comes quite naturally, but for countless others, it does not. To these, Gary gave companions—not just friends, but fellow adventurers, sharing dangerous journeys and exotic quests.

Acclaimed science fiction writer Jay Lake found this concept of companionship through role-playing games especially true during his early years. "At boarding school, if you're good and fast with homework, and deeply socially and athletically inept otherwise, there's not a lot to do. I'd been to seven schools in nine years on three continents when I hit Choate Rosemary Hall. I possessed the kind of poor social skills that are almost hip today, but were a recipe for meat-grinder misery in the 1970s when too-smart, too-isolated kids didn't have ready access to the kind of virtual retreats we have today in gaming, programming and online life. Geek culture at the teen level didn't exist yet, except as a special class of victimhood. Combine that with a raging case of clinical depression, and I was a disaster waiting to happen," says Lake. "The alternate worlds and wild imagination of *D&D* gave me and my fellow misfits an outlet."[6]

The bonds built between fellow gamers are indeed unique. Not only do they share imaginary adventures and a fair share of make-believe peril, but they reveal facets of their personalities that most mainstream friendships would never see. How many modern friends can say that together they have stormed dungeons, slain dragons, and been brought to the brink of death and back countless times? Though these experiences are imaginary, they are derived from a part of each gamer's personality, a part that most people would never let anyone see—the dreamer inside. These unabashed and unashamed group imagination exercises no doubt form the basis for deep and long lasting real-life relationships.

Gary Gygax believed friendship to be a sacred bond and blessing. As one who created games for a living, he understood gaming to be a means of fellowship, and he gave the topic a fair amount of study and contemplation. He would speak affectionately of an essay about friendship by Ralph Waldo Emerson that he read in his beloved "Little Leather Library,"[7] bequeathed to him by his chess-loving grandfather. Emerson's "Essay VI: Friendship" explains, "The only reward of virtue is virtue; the only way to have a friend is to be one . . . The essence of friendship is entireness, a total magnanimity and trust." Emerson would expound on this topic in his memoirs: "It is one of the blessings of old friends that you can afford to be stupid with them." These words well articulate not only the general concept of friendship, but specifically the sort of bonds formed through gaming.

D&D historian Paul Stormberg noted how Gary and many of his other early wargaming companions, such as Dave Arneson, Dave Wesley, and Jeff Perren, were only children—or, in Gary's case, effectively an only child, with a much older half brother and sister. Stormberg concludes that these early gamers were in essence "only children looking for brothers,"[8] seeking to build community and even family through their shared love of gaming. For Gary, RPGs served as "a ticket to worlds of adventure for you and your friends."[9]

Of Gary's contribution to friendships, his widow, Gail Gygax, says it best: "Gary led players on a journey of mutual respect and friendship through which they developed lifelong relationships, all thru the guise of a game."[10]

+42

The Butterfly Effect

IT IS MORE THAN the geeks of the world who owe Gary Gygax a debt of gratitude. A complete list of beneficiaries cannot easily be derived, but one also need not look far to see his exceptional contribution. Both the genres of fantasy and science fiction owe a great deal to Gygax. Beyond having his own character on *Futurama*, numerous books, movies, and video games have drawn inspiration either directly or indirectly from him and his games. To be sure, these media all exist independently of Gary and any work that he did. But, as Gary knew, there is a big difference between having an idea and realizing that idea. Gary's ability to accomplish the latter—whether it was assembling the disparate gaming mechanics that comprised role-playing games or organizing national gaming conventions—may have been his biggest strength. He knew how to put the pieces together to make something understandable, accessible, clear, and ultimately successful. Many have great ideas, but few combine these ideas with a vision to achieve them. Gary did, and because his work encouraged personal creativity, his contributions inspired and enabled countless other to do the same—to put the pieces together.

The influence of Ernest Gary Gygax and his creation *Dungeons & Dragons* on pop culture simply cannot be overstated. Just as Tolkien brought the fantasy genre into the mainstream, Gygax brought role-playing games and their derivative concepts to the masses.

D&D effectively created the role-playing-game industry, so it would not be a stretch to conclude that clear-cut *D&D* derivative games, and in fact all RPGs, came from this influential work. *Tunnels & Trolls* (Flying Buffalo, 1975), *Traveller* (GDW, 1977), *Call of Cthulhu*

(Chaosism, 1981), *Paranoia* (West End Games, 1984), *DC Heroes* (Mayfair Games, 1985), *Warhammer Fantasy Roleplay* (Games Workshop, 1986), *Star Wars* (West End Games, 1987), *Amber* (Phage Press, 1991), *Vampire the Masquerade* (White Wolf Publishing, 1991), *Deadlands* (Pinnacle Entertainment Group, 1996), *HackMaster* (Kenzer & Company, 2001), *Castles & Crusades* (Troll Lord Games, 2004), *Pathfinder* (Paizo Publishing, 2009), *Dungeons & Dragons 5th Edition* (Wizards of the Coast, 2014), and numerous others were either directly or indirectly inspired by the advent of *D&D*. "There's a reason why nearly every big-name American game designer will cite *D&D* as a formative influence," wrote *D&D 5th Edition* co-designer Rodney Thompson, "because the principles of *D&D* help form the foundation upon which modern game design is built."[1]

Ancillary to Gary's game design work was, of course, his 1968 founding of the Lake Geneva Wargames Convention, later known exclusively as Gen Con. Once a small get-together for an eclectic and disparate group of wargamers, Gen Con is today the nation's largest RPG and table-gaming convention, boasting more than fifty thousand attendees per year. Not only is Gen Con a legendary institution in its own right, but it inspired and effectively set the standard for other "cons" to follow, such as the renowned San Diego Comic-Con, which plays host to more than 120,000 people each year. Unsurprisingly, these cons feature a significant overlap of attendees, despite featuring a wide variety of geek-interest themes, including comics, RPGs, and cosplay, but Gen Con led the way, serving as the first notable convention of this type in the United States. According to friend and early TSR designer Mike Carr, Gen Con has for decades "entertained countless individuals and been the source of wonderful experiences, new friendships and cherished memories. To have founded such a successful and joyous event— I'd say THAT is a legacy of the highest order!"[2]

Even after his death, Gary continues to build the gaming community—most recently with a convention he didn't mean to create, Gary Con. Arranged by Gary's two eldest sons, Gary Con began as an informal gaming get-together following Gary's funeral in 2008. Since then, the annual Lake Geneva event has grown into a popular and highly organized "living memorial"[3] to *D&D*'s creator, with roughly nine hundred attendees per year, and growing.

Also relevant to Gary's legacy are the number of RPG companies that popped up over the years. Common hobbies such as reading don't usually inspire such a large number of participants to start a publishing company or open a bookstore, but the unique do-it-yourself nature of RPGs inspires their participants to not only play but to create. By the end of the 1970s dozens of RPG and related gaming companies had opened their doors, and today there are hundreds. *D&D* inspired and enabled the people who started these companies, all individuals who were once recreational gamers and enthusiasts, to take their interest to the next level. This not only triggered a virtual flood of ideas and creativity in the gaming world but, from a pragmatic standpoint, also created jobs and opportunities for many others. Thus, *D&D* started a butterfly effect of a scope and magnitude that cannot be underestimated creatively, socially, or economically.

Transitioning from the tabletop to the outdoors, live action role-playing games, or LARPs, are yet another phenomenon that owes at least some of its provenance to Gary Gygax, as evidenced by its name alone. Beginning as a culture that predated *D&D* with groups like the Society for Creative Anachronism (SCA), it was in its earliest form an activity that involved participants in period garb reenacting medieval and Renaissance culture. What has changed in the culture since the promulgation of *D&D* is a gaming or competitive element among many of these groups. LARPers are now an international community estimated to be in the hundreds of thousands worldwide, and many embody their characters both physically and behaviorally while participating in various role-playing games that have been retrofitted to suit live-action settings. Ironically, these activities are not dissimilar to the kind of gaming William Dear had speculated about in the case of James Dallas Egbert—minus the psychological dangers, of course.

Today, LARPs are as varied as the role-playing games that inspired them, ranging from physical group storytelling to combat-focused reenactments. In one popular example, True Dungeon, organizers create a "live-action, walk-through Dungeons & Dragons adventure,"[4] where participants navigate through a physical dungeon populated with tangible treasure, artifacts, animatronic monsters, and actors who serve as enemies and nonplayer characters (NPCs). Held annually at Gen Con, True Dungeon has become its biggest single event, impressing even Gary, who said, "When I started Gen Con more than three decades ago I did it in a true spirit of wanting to share with fellow gamers the true fun of getting together and enjoying ourselves. And True Dungeon is the epitome of that very thing."[5] Other popular LARPs include the Darkon Wargaming Club and NERO LARP, which feature simulated combat using foam-coated weapons. In MagiQuest, the most commercially successful LARP, players buy and use an interactive electronic wand that enables participants to solve puzzles and defeat monsters while tracking their gold and experience. Since opening in 2005, MagiQuest has expanded to fifteen commercial locations in the United States and Japan and sold more than eight hundred thousand wands.[6]

Along the same lines as table RPGs and LARPs, without *D&D* there clearly would be no basis for computer role-playing games (CRPGs) or massively multiplayer online role-playing games (MMORPGs or MMOs). As with the others, the relationship between these institutions and RPGs is self-evident, each ending its categorical title with "role-playing game." Where traditional tabletop RPGs never fully broke into the mainstream, both CRPGs (also synonymous with role-playing video games) and MMORPGs have become legitimate pop culture phenomena. According to authors Brad King and John Borland, *D&D* put this industry into motion by attracting "a community of, mostly, young men who were at the same time discovering the power and creativity offered by computer programming. In seeking to combine these two loves, this group of programmers, developers, and game players would over time profoundly shape an industry that would ultimately come to rival Hollywood in terms of scope and influence."[7]

Beginning as simple *D&D*-inspired text-based adventure games like *Zork*, early programmers used these concepts to create some of the earliest online games and communities called multi-user dungeons (MUDs). These adventure games and MUDs are the acknowledged ancestors of titles like *Might and Magic*, *Final Fantasy*, *Diablo*,

The Elder Scrolls, World of Warcraft, EverQuest, Star Wars: The Old Republic, Ultima, Eve Online, and even Nintendo's *The Legend of Zelda.* These are just some of the leading CRPGs and MMORPGs of the past few years and are very much part of the social mainstream, not to mention a multibillion-dollar industry.

"Gary Gygax was pivotal to the development of the gaming industry, and to my own career," said Richard Garriott, creator of the immensely popular *Ultima* series. "Millions upon millions of players around the world live and play in imaginary worlds built on the back of what Gary first conceived."[8]

With over ten million subscribers by itself, *World of Warcraft (WoW)* is as popular as some of the biggest shows on television. But unlike broadcast TV shows, which passively get an hour or so per week of a viewer's time, *WoW* and its counterparts often rack up hours of immersive and applied activity from individual subscribers, arguably providing a more valuable media platform to its users. Today one would be hard-pressed to spend any meaningful time on the Internet without seeing ads, pop-ups, or banners for an MMORPG. Ironically, many of the users and participants of these CRPGs and MMOs wouldn't necessarily categorize themselves as "role-playing gamers," and may not even realize that the mechanics of these games are derived from traditional tabletop RPGs.

This is not to ignore *D&D*'s impact on other video game types, most notably first-person shooters. The same way that Gary essentially created the RPG industry, John Carmack and John Romero created this monstrously successful genre of video game with their release of *Castle Wolfenstein* and their subsequent release of the legendary *Doom.* Notably, Carmack and Romero were prolific *Dungeons & Dragons* players, and one need not look far in their games to see *D&D*'s proverbial fingerprints all over them, whether it be the dungeon/maze element to their design or the monsters that you fight. Romero has even suggested that the idea for *Doom* may have come directly from one of their recent *D&D* sessions where "demons had overrun the entire planet and destroyed the whole game."[9]

With millions of copies sold for some of the larger franchises, first-person shooters have, so far, been the games of the twenty-first century.

With titles such as *Call of Duty*, *Halo*, and *Medal of Honor*, these games control a massive share of the video game industry—a trend recently demonstrated by the long-awaited release of Activision Blizzard's first-person shooter MMO, *Destiny*. The game achieved over $325 million in sales in its first five days—a feat rarely if ever accomplished in any established form of entertainment.

Going yet another step, massively popular virtual worlds, such as *Second Life* and *Habbo*, would have lacked the foundations for development without *D&D*. In fact, the entire concept of assuming an "avatar" has its origins deeply rooted in the earliest RPGs—namely, *D&D*. At its peak hosting over twenty million registered users, *Second Life* includes all of the elements of a traditional MMORPG with the exception of an obvious gaming objective. Nonetheless, without the foundational MMORPG interfaces, developed originally for *Neverwinter Nights*, *Ultima Online*, and *EverQuest*, to name a few, there would be no technical or intellectual structure for an institution such as *Second Life*. None of the creators of those MMORPGs would dispute finding a major part of their inspiration in *D&D* or a *D&D* derivative.

And what about online social networks and social media? Shortly after Gary's death, *Wired* editor and *New York Times* contributor Adam Rogers wrote, "Gary Gygax died last week and the universe did not collapse. This surprises me a little bit, because he built it."[10] He goes on to credit Gygax and *D&D* with laying the foundation for "the social and intellectual structure of our world."[11] And while it may be far-reaching to ascribe all things social media, and indeed their success, to Gary Gygax and *Dungeons & Dragons*, it is important to acknowledge that these technologies use concepts and platforms that were originally unique to RPGs. Drawing their lineage from early online networks like MUDs, sites like Facebook, Twitter, Google+, and OKCupid require participants to build a unique persona that will be "played" by its user. As I believe most would acknowledge, this persona is part real and part imaginary—effectively, the side created for public presentation. Any gamer could tell you that their RPG characters are just that: a component of his or her personality or intellect that is given life by the character.

Brad King and John Borland perhaps sum up this phenomenon best in their book *Dungeons & Dreamers*: "From pencil, paper, and dice came digital swords and magic spells, chain-guns and rocket launchers, clans and guilds, and, ultimately, rich virtual worlds filled with people who, in many cases, wanted to do nothing but talk."[12]

Moving from the desktop to the big screen, movies (and often the actors who star in them) have found tremendous inspiration through *Dungeons & Dragons*. Ignoring titles such as the unintentionally hilarious 1981 TV movie *Mazes and Monsters*, starring Tom Hanks, or the 1999 *Dungeons & Dragons*, a feature film starring Marlon Wayans and Jeremy Irons that Gary found to be without a "single redeeming feature,"[13] many movies and television shows have utilized concepts and ideas directly from *D&D*. This is not to ignore the obvious yet notable 1983 CBS cartoon *Dungeons & Dragons* starring Don Most and the legendary Frank Welker, but looking a little deeper, we find others.

Dungeons & Dragons was the game of choice for Elliott and his friends in the 1982 Steven Spielberg blockbuster *E.T. the Extra-Terrestrial*. It is known that Spielberg himself ran a module for the young cast ahead of filming in order to build a sense of family among the group.[14] Others, like celebrated actor, director, and writer Jon Favreau, while not using the game explicitly on-screen, credits the game with providing him "a really strong background in imagination, storytelling, understanding how to create tone and a sense of balance."[15]

D&D, however, has not always been portrayed in a favorable light by these entertainment media. It is said that imitation is the best form of flattery, and this too may apply to mockery. The word *mockery* applies, as few genres have continued to be so mocked, scorned, and abused as *Dungeons & Dragons* and its geeky gaming constituency on television or in the movies. And yet, whether it be through outrageous claims of devil worship or being ridiculed on television shows or movies, these have only managed to contribute to the appeal and notoriety of the otherwise esoteric game. A good example may be the episode entitled "Advanced Dungeons and Dragons" on the popular NBC sitcom *Community*. The show's extreme portrayals of both the game and its players not only exaggerate its sometimes outrageous nature, but an informed observer might note that some of the cast and crew seem more than casually familiar with its concepts.

Judd Apatow and Paul Feig used a session of *Dungeons & Dragons* to close out their short-lived but much beloved 1999 series *Freaks and Geeks*—a show that launched the careers of a who's who of prominent Hollywood actors, including James Franco, Seth Rogen, Jason Segel, Linda Cardellini, Martin Starr, Busy Philipps, and John Francis Daley, among others. In the series finale, entitled "Discos and Dragons," the show's geeky protagonists (the geeks) come together with James Franco's bad-boy hipster character (the freak) over a game of *D&D*, leaving the geeks to wonder, "Does him wanting to play with us again mean that he's turning into a geek, or we're turning into cool guys?"[16] *That 70's Show* features a similarly memorable session of *D&D* that includes legendary shock rocker Alice Cooper, while Joss Whedon features the game in the series finale of *Buffy the Vampire Slayer*. Now in its eighth season, the wildly successful *The Big Bang Theory* features the lead characters in a co-ed session of *D&D* in the show's sixth season, while in its eighth season Sheldon speaks of a desire to make a pilgrimage to Gary Con. The show's astonishing success serves as perhaps the best evidence of pop culture's current love affair with geek culture.

The extraordinary success of the *Lord of the Rings* movie trilogy and the more recent *Game of Thrones* television series are but a couple of examples of how inundated popular culture has become with the formerly esoteric world of fantasy. To be sure, Gygax did not create the fantasy genre, but he certainly popularized it in a very personal way that not only bolstered its audience but also multiplied its creators and innovators. Luke Gygax, Gary's youngest son by his first wife, Mary Jo, wonders, "Would Lord of the Rings or Harry Potter been made into movies had the market not been prepped for it by Dungeons & Dragons?"[17] Gary's *Lejendary Adventures* co-designer Chris Clark agrees, pointing out that if you look in *TV Guide* from 1974 "you'll see Star Trek; you won't see any fantasy . . . that's not the case anymore, is it?"[18] Who or what was carrying the fantasy torch through the 1970s, '80s, and '90s? Who was providing the fundamental structure for fantasy characters, settings, and plots? According to RPG scholar Michael Tresca, "Dungeons & Dragons acted as a translation of sorts for the fantasy genre."[19] Whether it was a translation or an inspiration, there can be little doubt that Gary's creation popularized and influenced the fantasy genre as we know it today.

There are, of course, many clear-cut derivations of *D&D* in the world of fantasy and science fiction. Without Gary Gygax, there always were and always would be fans of these genres, but never to the extent of immersion or popularity that they eventually reached. These genres are, frankly, too abstract and require too much investment for the average person to undertake. But *Dungeons & Dragons*, and role playing in general, provided a new level of personalization for these worlds. It created an atmosphere of do-it-yourself fantasy and science fiction storytelling that, according to Jay Little, designer of Fantasy Flight Games' *Star Wars: Edge of the Empire Roleplaying Game*, "created a new way for fans to interact with fantasy literature and culture."[20] Now anyone could be part of the story, and anyone could begin to fill in the blanks regarding the background and characters of these fantastical worlds. Here too, RPGs created a foundation with which millions could begin to contribute to the story.

Fittingly, one such example is the *Star Wars* saga. Pennsylvania-based West End Games started in 1974 as a board game company but began developing role-playing games in the early 1980s based on their immense popularity. By 1986, they had managed several RPG successes, including *Paranoia* and *Ghostbusters: A Frightfully Cheerful Roleplaying Game*. In 1987, they decided to take a gamble on what would be an expensive but potentially lucrative license—*Star Wars*.

To date, more credible *Star Wars* background information and details have emerged from this gaming system than from any other source apart from George Lucas and the past and present owners of the intellectual property, Lucasfilm and now Disney. Countless characters, weapons, planets, aliens, and plot lines surfaced from this collection of source books and adventure modules and became officially accepted as *Star Wars* canon, providing substantial material used in the second trilogy of films, as well as the foundation for what fans term the *Star*

Wars Expanded Universe. As such, West End Games and the players of the *Star Wars* RPG filled in many of the blanks ahead of numerous comics, books, video games, and animated series. Ultimately, this effort would not have been possible without RPGs. And without Gary Gygax, there would be no RPGs.

From the role-playing games to live-action role playing, from geek conventions to gaming companies, from video games and virtual worlds to online social networks, from books and movies to television shows, Gary's game has made—and continues to make—its mark.

All hail Gary Gygax, the King of the Nerds.

+43

The Road Goes Ever On

ALTHOUGH GARY DIED IN 2008, his story is still unfinished. Perhaps the best evidence of Gary's impact is the enduring success of his seminal gaming masterpiece, *Dungeons & Dragons*, now in its fifth edition.

Since officially parting ways with Gary in 1986, *D&D* embarked on a journey that proved every bit as rocky as its creator's. Under Lorraine Williams, TSR embraced a company culture less intent on crediting individuals with the products they worked on, instead ascribing this creative output to the corporation. While this is a common practice in many businesses, TSR once had a unique creative culture built on its developers and designers receiving significant individual recognition and, in previous years, a share in their product's successes through royalties. The company quickly lost much of its best talent a couple of years after Gary's departure, including bestselling authors Margaret Weis and Tracy Hickman, as well as celebrated illustrator Larry Elmore—the creative team behind TSR's bestselling *Dragonlance* novels. This was on top of losing Gary himself as well as Frank Mentzer and Kim Mohan, who joined his New Infinities team. Still, many talented staffers stayed on and produced worthy materials, like Ed Greenwood's *Forgotten Realms* campaign materials, but also suffered through precarious projects such as a series of *Buck Rogers* game products, an intellectual property still owned by and licensed from the family of Lorraine Williams. In fact, when Elmore heard about the *Buck Rogers* line shortly before his departure, he recalls commenting to a co-worker that "you couldn't sell that game in a gold-plated box!"[1]—a sentiment shared by much of TSR's creative staff, including VP for creative services Jim Ward. After announcing a new version of

Buck Rogers XXVC role-playing game at the 1993 GAMA show, Ward famously remarked, "We're going to keep making it until you buy it."[2]

After TSR's lukewarm release of *2nd Edition* in 1989, the company seemed to maintain a growth strategy of one step forward, two steps back. The positives included popular campaign settings such as the vampire-themed *Ravenloft*; a series of class-specific *Player's Handbook Rules Supplements* (often referred to as "splatbooks"), and a lucrative license for a series of *AD&D* computer role-playing games produced by Strategic Simulations, Inc. (SSI). These successes, however, were outweighed by puzzling business moves like the buyouts of Gary's *Dangerous Journeys* and Mayfair's *Role Aids* lines, expensive deals that acquired products that barely saw the retail shelves; a series of pricey lawsuits; and the overproduction of fantasy novels that were steadily declining in quality and appeal. These suspect decisions culminated in TSR's costly and ultimately unsuccessful bets on *Spellfire: Master the Magic* and *Dragon Dice*, products meant to compete with the wildly successful *Magic: The Gathering* collectible card game (CCG).[3] These failures, combined with the return of millions of dollars of inventory from its distributor, Random House, and mounting pressures from creditors, ultimately spelled certain doom for TSR.

By 1997, TSR was $30 million in debt and game production had halted. At this point, Williams had little choice but to pursue offers from competitors, which came in the form of Five Rings Publishing, maker of the *Legend of the Five Rings* CCG. Early in the due diligence phase of the prospective deal, Five Rings principal Ryan Dancey "found a dead company" that was "rotten to the core."[4] Over the course of several trips to TSR's Lake Geneva headquarters, Dancey discovered a once-great brand that had resorted to using copyright interests to secure its many debts, along with "a warehouse packed from floor to 50-foot ceiling with products valued as though they would they would soon be sold to a distributor with production stamps stretching back to the late 1980s," including "stacks and stacks of 1st edition rulebooks."[5] Still, Dancey was convinced that *Dungeons & Dragons* could be saved, and he recommended the purchase to Five Rings CEO Bob Abramowitz, who subsequently negotiated an option to buy TSR. Five Rings, however, was not nearly large enough to fund such an acquisition, so it approached CCG competitor and industry leader Wizards of the Coast for an investment. Fortunately, Wizards founder and CEO Peter Adkison was a longtime role-playing gamer and understood the intrinsic value of the TSR brand, but instead of arranging the investment, he made a counteroffer—to purchase both TSR and Five Rings Publishing outright. It turned out that Adkison had broached the subject of acquisition with TSR two years earlier, to no avail. Now the deal had come right to his doorstep, and it proved timely for Wizards, as there had been a growing concern among leadership that the company had become a "one-hit wonder" with its *Magic: The Gathering* CCG. Owning TSR would give Wizards the name recognition and diversification it was looking for. With Five Rings now serving as broker to the deal, Wizards acquired TSR and all of its intellectual property for roughly $30 million, the vast majority used to pay off its creditors.[6] As with Adkison's other business dealings, including his later repurchase of Gen Con for under $1 million, everything he touched turned to gold. Just two years later, in 1999, Adkison turned around and sold Wizards to leading toymaker Hasbro for nearly $500 million.

Wizards of the Coast, now operating as a subsidiary of Hasbro, has carried the *D&D* torch ever since. During its tenure with *D&D*, Wizards has released three major revisions to the game, *3rd Edition*, *4th Edition*, and *5th Edition* (known in the industry as 3E, 4E, and 5E, respectively), all with varying levels of success. Released in 2000, *3rd Edition* sought to clean up many of the game's mechanics by adapting it to the "d20 System," predicated on the use of the twenty-sided die but retaining the other polyhedral dice for secondary results such as damage. However, whatever complexities they saved with dice mechanics they made up for with character customization, which added a series of character-specific skills and feats, making the game both story focused and complex. Also notable is that *3rd Edition* was published under the Open Gaming License (OGL), a system meant to build popularity and engender community by allowing its supporters to develop their own d20-derivative games and supplements without paying licensing fees. Whatever its strengths and weaknesses, *D&D*'s *3rd Edition* rejuvenated the brand and was a commercial success, as were Wizard's other games based on the same d20 System, including its 2000 release of the *Star Wars Roleplaying Game.*

In the following years, Wizards developed other *D&D* versions, including an edition informally called "3.5," a moderate revision to the *3rd Edition* rules in 2003, and the 2008 release of *4th Edition*, which streamlined some elements of character creation and development, but ramped up the complexity of the combat system. By this time, the game's mechanics had begun to emulate the many computer role-playing games on the market, prioritizing character customization and sensational combat maneuvers achieved through a system of class-specific "powers," in addition to its skills and feats. Like its *2nd Edition* counterpart, this game was met with only moderate success, and soon thereafter many fantasy role-playing gamers gravitated toward Paizo Publishing's 2009 *Pathfinder*, ironically a revised and modified version of *D&D*'s *3rd Edition* (and 3.5) rules, developed under the d20 Open Gaming License.

With *D&D* suffering from what many gamers and Wizards staffers called "edition wars,"[7] it began to look as though the game might eventually fade into relative obscurity and become just another fantasy role-playing game. But Wizards is a company that prides itself on being responsive to its audience. Many fans were unhappy that *D&D* edition 3.5 had so quickly been abandoned and that *4th Edition* was not readily compatible. Others complained that the combat mechanics for *4th Edition* had become too complicated and cumbersome, especially at higher levels. Taking these comments to heart, Wizards embarked on a simpler, universally compatible system called *Dungeons & Dragons 5th Edition*. Released at Gen Con 47 in 2014, the *Player's Handbook* for *5th Edition* quickly became a bestseller, not just among role-playing games but among all books, achieving number one bestseller status on Amazon (all books) and reaching number one on the *Wall Street Journal* and *Publisher's Weekly* hardcover nonfiction lists. The subsequent releases of the *Monster Manual* and *Dungeon Master's Guide* for that edition attained similarly impressive results. *D&D*'s newest version is an unqualified success. Ironically, much of *5E*'s success is due to returning to many of the original concepts that Gary had laid out in his early *D&D* products—back to the basics. "The designers of *5E* have ruthlessly hacked off much of the complexity that can put off new role-players, arriving at an elegant system that owes much more to classic *D&D* than it does to the previous edition,"[8] said one reviewer. Wizards designer Rodney Thompson explained more methodically, "We wanted our players to be able to trust the Dungeon Master as much as we did, and a big thing we could do to make that happen is to have the system function in a way that makes those judgment calls seem natural and expected . . . If you look back at older editions of *D&D*, especially those that Gygax and Arneson had a hand in crafting, you can see that they had that same kind of trust in the DM."[9]

While *D&D* is a bestseller again, some things around the game have never changed, including controversy and litigation. Even after decades of credible defense, most notably that of Michael Stackpole's writings, *D&D* still suffers from some of its earliest stigmas. In 2010, the Seventh Circuit U.S. Court of Appeals upheld the ban of *D&D* from a Wisconsin prison, its officials arguing that the game could promote "competitive hostility, violence, addictive escape behaviors, and possibly gambling,"[10] and ultimately "foster an inmate's obsession with escaping from the real-life correctional environment."[11]

More recently, *D&D* has attracted national attention from a lawsuit related to the making of a documentary about the game. Beginning with a 2012 Kickstarter campaign that raised over $195,000, filmmakers Anthony Savini, Andrew Pascal, and James Sprattley embarked on what was meant to be the highest-quality, most comprehensive *D&D* documentary to date, entitled *Dungeons & Dragons: A Documentary*. After conducting extensive research and undertaking numerous on-camera interviews, the documentary seemed poised for success and was on schedule to meet its summer 2014 release date, in time to commemorate the game's fortieth anniversary. But, as of this writing, no documentary has been released. Instead, the trailer for a second and competing documentary called *The Great Kingdom* popped up on the scene in January 2014, produced by two of original documentary's three partners, Andrew Pascal and James Sprattley. Apparently a creative rift occurred between Savini and his two partners early in the first film's development and the producers parted ways. Savini subsequently filed a lawsuit in New York State's Supreme Court against his former partners that includes a range of charges from breach of fiduciary duty to fraudulent inducement to unfair competition.[12] And for the time being, the court agrees: "It has been demonstrated that completion of the partnership film is being undermined, and its commercial value potentially diluted, by defendants' solicitation of funding for, and advertising of, its competing film,"[13] wrote Justice Carolyn E. Demarest, who has granted Savini's injunction and put *The Great Kingdom* on indefinite hold.

Lawsuits and *D&D* have been inexplicably linked since the game's earliest days. Some liken this relationship to a curse, including defendant Andrew Pascal, who explains, "Gamers are very territorial and they're very opinionated, and so because of that there's sort of a natural inclination to form factions and form groups and rivalries and things like that."[14] Whatever the case, it's hard not to see the parallels between the development of the game and the documentary, whose tagline reads, "A cautionary tale of an empire built by friends and lost through betrayal, enmity, poor management, hubris and litigation."[15]

For those who know, play, and love *D&D*, this is nothing new—it's like déjà vu all over again.

✝44

A Man for All Seasons

GARY GYGAX WAS so many things to so many people: an innovator, a friend, colleague, and family man. Late one night shortly after Gary had passed, Gary's first son, Ernie, was reminiscing with Gary's friend and Troll Lord Games publisher, Steve Chenault. After a time, when Steve rested his feet on the table, Ernie looked at Steve's boots and said, "You know, my dad was a cobbler."[1] This phrase puzzled Chenault for the remainder of the evening and for several days thereafter. He then quite suddenly realized that Gary "was the guy who made boots for all of us. He gave us boots and told us to adventure,"[2] explained Chenault.

Gary Gygax was indeed a cobbler of tales, a cobbler of adventure, and a cobbler of friendship. He discovered the recipe for bringing a diverse group of individuals together and allowing them to find common ground. "He showed us the potential for games to bring humanity together,"[3] said *D&D* historian Paul Stormberg when asked about Gary's legacy. One can only imagine how odd the scene must have looked in the days of Gary's local gaming group, the Lake Geneva Tactical Studies Association: a few guys in their mid-thirties, including a professor of statistics; a couple of guys in their early twenties; a young teenager; and a ten-year-old. Despite the significant differences that existed in their respective lives, on the gaming table they could all come together for a common purpose by which they were united.

Gary's old friend and employee Tim Kask equates Gary to a farmer who "cleared the trees, pulled the stumps, plowed the fields and sowed the first seeds"[4] of extraordinary creativity for others to cultivate. As Gary describes it himself in the original *Advanced Dungeons & Dragons*

Player's Handbook, "So at best I give you parameters here, and the rest is up to the individuals who are the stuff *D&D* is made of."⁵

Whether it be as a cobbler, farmer, gamer, or father, Gary Gygax's legacy lives on through his family, his friends, the games he invented, and the culture of geeks who played the game and subsequently took over the world—a world that he prepared for imagination. This is Gary's empire of imagination.

Though not easily quantifiable, Gary's contributions to the world we know can only be described as extraordinary. True to his humble nature, he probably would have been quite surprised by this. After all, his focus wasn't wealth, power, or worldly success. He just wanted to play games. He just wanted others to love and play games, as he did.

As usual, the legendary person who inspired this book best speaks for himself: "The books I write because I want to read them, the games because I want to play them, and stories I tell because I find them exciting personally . . . I would like the world to remember me as the guy who really enjoyed playing games and sharing his knowledge and his fun pastimes with everybody else."⁶

Acknowledgments

EMPIRE OF IMAGINATION was an incredible three-year journey that would not have been possible without an extraordinary amount of external love, help, and support. While the following words cannot fully express the amount of gratitude I feel, please accept this as my attempt to acknowledge these exceptional contributions.

First and foremost, thank you God for inspiring me with this crazy idea, and then granting me the energy and inspiration to make it happen. Through this process, I hope I have lived up to Gary's favorite Bible passage to "let your light shine before others, that they may see your good deeds and glorify your Father in heaven."

Thank you to my spectacularly loving and supportive family (both immediate and extended), who encouraged, empowered, and ultimately enabled me to complete this exciting journey. Limitless thanks to my wife and children for putting up with my particularly intolerable moments as I scrambled to create time to make this project happen. Also, a heartfelt thank-you to my parents: my dad, who supported every part of the project from its earliest stages and served as my first editor (along with the help of Corinne Pardon), and my mom, who picked up so many pieces in my life throughout, allowing me to take the project across the finish line. Lastly, thank you to my brother, Sam, who originally inspired my interest in the subject and served as our longtime Dungeon Master—quite possibly the world's greatest.

Thank you to the professional team that allowed this project to take flight. First, a grand thank-you to my agent, the great Jacques de Spoelberch, for taking a chance on an unknown like myself and being such an incredible advocate for the project. Next, a tremendous thanks to my editor, the incomparable Rob Galloway, who believed in the project and put himself on the line to acquire it. He then contributed his exceptional editorial talent to truly make the book what it is today. Then to the good folks at Bloomsbury for believing in the project and devoting your significant time, talents, and resources to the project, especially George Gibson, Patti Ratchford, Gleni Bartels, Summer Smith, Megan Ernst, Callie Garnett, and Derrick Kennelty-Cohen—thank you!

A huge and special thanks to members of the Gygax family, who generously shared with me their memories and insights around Gary, which, perhaps more than anything else, made this project possible. I was literally driven to tears at times, overwhelmed by the commitment, helpfulness, and generosity of the Gygaxes—a wonderful testament to how much Gary was loved and to the quality of people that he raised. My love and thanks go out to them.

Thank you to the Council, my oldest friends and gaming group that fostered in me the interest, creativity, and support to complete this project—love you guys!

Thank you to the University of Chicago, which through the Graham School master's program inspired me, and indeed required me, to rise to the next level of intellectual curiosity and study. Special thanks to Dr. David Bevington, who served as my faculty advisor and provided me excellent advice on early versions of the manuscript when it was still a master's project. Beyond being the world's preeminent authority on Renaissance drama, Dr. Bevington is also an all-around great guy.

A major thanks to TSR art legend Jeff Easley, who not only was kind enough to allow me to interview him but also provided the spectacular cover art. Thank you, Jeff, for lending us your spectacular talents and for your endless patience as you dealt with the rambling critiques of a nonartist like myself. My hearty thanks also to Stephen Sullivan, another TSR legend, for lending his talents to the awesome endpaper maps.

Thank you to Paul Stormberg, preeminent *D&D* historian and owner of The Collector's Trove. Paul not only shared his amazing insights about Gary in an interview but also later graciously signed on to support the work as a research consultant, providing numerous details and insights that otherwise would have been impossible to find. No matter how much I think I know about the subject of RPGs, I am continually humbled when I talk to Paul.

Finally, my infinite thanks to the following individuals who generously and graciously gave me their time through interviews and correspondence, sharing their unique industry insights and one-of-a-kind experiences with Gary (listed alphabetically): Peter Adkison; Mike Carr; Stephen Chenault; Chris Clark; Curt Duval of Games Plus, who allowed me to peruse his spectacular collection of early and original gaming and role-playing materials; Larry Elmore; Harold Johnson; Tim Kask; Jay Little; Millie Marmur; Frank Mentzer; Jeff Perren; Jon Peterson, author of *Playing at the World*, the RPG history bible as far as I'm concerned; Jon Pickens; Ciro Alessandro Sacco for his spectacular "The Ultimate Interview with Gary Gygax"; Rodney Thompson; Jim Ward; and, last but certainly not least, Dave Wesley. You all are the stuff that *Empire of Imagination* is made of—thank you!

Appendix A
Gary Gygax Timeline

July 27, 1938: Ernest Gary Gygax was born to Ernest and Almina "Posey" Gygax in Chicago, Illinois.

1943: Gary learns pinochle.

1944: Gary learns chess from his maternal grandfather, Hugh Burdick.

Summer 1946: Gary is involved in a brawl with kids from another neighborhood, and his father moves his family to Lake Geneva, Wisconsin, his mother's hometown.

Summer 1947: Gary experiences an unexplained "poltergeist" incident in his grandparents' house.

Fall 1949: Gary explores the Oak Hill Sanatorium with friends—the first of many such adventures.

November 1949: Gary has a second "poltergeist" experience while home alone reading "The Fall of the House of Usher" in his grandparents' parlor.

Summer 1950: Having recently read Robert E. Howard's *Conan the Conqueror*, Gary develops a great interest in pulp magazines.

Summer 1953: Fifteen-year-old Gary takes his father's car out for a joy ride and crashes it. Gary never drives again.

January 1956: Gary's father, Ernest, passes away at the age of seventy-two.

Spring 1956: Gary drops out of high school and joins the Marines.

1957: Gary gets a job as a shipping clerk at Kemper Insurance in Chicago.

1958: Gary begins playing an Avalon Hill wargame called *Gettysburg.*

September 14, 1958: Gary marries childhood friend Mary Jo Powell.

September 2, 1959: Gary's first son, Ernest "Ernie" Gary Gygax Jr., is born.

1960: Gary, Mary Jo, and Ernie move to Chicago, Illinois.

August 1, 1961: Gary's first daughter, Mary Elise Gygax, is born.

1962: Gary gets a job as an insurance underwriter at Fireman's Fund Insurance of Chicago.

April 17, 1963: Gary's childhood friend Tom Keogh passes away.

Late 1963: Gary moves back to Lake Geneva and rents a home at 330 Center Street.

October 20, 1964: Gary's second daughter, Heidi Jo Gygax, is born.

September 1966: Gary joins a small, national wargaming group called the United States Continental Army Command (USCAC). He begins writing columns in several wargaming newsletters and periodicals (fanzines).

December 16, 1966: Gary's third daughter, Cindy Lee Gygax, is born.

1967: Gary becomes increasingly involved with the USCAC and cofounds a successor group called the International Federation of Wargaming (IFW).

July 1967: Gary helps organize an IFW wargaming convention in Malvern, Pennsylvania, but the event has low attendance and is unsuccessful.

1968: Gary founds a specialty group of the IFW called the War Game Inventors Guild. He regularly publishes new games and game variants through this group and IFW periodicals.

August 24, 1968: Gary organizes and hosts the inaugural Lake Geneva Wargames Convention (Gen Con).

August 23, 1969: Gary meets Minneapolis wargamer Dave Arneson at Gen Con II.

Late 1969: Gary builds a six-by-ten-foot sand-topped gaming table in his basement to facilitate large-scale miniatures wargames.

Late 1969/early 1970: Gary organizes a group of local gamers called the Lake Geneva Tactical Studies Association (LGTSA).

March 1970: Gary forms a specialty group of the LGTSA focused on the medieval period called the Castle & Crusade Society (C&CS). He supports the group through a monthly periodical called *Domesday Book*.

Late October 1970: Gary loses his job as an insurance underwriter at the Fireman's Fund of Chicago.

November 7, 1970: Gary's second son, Lucion "Luke" Paul Gygax, is born.

Early 1971: Gary begins developing and editing games for boutique game publisher Guidon Games.

March 1971: Gary coauthors a medieval miniatures wargame game called *Chainmail* with LGTSA member Jeff Perren, published through Guidon Games.

Mid-1971: To supplement his meager game design earnings, and in an effort to make ends meet, Gary begins cobbling shoes out of his basement.

1971–1972: Gary collaborates with Dave Arneson and Mike Carr on a naval miniatures rules set called *Don't Give Up the Ship*, published through Guidon Games.

November 1972: Dave Arneson comes to Lake Geneva to demonstrate to Gary and other LGTSA members a game based on *Chainmail* called *Blackmoor* that he has been playing with his Twin Cities gaming group. Gary believes the game has potential and asks Arneson for his notes.

Late 1972/early 1973: Gary begins drafting formalized rules for the *Blackmoor* game and playtests them with his local group. Gary and Arneson use a working title of *The Fantasy Game.*

October 1973: Gary and Don Kaye form a partnership called Tactical Studies Rules (TSR) to produce Gary and Arneson's new game, now called *Dungeons & Dragons (D&D).* They count on their first publication, *Cavaliers and Roundheads,* coauthored by Gary and his *Chainmail* collaborator Jeff Perren, to raise enough capital to produce *D&D.*

December 1973: Gary becomes anxious to produce *D&D* immediately; in order to quickly raise the necessary capital, Gary and Kaye bring in a third, equal partner, Brian Blume.

January 1974: TSR publishes its first one thousand copies of *D&D.*

January 4, 1974: Gary, acting on behalf of the partnership, signs a royalty contract with Dave Arneson listed as coauthor. Each gets a 10 percent royalty on copies sold.

January 31, 1975: Gary's longtime friend and TSR's one-third partner, Don Kaye, unexpectedly dies of a heart attack.

April 1975: Gary launches TSR's in-house gaming periodical, called the *Strategic Review.*

Summer 1975: Due to the success of *D&D,* Gary sells his cobbling equipment and becomes TSR's first full-time employee.

Fall 1975: The partnership of TSR is reorganized as TSR Hobbies, Inc. and a third investor, Melvin Blume (Brian's father), is brought in to assist in buying out the Kaye shares and to enable continued production.

September 1975: TSR hires its first outside employee, Tim Kask.

Early 1976: TSR hires creative staff including Mike Carr, Dave Megarry, Dave Sutherland, Rob Kuntz, and *D&D* cocreator Dave Arneson.

April 1976: TSR acquires space in a house, which serves as its corporate offices and retail location, the Dungeon Hobby Shop.

June 1976: TSR debuts its gaming magazine, the *Dragon.*

November 1976: Dave Arneson's employment at TSR ends. Brian Blume's brother, Kevin, is hired to work in TSR's accounting department.

1977: TSR releases a popular revised boxed set of basic *D&D*.

1978: TSR releases the *Monster Manual* and the *Player's Handbook,* the first two core books of a version of the game called *Advanced Dungeons & Dragons (AD&D)*.

February 1979: Dave Arneson sues Gary and TSR for not paying him royalties on the new *AD&D* system.

July 1979: Gary purchases a twenty-three-acre horse farm and mansion in Clinton, Wisconsin, that he nicknames "Dragonlands."

August 1979: A *D&D*-playing Michigan State University student named James Dallas Egbert disappears. The private detective on the case theorizes that the game damaged the student's sense of reality, causing him to make fatal decisions. A media frenzy ensues that tarnishes the game's image but bolsters its sales and notoriety.

September 1979: TSR signs an exclusive book trade distribution agreement with the nation's largest publisher, Random House.

October 20, 1980: Gary's mother, Posey, dies of a heart attack.

1982: TSR is named by *Inc.* magazine as one of its top 100 fastest-growing companies.

March 1983: Gary and his wife, Mary Jo, separate.

Summer 1983: TSR splits into various subsidiaries. Gary is directed by the board to manage Dungeons & Dragons Entertainment Corp. in Los Angeles. Gary sets up his residence and headquarters at a lavish Beverly Hills estate formerly owned by Hollywood producer/director King Vidor.

September 17, 1983: CBS premieres *Dungeons & Dragons* the cartoon, which leads its Saturday morning time slot.

1984: Gary attempts to put together a *D&D* movie deal and gains the interest of Universal Studios and renowned Hollywood actors and directors.

Late 1984: Gary returns to Lake Geneva amid rumors of financial troubles at TSR and its imminent sale. He links Kevin Blume to the issues and gets him removed as president of the company.

March 18, 1985: Gary exercises a long-held stock option and gains majority interest in TSR.

April 1, 1985: Gary hires Lorraine Williams to help manage TSR and regain its financial footing.

June 1985: TSR releases *AD&D Unearthed Arcana*, which sells ninety thousand copies in its first month. This, paired with other strong-performing product lines like *Marvel Super Heroes*, *D&D Dragonlance*, and Gary's bestselling *Greyhawk* novel, *Saga of Old City*, brings the company back to reasonable financial health.

October 22, 1985: Gary is ousted from TSR after Lorraine Williams purchases a majority interest in the company from the Blume brothers.

1986: Gary takes Williams and the Blume brothers to court, claiming their deal violated the shareholder agreement. Gary loses and sells his remaining TSR interest to Williams.

August 2, 1986: Gary's third son, Alexander Hugh Hamilton Gygax, is born to girlfriend and former TSR assistant Gail Carpenter.

October 1986: Gary starts a new gaming and publishing company called New Infinities Productions. Gary writes novels for the company, while its design staff, Frank Mentzer and Kim Mohan, work on games.

1987: TSR sues New Infinities for copyright infringement over its publishing of an adventure module that was originally developed at TSR.

August 15, 1987: Gary marries Gail Carpenter on what would have been his parents' fiftieth wedding anniversary.

1989: New Infinities files for bankruptcy and goes out of business.

1992: Gary develops a new role-playing gaming system called *Dangerous Dimensions*. Games Designers' Workshop (GDW) publishes the paper game, while NEC and JVC acquire its video game rights. TSR sues over trademark confusion.

Late 1992: To avoid litigation with TSR, Gary changes the name of *Dangerous Dimensions* to *Dangerous Journeys*. TSR persists in its litigation against Gary and GDW, this time for copyright infringement. NEC and JVC drop out of the deal.

March 18, 1994: Gary and GDW settle with TSR, which purchases and shelves all of the *Dangerous Journeys* rights and products.

1994–1996: Gary develops a number of computer and video game role-playing game (CRPG) concepts and sells the rights to a couple of them.

1996: Gary begins testing a tabletop RPG version of one of his earlier CRPG concepts with his local gaming group. The game is called *Lejendary Adventures*.

1997: With bankruptcy looming, TSR is acquired by *Magic: The Gathering* maker Wizards of the Coast. Gary receives a generous buyout of his residual rights from Wizards founder Peter Adkison.

1998–1999: In the wake of TSR's bankruptcy and acquisition, Gary teams up with Chris Clark of Inner City Games to develop a couple of generic fantasy RPG modules.

1999: Gary and Chris Clark form a partnership called Hekaforge Productions and publish Gary's *Lejendary Adventures* RPG.

May 21, 2000: Gary is featured on an episode of Fox's hit animated show *Futurama*, alongside Al Gore, Stephen Hawking, and Nichelle Nichols.

2001: Gary begins working on a number of generic RPG products with Arkansas-based Troll Lord Games.

2002–2003: Gary is named as number eighteen on *GameSpot* magazine's "30 Most Influential People in Gaming," number thirty-seven on *SFX* magazine's "50 Greatest SF Pioneers," and number one on *Sync* magazine's "50 Biggest Nerds of All Time."

July 27, 2003: Gary hosts all of his children and grandchildren at his Lake Geneva home in celebration of his sixty-fifth birthday.

April 1 and May 4, 2004: Gary suffers back-to-back strokes, leaving him in poor health and unable to work his usual long hours.

2005: Troll Lord Games picks up Gary's *Lejendary Adventures* system and publishes *Lejendary Adventures Essential Rulebook*. A number of related products follow.

Late 2005: Gary is diagnosed with an abdominal aortic aneurysm, a ballooning of the largest artery leading into the heart.

March 4, 2008: Gary dies of an abdominal aortic aneurysm.

Appendix B
Gary Gygax: A Life's Work

Role-Playing Games

Dungeons & Dragons (D&D), role-playing game with Dave Arneson (TSR 1974)

Greyhawk, *D&D* supplement with Rob Kuntz (TSR 1975)

Eldritch Wizardry, *D&D* supplement with Brian Blume (TSR 1976)

Boot Hill, role-playing game with Brian Blume (TSR 1975)

Lost Caverns of Tsojcanth, *D&D* adventure module (TSR 1976 & 1982)

Dungeon Geomorphs (3 sets), *D&D* accessories (TSR 1976–1977)

Outdoor Geomorphs, *D&D* accessory (TSR 1977)

Monster Manual, *Advanced Dungeons & Dragons (AD&D)* role-playing game rule book (TSR 1977)

Players Handbook, *AD&D* role-playing game rule book (TSR 1978)

Steading of the Hill Giant Chief, *AD&D* adventure module (TSR 1978)

Glacial Rift of the Frost Giant Jarl, *AD&D* adventure module (TSR 1978)

Hall of the Fire Giant King, *AD&D* adventure module (TSR 1978)

Descent into the Depths of the Earth, *AD&D* adventure module (TSR 1978)

Shrine of the Kuo-Toa, AD&D adventure module (TSR 1978)

Vault of the Drow, AD&D adventure module with *Descent into the Depths of the Earth* and *Shrine of Kuo-Toa* (TSR 1978)

Tomb of Horrors, AD&D adventure module (TSR 1978)

Dungeon Masters Guide, AD&D role-playing game rule book (TSR 1979)

Village of Hommlet, AD&D adventure module (TSR 1979)

Keep on the Borderlands, D&D adventure module (TSR 1979)

World of Greyhawk, AD&D supplement (TSR 1980)

Expedition to the Barrier Peaks, AD&D adventure module (1980)

Dungeons & Dragons Expert Rulebook, role-playing game rule book (TSR 1981)

Dungeons & Dragons Expert Set, role-playing game boxed set (TSR 1981)

Legion of Gold, Gamma World adventure module with Luke Gygax and Paul Ritchie III (TSR 1981)

Forgotten Temple of Tharizdun, AD&D game adventure module (TSR 1982)

Monster Manual II, AD&D supplement (TSR 1983)

Dungeons & Dragons Set 2: Expert Rules, role-playing game boxed set (TSR 1983)

Dungeonland, AD&D adventure module (TSR 1983)

Land Beyond the Magic Mirror, AD&D adventure module (TSR 1983)

Mordenkainen's Fantastic Adventure, AD&D adventure module with Rob Kuntz (TSR 1984)

The Book of Marvelous Magic, D&D supplement with Frank Mentzer (TSR 1984)

Isle of the Ape, AD&D adventure module (TSR 1985)

Unearthed Arcana, AD&D supplement (TSR 1985)

Temple of Elemental Evil, AD&D adventure module with Frank Mentzer (TSR 1985)

Dungeons & Dragons Set 4: Master Rules, role-playing game boxed set with Frank Mentzer (TSR 1985)

Oriental Adventures, AD&D supplement with David Cook and François Froideval (TSR 1985)

Queen of the Spiders, AD&D adventure module (TSR 1986)

Cyborg Commando, role-playing game with Frank Mentzer and Kim Mohan (NIPI 1987)

Mythus, Dangerous Journeys (DJ) role-playing game rule book (GDW 1992)

Mythus Magick, DJ supplement with Dave Newton (GDW 1992)

Epic of Aearth, DJ supplement (GDW 1992)

Necropolis, DJ adventure module (GDW 1992)

Mythus Bestiary, DJ supplement with Dave Newton and Michele Newton (GDW 1993)

Mythus Prime, DJ supplement with Dave Newton (GDW 1994)

Uninvited Guests, generic adventure module with Lester Smith and Bryan Winter (DG 1997)

A Challenge of Arms, generic adventure module with Chris Clark (ICG 1998)

The Ritual of the Golden Eyes, generic adventure module with Chris Clark (ICG 1999)

Weyland Smith & Company Giant Fun Catalog, generic supplement (HF 1999)

Lejendary Rules for All Players, *Lejendary Adventure (LA)* role-playing game rule book (HF 1999)

Beasts of Lejend, LA role-playing game rule book (HF 2000)

Lejend Master's Lore, LA role-playing game rule book (HF 2000)

Forlorn Corners, LA adventure module (HF 2001)

Lejendary Earth Gazetteer, *LA* supplement (HF 2002)

Necropolis, d20 adventure module (NG 2002)

The Slayer's Guide to Dragons, d20 supplement (MP 2002)

The Slayer's Guide to Undead, d20 supplement with John Creffield (MP 2002)

Gary Gygax's The Canting Crew, the Criminal Underclass: Gygaxian Fantasy Worlds, Volume I, generic supplement (TLG 2002)

The Hermit, d20/*LA* adventure module (TLG 2002)

Gary Gygax's World Builder: Gygaxian Fantasy Worlds, Volume II, generic supplement with Dan Cross (TLG 2003)

Gary Gygax's Living Fantasy: Gygaxian Fantasy Worlds, Volume III, generic supplement (TLG 2003)

Noble Knights and Dark Lands, *LA* supplement with Chris Clark (HF 2003)

Terekaptra: The Lost City of Utiss, *LA* adventure module with Chris Clark (HF 2004)

Hall of Many Panes, d20 adventure module (TLG 2005)

Lejendary Adventures Essentials Rulebook, *LA* rule book (TLG 2005)

The Exotic Realms of Hazgar, *LA* supplement with Chris Clark (HF 2006)

Castle Zagyg: Yggsburgh, Castles & Crusades (C&C) supplement, (TLG 2005)

Castle Zagyg: Dark Chateau, C&C adventure module (TLG 2005)

Castle Zagyg: Class Options & Skills for Yggsburgh, C&C supplement (TLG 2006)

Castle Zagyg: The Outs Inn, C&C supplement (TLG 2006)

Castle Zagyg: Yggsburgh Player's Maps, C&C supplement (TLG 2006)

Castle Zagyg: The East Mark Gazetteer, C&C supplement and adventure module with Jeff Talanian (TLG 2007)

More Beasts of Lejend, LA supplement (TLG 2007)

A Problem of Manors, LA module with Chris Clark (TLG 2007)

Castle Zagyg: The Upper Works, C&C supplement (TLG 2008)

Miniatures Games

Untitled Miniatures Rules, ancient period miniature wargame (IFWM 1969)

LGTSA Medieval Miniatures Rules, miniature wargame with Jeff Perren (PF/DB/SIM 1970)

Chainmail, medieval miniatures wargame with Jeff Perren (GG 1971)

Tractics, World War II miniatures wargame with Michael Reese and Leon Tucker (GG 1971)

Don't Give Up the Ship, naval miniatures wargame with Dave Arneson and Mike Carr (GG 1972)

Cavaliers and Roundheads, English Civil War miniatures wargame with Jeff Perren (TSR 1973)

Warriors of Mars, fantasy miniatures wargame with Brian Blume (TSR 1974)

Classic Warfare, ancient period miniatures wargame (TSR 1975)

Swords & Spells, D&D miniatures supplement (TSR 1976)

Diplomacy Games/Variants

Napoleonic Diplomacy II, Diplomacy variant (TGD 1969)

Crusadomacy, Diplomacy variant (DB 1970)

Khanomacy, Diplomacy variant (SP 1970)

Rajomacy, Diplomacy variant (SP 1970)

Hyborian Age Diplomacy (Conanomacy), *Diplomacy* variant (SN
  1972)

War, Board, and Chess Games/Variants

Little Big Horn, board wargame based on the historic Custer battle
  (WGIG 1968, TSR 1976)

Overlord: The Battle for France, board wargame variant of Avalon
  Hill's *D-Day* with Bill Hoyer (ST 1968)

Arbela, Alexander the Great–themed board wargame with Dane
  Lyons (WGIG 1968)

The Caucasus Extension, World War II–era board wargame variant
  of Avalon Hill's *Stalingrad* (IW 1969)

France 1940, World War II–era board wargame (GDB 1969)

Arsouf, Crusades-era board wargame (PF 1969)

War of the Empires, play-by-mail strategy wargame with Tuillo
  Proni (SP 1969)

Dark Ages, Medieval Conflict on Alternate World "Entropy,"
  strategy wargame with referee and miniatures component (DB
  1970)

Alexander the Great, board wargame with Don Lowry (GG 1971,
  AH 1974)

Dunkirk: The Battle of France, World War II–era board wargame
  (GG 1971)

Alexander's Other Battles, extensions to *Alexander the Great* board
  wargame (GG 1972, AHG 1974)

Victorious German Arms, alternate World War II history for
  wargames with Terry Stafford (TKG 1973)

Dragonchess, chess variant (TSR 1985)

Fidchell, Dangerous Journeys chess variant (GDW 1992)

Novels and Books

Hero's Challenge: Sagard the Barbarian: The Crimson Sea, choose-your-own-adventure book with Flint Dille (TSR 1985)

Hero's Challenge: Sagard the Barbarian: The Green Hydra, choose-your-own-adventure book with Flint Dille (TSR 1985)

Hero's Challenge: Sagard the Barbarian: The Ice Dragon, choose-your-own-adventure book with Flint Dille (TSR 1985)

Hero's Challenge: Sagard the Barbarian: The Fire Demon, choose-your-own-adventure book with Flint Dille (TSR 1986)

Saga of Old City, AD&D novel (TSR 1985)

Artifact of Evil, AD&D novel (TSR 1986)

City of Hawks, AD&D novel (NIPI 1987)

Night Arrant, AD&D novel (NIPI 1987)

Sea of Death, AD&D novel (NIPI 1987)

Role-Playing Mastery, how-to RPG book (PP 1987)

Dance of Demons, AD&D novel (NIPI 1988)

Come Endless Darkness, AD&D novel (NIPI 1988)

Master of the Game, how-to RPG book (PP 1989)

The Anubis Murders, *Dangerous Journeys* novel (PR 1992)

The Samarkand Solution, *Dangerous Journeys* novel (PR 1993)

Death in Delhi, *Dangerous Journeys* novel (PR 1993)

Horsemen of the Apocalypse, essays on role playing (JRG 2000)

Infernal Sorceress, *Dangerous Journeys* novel (PG 2009)

Magazine/Fanzine Contributions (Representing Hundreds of Columns, Games, and Variants)

AFV-G2

Alarums & Excursions

Avalon Hill General

Bleak December

Campaign

Canadian Wargamer

The Cardboard Commander

The Courier

The Crusader

Domesday Book

*The Dragon (Dragon, Dragon Magazine, Dragon Annual, Best of
Dragon)*

El Conquistador

Europa

Europe '44

Great Plains Game Players Newsletter

IFW Monthly

IFW Quarterly

Imagine

International Wargamer

Journeys: Journal of Multidimensional Roleplaying

Kipple

La Vivandière

Liaisons Dangereuses

Little Wars

Lowry's Guidon

Mythic Masters

New War Reports

Panzerfaust

Polyhedron

Random Events

Realms of Adventure

SF & F Journal

Shadis

Space/Fantasy Gamer

The Spartan

Spartan International Monthly

The Strategic Preview: T.S.R. Jobbies

The Strategic Review

Strategy & Tactics

Supernova

Tactics & Variants

Thangorodrim

Tricolor

Troll

Wargamer's Digest

Wargamer's Newsletter

White Dwarf

Key

AH: Avalon Hill

AHG: Avalon Hill General

DB: Domesday Book

DG: Destination Games

GDB: IFW Game Design Bureau

GG: Guidon Games

GDW: Games Designers' Workshop

HP: Hekaforge Productions

IFWM: International Federation of Wargaming Monthly

ICG: Inner City Games

IW: International Wargamer

JRG: Jolly Roger Games

MP: Mongoose Publishing

NG: Necromancer Games

NIPI: New Infinities Productions, Inc.

PF: Panzerfaust

PG: Paizo Games

PP: Putnam/Perigee

PR: Penguin/Roc

SIM: Spartan International Monthly

SN: Supernova

SP: Self-published

ST: Spartan

TGD: Thangorodrim

TKG: TK Graphics

TLG: Troll Lord Games

TSR: Tactical Studies Rules; TSR Hobbies, Inc.; TSR, Inc.

WGIG: War Game Inventors Guild

References and Selected Bibliography

Selected Interviews and Direct Correspondence

Adkison, Peter. Personal communication: In-person interview, December 28, 2014.

Carr, Mike. Personal communication: E-mail interview and phone correspondence, January 11, 2015.

Chenault, Stephen. Personal communication: Phone interview, February 13, 2013.

Clark, Chris. Personal communication: Phone interview, November 21, 2014.

Easley, Jeff. Personal communication: Phone interview, August 28, 2014.

Elmore, Larry. Personal communication: Phone interview, October 3, 2014.

Gygax, Elise. Personal communication: Phone interview, May 11, 2013.

Gygax, Ernest (Ernie). Personal communication: In-person interview, April 27, 2013 and August 30, 2014.*

Gygax, Luke. Personal communication: Phone interview, April 5, 2013.

Gygax-Walker, Mary. Personal communication: Phone interview, April 28, 2013.*

Johnson, Harold. Personal communication: In-person meeting, March 17, 2013.

Kask, Tim. Personal communication: Phone interview, February 6, 2013 and September 30, 2014.

Little, Jay. Personal communication: E-mail interview, December 15, 2014.

Marmur, Mildred. Personal communication: E-mail interview, January 23, 2015.

Mentzer, Frank. Personal communication: Phone interview, April 16, 2013.

Perren, Jeff. Personal communication: In-person interview, April 12, 2015.

Peterson, Jon. Personal communication: In-person meeting, March 17, 2013.

Pickens, Jon. Personal communication: In-person meeting, March 17, 2013.

Stormberg, Paul. Personal communication: Phone interview, August 20, 2014* and as a research consultant, February/March 2015.

Thompson, Rodney. Personal communication: E-mail interview, October 15, 2014.

Ward, James. Personal communication: Phone interview, April 16, 2014.

Wesely, David. Personal communication: Phone interview, April 4, 2014.

* Plus follow-up e-mail correspondence

Selected Bibliography

Alsop II, S. 1982. "Tsr Hobbies Mixes Fact and Fantasy." *Inc.*, February 1.

Appelcline, S. 2014a. *Designers & Dragons: The '70s*. Silver Spring: Evil Hat Productions, LLC.

———. 2014b. *Designers & Dragons: The '80s*. Silver Spring: Evil Hat Productions, LLC.

———. 2014c. *Designers & Dragons: The '90s*. Silver Spring: Evil Hat Productions, LLC.

———. 2014d. *Designers & Dragons: The '00s*. Silver Spring: Evil Hat Productions, LLC.

Arneson, D. 1975. *Dungeons & Dragons: Rules for Fantastic Medieval Wargames Campaigns Playable with Paper and Pencil and Miniatures Figures—Book V—Blackmoor*. Lake Geneva: Tactical Studies Rules

Barton, M. 2008. *Dungeons & Desktops: The History of Computer Role-Playing Games*. Wellesley: A K Peters, Ltd.

Bartyzel, M. 2014. "8 Glorious TV Homages to the Geekery of Dungeons & Dragons." *Film School Rejects Blog*, July 3. Retrieved from http://film schoolrejects.com/features/eight-homages-geekery-dungeons-dragons.php.

Borrelli, C. 2014. "Does Late Dungeons & Dragons Creator Gary Gygax Deserve a Statue?" *Chicago Tribune*, March 26.

Borsuk, A. J. 1985. "The Dungeon Master: For E. Gary Gygax the Pitfalls of Success Are Not Unlike His Popular Game, Dungeons & Dragons." *Milwaukee Journal*, March 10.

Boucher, G. 2008. "Jon Favreau Is the Action Figure Behind 'Iron Man.'" *Los Angeles Times*, May 5.

Carpio, J. 2013. "The Cosmology of Role-Playing Games." *Gygax*, February.

Chenault & Gray, LLC. 2008. "Troll Lord Games Forum." Trolllord.com. Retrieved from http://www.freeyabb.com/phpbb/viewtopic.php?mforum= trolllordgames&t=4373&postdays=0&postorder=asc&start=0&mforum= trolllordgames.

Cover, J. G. 2010. *The Creation of Narrative In Tabletop Role-Playing Games.* Jefferson: McFarland.

Craig, S. 1986. "Wunderkinds." *Orange Coast Magazine*, April.

Crigger, L. 2008. "Chasing *D&D*: A History of RPGs." 1UP.com, IGN Entertainment Games, April. Retrieved from http://www.1up.com/features/chasing-history-rpgs.

Dancey, R. 2001. "Ryan Dancey on the Acquisition of TSR." Retrieved from http://insaneangel.com/insaneangel/RPG/Dancey.html.

De Smet, A. 2004. "Visiting TSR." *High Programmer.* Retrieved from http://www.highprogrammer.com/alan/rants/tsr.html.

Entertainment Weekly. 1992. "Down the Tubes." *Entertainment Weekly,* December 25.

EN World RPG News & Reviews. 2002. "Q&A with Gary Gygax—Part I." Enworld.org. Retrieved from http://www.enworld.org/forum/showthread.php?t=22566.

———. 2003a. "Q&A with Gary Gygax—Part II." Enworld.org. Retrieved from http://www.enworld.org/forum/showthread.php?t=38912.

———. 2003b. "Q&A with Gary Gygax—Part III." Enworld.org. Retrieved from http://www.enworld.org/forum/showthread.php?t=46861.

———. 2003c. "Q&A with Gary Gygax—Part IV." Enworld.org. Retrieved from http://www.enworld.org/forum/showthread.php?t=57832.

———. 2003–4. "Q&A with Gary Gygax—Part V." Enworld.org. Retrieved from http://www.enworld.org/forum/showthread.php?t=71486.

———. 2004. "Q&A with Gary Gygax—Part VI." Enworld.org. Retrieved from http://www.enworld.org/forum/showthread.php?t=76849.

———. 2004–5. "Q&A with Gary Gygax—Part VII." Enworld.org. Retrieved from http://www.enworld.org/forum/showthread.php?t=104817.

———. 2005a. "Q&A with Gary Gygax—Part VIII." Enworld.org. Retrieved from http://www.enworld.org/forum/showthread.php?t=121380.

———. 2005b. "Q&A with Gary Gygax—Part IX." Enworld.org. Retrieved from http://www.enworld.org/forum/showthread.php?t=125997.

———. 2006a. "Q&A with Gary Gygax—Part X." Enworld.org. Retrieved from http://www.enworld.org/forum/showthread.php?t=161566.

———. 2006b. "Q&A with Gary Gygax—Part XI." Enworld.org. Retrieved from http://www.enworld.org/forum/showthread.php?t=167680.

———. 2006–7. "Q&A with Gary Gygax—Part XII." Enworld.org. Retrieved from http://www.enworld.org/forum/showthread.php?t=171753.

———. 2007–8. "Q&A with Gary Gygax—Part XIII." Enworld.org. Retrieved from http://www.enworld.org/forum/showthread.php?t=193204.

Ewalt, D. M. 2013. *Of Dice and Men: The Story of Dungeons & Dragons and the People Who Play It*. New York: Scribner.

———. 2011. "How to Get Started with Dungeons & Dragons." *Forbes*, February 14.

Florio, V. 2010. "Interview with Mike Carr." *The Save or Die Podcast*, December 4. Retrieved from http://saveordie.info/?p=333.

Furino, G. 2014. "Dungeons & Dragons Is Officially Cool Again." *Vice*, August 20. Retrieved from http://www.vice.com/read/dungeons-dragons-is-officially-cool-again-115.

Gilsdorf, E. 2009. *Fantasy Freaks and Gaming Geeks: An Epic Quest for Reality Among Role Players, Online Gamers, and Other Dwellers of Imaginary Realms*. Guilford: Lyons Press.

———. 2014. "A Game as Literary Tutorial: Dungeons & Dragons Has Influenced a Generation of Writers." *New York Times*, July 13.

Gray, S. 2008. "Gary Gygax." *Times* (London), March 6.

Gygax, E. 2013. "The Gygax Family Storyteller." *Gygax*, February.

Gygax, G., ed. 1975. *The Strategic Review*. No. 4. Lake Geneva: TSR Hobbies, Inc.

Gygax, G. 1977. *Monster Manual: Advanced Dungeons & Dragons*. Lake Geneva: TSR Hobbies, Inc.

———. 1978. *Players Handbook: Advanced Dungeons & Dragons*. Lake Geneva: TSR Hobbies, Inc.

———. 1979. *Dungeon Master's Guide: Advanced Dungeons & Dragons*. Lake Geneva: TSR Hobbies, Inc.

———. 1985. *Unearthed Arcana: Advanced Dungeons & Dragons*. Lake Geneva: TSR Hobbies, Inc.

———. 2005. "How It All Happened: The Inspiration for the *D&D* Game, Its Creation, Gen Con's Founding, How TSR Came into Being, and Its Early Days—Way Back When . . ." *Crusader: The Journal of the Intrepid Adventurer*, July.

———. 2006a. "How It All Happened: The Inspiration for the *D&D* Game, Its Creation, Gen Con's Founding, How TSR Came into Being, and Its Early Days—Live Action RPGing in 1947." *Crusader: The Journal of the Intrepid Adventurer*, Winter.

———. 2006b. "How It All Happened: The Inspiration for the *D&D* Game, Its Creation, Gen Con's Founding, How TSR Came into Being, and Its Early

Days—Knightly Combat and Military Play." *Crusader: The Journal of the Intrepid Adventurer,* Spring.

———. 2007a. "How It All Happened: The Inspiration for the *D&D* Game, Its Creation, Gen Con's Founding, How TSR Came into Being, and Its Early Days—Older Boys." *Crusader: The Journal of the Intrepid Adventurer,* Winter.

———. 2007b. "How It All Happened: The Inspiration for the *D&D* Game, Its Creation, Gen Con's Founding, How TSR Came into Being, and Its Early Days—Wild Bookworms." *Crusader: The Journal of the Intrepid Adventurer,* Summer.

———. 2007c. "How It All Happened: The Inspiration for the *D&D* Game, Its Creation, Gen Con's Founding, How TSR Came into Being, and Its Early Days—Variety Is the Spice . . ." *Crusader: The Journal of the Intrepid Adventurer,* August.

———. 2008a. "How It All Happened: The Inspiration for the *D&D* Game, Its Creation, Gen Con's Founding, How TSR Came into Being, and Its Early Days—Ghostly Happenings . . ." *Crusader: The Journal of the Intrepid Adventurer,* March.

———. 2008b. "How It All Happened: The Inspiration for the *D&D* Game, Its Creation, Gen Con's Founding, How TSR Came into Being, and Its Early Days—Ghostly Happenings . . . Part II." *Crusader: The Journal of the Intrepid Adventurer,* May.

———. 2008c. "How It All Happened: The Inspiration for the *D&D* Game, Its Creation, Gen Con's Founding, How TSR Came into Being, and Its Early Days—Risky Things." *Crusader: The Journal of the Intrepid Adventurer,* July.

———. 2008d. "How It All Happened: The Inspiration for the *D&D* Game, Its Creation, Gen Con's Founding, How TSR Came into Being, and Its Early Days—Risky Things Part II." *Crusader: The Journal of the Intrepid Adventurer,* August.

———. 2008e. "How It All Happened: The Inspiration for the *D&D* Game, Its Creation, Gen Con's Founding, How TSR Came into Being, and Its Early Days—Oak Hill Sanatorium." *Crusader: The Journal of the Intrepid Adventurer,* September.

———. 2008f. "How It All Happened: The Inspiration for the *D&D* Game, Its Creation, Gen Con's Founding, How TSR Came into Being, and Its Early Days—Miscellaneous Make-Believe." *Crusader: The Journal of the Intrepid Adventurer,* October.

———. 1987. *Role-Playing Mastery*. New York: Perigee Books.

Gygax, G., and D. Arneson. 1974a. *Dungeons & Dragons: Rules for Fantastic Medieval Wargames Campaigns Playable with Paper and Pencil and Miniatures Figures—Book I—Men & Magic*. Lake Geneva: Tactical Studies Rules.

———. 1974b. *Dungeons & Dragons: Rules for Fantastic Medieval Wargames Campaigns Playable with Paper and Pencil and Miniatures Figures—Book II—Monsters & Treasure*. Lake Geneva: Tactical Studies Rules.

———. 1974c. *Dungeons & Dragons: Rules for Fantastic Medieval Wargames Campaigns Playable with Paper and Pencil and Miniatures Figures—Book III—The Underworld & Wilderness Adventures*. Lake Geneva: Tactical Studies Rules.

Gygax, G., and R. Kuntz. (1975). *Dungeons & Dragons: Rules for Fantastic Medieval Wargames Campaigns Playable with Paper and Pencil and Miniatures Figures—Book IV—Greyhawk*. Lake Geneva: Tactical Studies Rules.

Gygax, G., and J. Perren. 1971. *Chainmail: Rules for Medieval Miniatures*. Evansville: Guidon Games.

Gygax, G., and Sacco, A. 2002. "The Ultimate Interview with Gary Gygax." *The Kyngdoms*. Retrieved from http://www.thekyngdoms.com/interviews/garygygax.php.

Heinsoo, R., A. Collins, and J. Wyatt. 2008. *Dungeons & Dragons Player's Handbook: Arcane, Divine, and Martial Heroes*. Renton: Wizards of the Coast, Inc.

Hulse, E. 2009. *The Blood 'n' Thunder Guide to Collecting Pulps*. Morris Plains: Murania Press.

Jeffries, A. 2014. "The Case of the Dueling 'Dungeons & Dragons' Documentaries." *The Verge*, July 15. Retrieved from http://www.theverge.com/2014/7/15/5901199/the-case-of-the-dueling-dungeons-dragons-documentaries.

Kask, T. 2008. "Interview: Tim Kask (Part I)." *Grognardia*, September 18. Retrieved from http://grognardia.blogspot.com/2008/09/interview-tim-kask-part-i.html

Kask, T., ed. 1975. *The Strategic Review*. No. 5. Lake Geneva: TSR Hobbies, Inc.

———. 1977. *The Dragon*. No. 7. Lake Geneva: TSR Hobbies, Inc.

———. 1977. *The Dragon*. No. 11. Lake Geneva: TSR Hobbies, Inc.

Kelly, K. 2015. *Hawk & Moor Trilogy: The Unofficial History of Dungeons & Dragons*. Amazon Digital: Wonderland Imprints.

King, B., and J. Borland. (2014). *Dungeons & Dreamers: A Story of How Computer Games Created a Global Community.* 2nd ed. Pittsburgh: ETC Press.

Kushner, D. 2008. "Dungeon Master: The Life and Legacy of Gary Gygax." *Wired*, March 10.

Kutalik, C. 2011. "No Borders: A Conversation with Rob Kuntz." *Hill Cantons Blog*, August 15. Retrieved from http://hillcantons.blogspot.com/2011/08/no-borders-or-limits-conversation-with.html.

La Farge, P. 2006. "Destroy All Monsters." *The Believer*, September. Retrieved from http://www.believermag.com/issues/200609/?read=article_lafarge.

Lake Geneva Public Library. 2013. "Know Us." Retrieved from www.lakegeneva.lib.wi.us/knowus.htm.

Lynch, S. 2001. "Interview with Gary Gygax, Part 1 of 3." RPGnet, May 1. Retrieved from http://www.rpg.net/news+reviews/columns/lynch01may01.html.

Michaud, Jon. 2014. "Dungeons & Dragons Saved My Life." *New Yorker*, July 16.

Mills, B. K. 1980. "If Students' Tails Are Dragon and Their Minds in the Dungeon Lately, Blame Gamesman Gary Gygax." *People*, January 14.

Newman, T. 2013. "How to Talk to Your Parents About *D&D*." *Monkey in the Cage*, January. Retrieved from http://www.monkeyinthecage.com/2013/01/23/how-to-talk-to-your-parents-about-dnd.

Ortega, T. 2012. "Bill Dear Is Full of It and I Can Prove It." *Village Voice Blogs*, April 3. Retrieved from http://blogs.villagevoice.com/runninscared/2012/04/oj_simpson_bill_dear_full_of_it.php.

Peterson, J. 2012. *Playing at the World.* San Diego: Unreason Press.

———. 2014. "The Ambush at Sheridan Springs: How Gary Gygax Lost Control of Dungeons & Dragons." *Playing at the World Blog*, July 28. Retrieved from http://playingattheworld.blogspot.com/2014/07/how-gary-gygax-lost-control-of-tsr.html.

Rausch, A. 2004a. "Gamespy: Gary Gygax Interview—Part I." *Gamespy*, August 15. Retrieved from www.pc.gamespy.com/articles/538/538820p.1.html.

———. 2004b. "Gamespy: Gary Gygax Interview—Part 2." *Gamespy*, August 16. Retrieved from www.pc.gamespy.com/articles/538/538817p.1.html.

———. 2004c. "Gamespy: Dave Arneson Interview." *Gamespy*, August 19. Retrieved from http://pc.gamespy.com/articles/540/540395p1.html.

Roberts, C. S. 1983. "Charles S. Roberts: In His Own Words." Charles S. Roberts Awards. Retrieved from http://www.alanemrich.com/CSR_pages/Articles/CSRspeaks.htm.

Rogers, A. 2008. "Geek Love." *New York Times*, March 9.

RPGnet. 2012–13. "Verified 'Celebrity' Tabletop Role-Playing Gamers?" RPG .net, March 9. Retrieved from http://forum.rpg.net/showthread.php?631055-Verified-quot-celebrity-quot-tabletop-role-playing-gamers/page10.

Sandler, C. 2013. "Fantastic Fun: Sid Sackson, Gary Gygax, and the World of Gaming." National Museum of Play, January 2. Retrieved from http://www.museumofplay.org/blog/play-stuff/2013/01/fantastic-fun-sid-sackson-gary-gygax-and-the-world-of-wargaming.

Scheele, T. 2003. "Press Release from Washington About *D&D*." *Computers for Christ*, May 1. Retrieved from http://www.believersweb.org/view.cfm ?ID=663.

Shanafelt, S. 2005. "The Growing Chic of Geek: How Turning 30 Made Dungeons & Dragons Feel Young Again." *Mountain Xpress*, November 2. Retrieved from http://www.mountainx.com/article/9563/The-growing-chic-of-geek.

Sheppard, N. 1979. "Tunnels Are Searched for Missing Student." *New York Times*, September 8.

Smith, H. (n.d.). "The Dungeon Master: An Interview with Gary Gygax." Witchboy.net. Retrieved from http://www.witchboy.net/articles/the-dungeon-master-an-interview-with-gary-gygax.

Smith, M. 2014. "New Dungeons & Dragons Is a Worthy Hit." *Yahoo! Games— Plugged In Blog*, August 28. Retrieved from https://games.yahoo.com/blogs/plugged-in/new-dungeons---dragons-is-a-worthy-hit-215420322.html.

Stackpole, M. A. 1990. "The Pulling Report." Retrieved from http://www .rpgstudies.net/stackpole/pulling_report.html#Lies.

———. 1989. "Game Hysteria and the Truth." August 28. Retrieved from http://www.featherlessbiped.com/6696/RPGSATAN/rpgsatan.htm.

Milwaukee Journal. 1982. "Portions of Sunken Vessel Raised." September 28.

WTAE. 2013. "W. Pa Addiction Doc Charged in Drugs-for-Sex Plan." WTAE .com: Pittsburgh's Action News 4, August 20. Retrieved from http://www .wtae.com/news/local/w-pa-addiction-doc-charged-in-drugsforsex-plan/21546374.

Staggs, M. 2010. "Writers Reminisce About Dungeons & Dragons." *Suvudu*, February 16. Retrieved from http://suvudu.com/2010/02/writers-reminisce-about-dungeons-dragons.html.

Temple, E. 2013. "Sam Lipsyte Says He Became a Writer Because of Dungeons & Dragons." *Flavorwire*, March 6. Retrieved from http://flavorwire.com/newswire/sam-lipsyte-says-he-became-a-writer-because-of-dungeons-dragons.

Tresca, M. J. 2011. *The Evolution of Fantasy Role-Playing Games.* Jefferson: McFarland.

Winter, S. 2009a. "Lake Geneva and the Dungeon." Wizards of the Coast, LLC, October 2. Retrieved from http://community.wizards.com/wotc_huscarl/blog/2009/10/02/lake_geneva_and_the_dungeon.

———. 2009b. "Hotel Clair, Lake Geneva." Wizards of the Coast, LLC, September 9. Retrieved from http://community.wizards.com/wotc_huscarl/blog/2009/09/09/hotel_clair_lake_Geneva.

Wizards of the Coast. 1999. *Dragon Magazine Archive.* Renton: Wizards of the Coast, Inc.

———. 2003. "The History of TSR." Wizards of the Coast, LLC, September 9. Retrieved from http://www.wizards.com/dnd/dndarchives_history.asp.

———. 2004. *30 Years of Adventure: A Celebration of Dungeons & Dragons.* Renton: Wizards of the Coast, Inc.

Yee, V. 2014. "Dungeons, Dragons & Documentaries: A Film Conjures a Battle." *New York Times*, September 12.

Notes

Prologue: Memory Lane

1. From an April 27, 2013, interview with Ernie Gygax. Ernie has since retained a version of the "TSR 1" plate for his own car.

2. Quoted from a Gary post in *EN World RPG News & Reviews* 2003–2004.

3. Because she was twice widowed and once divorced, Gary's mother had many names, but "Posey" was the preferred name used by friends and family, according to the author's interviews with the Gygax family, including Mary Jo (phone interview, April 28, 2013, plus e-mail follow-up), Ernie (interviews, April 27, 2013, and August 30, 2014, plus e-mail follow-up), Luke (phone interview, April 5, 2013), and Elise (phone interview, May 11, 2013).

4. Quoted from Gygax 2007b. Gary wrote a series of such articles entitled "How It All Happened" from 2005 to 2008.

5. Ibid.

6. Ibid.

7. Quoted from a phone interview with Frank Mentzer, April 16, 2013. By the time Mentzer arrived in January 1980, TSR was considered a highly desirable company to work for among game designers and gamers alike, and for him a "dream come true."

8. Quoted from Borsuk 1985.

9. Quoted from a Gary post in *EN World RPG News & Reviews* 2002.

10. This scene is based on a phone interview with Mary Jo Gygax-Walker, April 28, 2013. While Mary Jo couldn't remember the exact words used, she noted that he broke into tears during their conversation, which was only the second time she had ever known him to cry. The fictionalized dialogue captures the essence of the conversation.

+1: *Midwestern Mischief*

1. This scene is based on multiple Gary accounts of this event, including those found in *EN World RPG News & Reviews* 2005b, 2007–2008.

2. Quoted from Gygax 2005.

3. Quoted from a Gary post in *EN World RPG News & Reviews* 2005b, 2007–2008.

4. Ibid.

5. These accounts are from the author's interviews with Gygax family members, including Elise (phone interview, May 11, 2013), Ernie (interviews, April 27, 2013, and August 30, 2014, plus e-mail follow-up), Luke (phone interview, April 5, 2013), and Mary Jo (phone interview, April 28, 2013, plus follow-up e-mails). Gary also mentions some of these details about his father in Borsuk 1985.

6. Quoted from a Gary post in *EN World RPG News & Reviews*, 2005b.

7. From an interview with Ernie Gygax, April 27, 2013.

+2: *Fright Night*

1. This scene is based on multiple Gary accounts of this event, including Gygax 2008a. This is a story he frequently told, likely indicating that he considered it a formative event.

2. Quoted from a Gary post in *EN World RPG News & Reviews* 2005b. *Fracas* was a term Gary liked to use when discussing the fight of the Kenmore Pirates. There were in fact two factions that lived on Kenmore Street: the Pirates on Gary's side, and the Indians on the other. These sides were friendly rivals but would unite when confronted by outside gangs.

3. Quoted from Gygax 2008a.

4. Ibid.

5. Ibid.

+3: *Checkmate*

1. This scene is based upon and serves as a composite of various accounts and details from Gary about his grandfather, Hugh Burdick.

2. A well-known fact about Gary that he frequently mentioned, likely indicating that he perceived his early introduction to games as formative to his later game development work. See Gygax and Sacco 2002; Kushner 2008.

3.   Quoted from Kushner 2008. In 2003, Kushner wrote *Masters of Doom*, a book about id Software and the popularization of first-person-shooter video games—an industry that drew much of its inspiration from *D&D*.

4.   Quoted from Alsop 1982.

5.   From author's interviews with Gygax family members, including Mary Jo (phone interview, April 28, 2013 plus follow-up e-mails), Ernie (interviews, April 27, 2013, and August 30, 2014, plus plus follow-up e-mails), and Luke (phone interview, April 5, 2013). There was, however, some disagreement in the accounts whether his shorter leg was caused by an accident or whether it was congenital.

+4: *Here, There Be Dragons*

1.   This scene is based on one of Gary's favorite stories, retold to the author in a phone interview with Stephen Chenault, February 13, 2013. Gary also references this account in *EN World RPG News & Reviews* 2005b, where he mentions that "after seeing The Thing, I was keeping well away from the darkly shadowed bushes along my route."

2.   Quoted from Gygax 2008b. Gary wrote a series of such articles entitled "How It All Happened" from 2005 to 2008. This particular article, entitled "Ghostly Happenings . . . Part II," was published posthumously in May 2008.

3.   Ibid.

4.   Ibid.

5.   Ibid.

6.   Quoted from Gygax and Sacco 2002.

+5: *Tomb of Horrors*

1.   Gary's bedroom contents are derived from several Gary interviews, articles, and posts, including Gygax 2006b, 2007a, and Gygax and Sacco 2002.

2.   Quoted from a Gary post in *EN World RPG News & Reviews* 2003a and Gygax 2005. Gary often mentioned the imaginative games that he played as a child as an important influence on the future development of *D&D*. He regularly used the phrase "Let's pretend" when describing his childhood games and considered *D&D* a formalized version of such games.

3.   This scene is based upon and serves as a composite of various accounts and details from Gary about the Oak Hill Sanitorium. One such account is found in Gygax 2008e.

4.   Quoted from Gygax 2008e.

5. Ibid.
6. Ibid.
7. Ibid.

+6: *No One at the Wheel*

1. This scene is based on details from an interview with Ernie Gygax, April 27, 2013. It was apparently commonplace for Gary to sneak his father's car out of the garage in this manner for joyrides. This scene serves as a composite of those events and a dramatization of the particular evening Gary wrecked his father's car.

2 From an interview with Ernie Gygax, August 30, 2014, and follow-up e-mails.

3. Quoted from a Gary interview in Borsuk 1985.

+7: *Low Times at Lake Geneva High*

1. Quoted from a Gary post in *EN World RPG News & Reviews* 2003a.

+8: *The Real World*

1. Gary's regrets regarding his father were mentioned frequently in the author's interviews with Gygax family members, including Elise (phone interview, May 11, 2013), Ernie (interviews, April 27, 2013, and August 30, 2014, plus follow-up e-mails), Luke (phone interview, April 5, 2013), and Mary Jo (phone interview, April 28, 2013 plus follow-up e-mails). Gary carried these feelings of regret and guilt for the rest of his life.

2. A Gary quote from Kushner 2008.

3 A Gary quote from a 1967 *New War Reports* fanzine referencing his love of pulps, as cited in Peterson 2012, 101.

+9: *Dueling Passions*

1. This scene is based on details from a phone interview with Mary Jo Gygax-Walker on April 28, 2013.

2. Quoted from ibid.

3. Quoted from an interview with Ernie Gygax, April 27, 2013.

4. A Gary quote from a 1967 *New War Reports* fanzine referencing his love of pulps and his selection of a wife, as cited in Peterson 2012, 101.

5. Roberts 1983.

6 Quoted from Gygax 2008f.

7 Quoted from a phone interview with Mary Jo Gygax-Walker, April 28, 2013.

+10: *Another Woman?*

1. This scene is based upon and serves as a composite of various accounts by Mary Jo Gygax-Walker (phone interview, April 28, 2013) and Ernie Gygax (interview, April 27, 2013).

2. From a phone interview with Mary Jo Gygax-Walker, April 28, 2013.

3. Quoted from a Gary post in *EN World RPG News & Reviews* 2003c.

+11: *The One That Got Away*

1. This scene and its dialogue is based on accounts from phone interviews with Elise Gygax on May 11, 2013, and with Ernie Gygax on April 27, 2013. Dialogue with corresponding citations are direct quotes from their accounts. This was among Gary's favorite stories and one he often told.

2. Ibid.

3. Ibid.

+12: *Sunday in the Park with Gary*

1. This scene is based on an account from a phone interview with Mary Jo Gygax-Walker, April 28, 2013.

2. The "Back 40" was a family term used for a forty-acre parcel of land owned by members of the Burdick family. This was Gary's favorite picnic location, according to the author's interviews with the Gygax family, including Elise (phone interview, May 11, 2013), Ernie (interviews, April 27, 2013, and August 30, 2014, plus follow-up e-mails), Luke (phone interview, April 5, 2013), and Mary Jo (phone interview, April 28, 2013 plus follow-up e-mails). According to an autobiographical article by Gary written for Troll Lord Games' *Crusader*, the land contained "wooded hills with a central lowland that was marshy; its northern end culminating in a natural spring that emptied into a small creek."

+13: Playing Games

1. This scene is based on an account from *Strategy & Tactics* and summarized in Peterson 2012, 13: "The night before the doors opened, feeling the strain and uncertainty of a party host, Gygax reportedly insisted that he would never run a convention again."

2. Quoted from an account in Avalon Hill's *General*, as cited in Peterson 2012, 10.

3. Ibid., 9.

4. Ibid., 24.

5. From an interview with Ernie Gygax, August 30, 2014, plus follow-up e-mails. Ernie estimated the number of guests to be between eight and twelve. In 1967, as a precursor to Gen Con 1, Gary hosted an all-day (and all-night) gaming session at his home for a group of roughly twenty regional gamers, which has come to be known as "Gen Con 0."

+14: Fateful Encounter

1. This scene and its dialogue is based on various accounts by Gary and Dave Arneson and depicts what is known about their first meeting at Gen Con II.

+15: Tactical Studies, Anyone?

1. This scene is based on an account from an interview with Ernie Gygax, April 27, 2013.

2. Quoted from an interview with Ernie Gygax, August 30, 2014, plus follow-up e-mails. This particular account about U.S. Army Intelligence also comes from him.

3. Quoted from the *IFW Monthly*, as cited in Peterson 2012, 27.

4. Kutalik 2011.

+16: Chainmail

1. Quoted from a phone interview with Mary Jo Gygax-Walker, April 28, 2013. The scene is based on her account of his layoff, with the jug of Gallo wine being one of its most memorable features.

2. Quoted from an article by Gary in Kask 1975.

3. It is well known that Gary was unhappy with his work at the Fireman's Fund of Chicago and his focus had gravitated more and more toward his gaming

hobbies. According to Mary Jo, after losing a promotion to his in-office rival he considered resigning, but they both decided it would be more beneficial to stay the course. In *Strategic Review* #5 he discusses his former job as "selling out creativity and independence (at least) for a buck." In the same article he 'fesses up to slacking at work but doesn't mention the firing. Interestingly, in many of Gary's later articles and interviews he seems to indicate that he voluntarily left the insurance industry rather than being terminated—perhaps an indication that he was somehow embarrassed or ashamed that he had lost his position.

4. Quoted from issue #112 of the *Wargamer's Newsletter,* as cited in Peterson 2012, 33.

5. From correspondence with Paul Stormberg, 2015.

6. Quoted from a phone interview with Mary Jo Gygax-Walker, April 28, 2013.

7. Quoted from Gygax and Perren 1971.

8. Quoted from Kushner 2008.

9. A notion explored in Barton 2008, 18.

10. According to Perren, from the author's April 12, 2015 interview, Gary allowed Jeff to have a majority of the royalties for the sales of *Chainmail* as compensation for Gary's purchase of Perren's elastolin miniatures collection.

11. Quoted from Gygax and Sacco 2002.

+17: Genesis

1. Quoted from Kushner 2008.

2. Quoted from *Panzerfaust* #53, as cited in Peterson 2012, 50.

+18: The Muse

1. Quoted from an article by Gary in Kask 1977a.

2. Quoted from a Gary post in *EN World RPG News & Reviews* 2003a.

3. Quoted from Gygax 1987.

+19: Bedtime!

1. This scene is based on several accounts of the first test session of *The Fantasy Game*. While early mechanics of the published game included the use of a "caller," who would declare actions for the entire party vs. each individual declaring their own actions, Ernie doesn't recall using one in this instance, remarking that "everything was so new and intense."

2.   Gary's many accounts of the first session of *D&D* include only Ernie and Elise in attendance. However, Ernie indicated in the author's 2014 interview that he believes Rob Kuntz was also part of the first test session, playing his fighter Robilar.

3.   Many of Gary's accounts do not mention Terry Kuntz playing in the second session, but his participation in this session is included in many others and is fairly well established.

4.   Quoted from Chaosium's *Different Worlds* #3, as cited in Peterson 2012, 75.

5.   Quoted from an article by Gary in Kask 1977a.

6.   Quoted from Kushner 2008. Over the years, there has been conflicting accounts as the origin of the *D&D* name, with attribution sometimes to Mary Jo and sometimes to Cindy. The Cindy version is far more prevalent, which is why it is used here.

+20: *Publishing: A Catch-22*

1.   This scene is based on multiple Gary accounts about when he approached Guidon Games to publish *Dungeons & Dragons*, claiming that it would sell fifty thousand copies.

2.   Quoted from 1973 issue of Avalon Hill's *General*, as cited in Peterson 2012, 79–80.

3.   Quoted from an article by Gary in Kask 1977b.

4.   Quoted from Gygax 2008f.

5.   Quoted from a 1999 Gary account used in Wizards of the Coast 2004.

+21: *The Art of Making Art*

1.   A notion explored in Peterson 2012, 109.

2.   Quoted from a 1999 Gary account used in Wizards of the Coast 2004.

3.   Quoted from a letter Gary wrote to IFW member George Phillies, as cited in Peterson 2012, 34.

4.   Quoted from Gygax 2008f.

5.   Ibid.

6.   Ibid.

7.   Ibid.

8.   Quoted from *Great Plains Game Players Newsletter* #9, as cited in Peterson 2012, 79.

+22: *Casualties of Wargaming*

1. Alsop 1982.

2. This scene is based on several Gary accounts, including one found in *EN World RPG News & Reviews* 2003c.

3. Quoted from a Gary post in *EN World RPG News & Reviews* 2003c.

+23: *A Makeshift Solution*

1. This fictionalized scene represents how the conversation between Brian Blume and Gary may have gone when Melvin was brought in to help fund the Kaye buyout.

2. Peterson 2014.

3. Ibid.

4. Peterson 2012, 496. As Peterson notes, the most reliable *D&D* sales and production numbers come from early *Dragon* accounts. Several of Gary's later accounts seem to be off the cuff and include much higher figures that are not well supported by period documentation.

5. Quoted from Gygax 1975.

+24: *Kask Strength*

1. This scene and its dialogue is based on a phone interview with Tim Kask, February 6, 2013, as well as Kask 2008.

2. A notion explored in Peterson 2012, 502.

3. Quoted from a phone interview with Tim Kask, February 6, 2013. Gary expresses concerns about negatively reviewing the games of competitors in the *Strategic Review* #3, stating "could one expect honest and fair reviews from a source directly connected with a competitor of the product being review? Certainly not." Gary clearly lightens on this stance a bit, but also goes to great efforts to ensure that the *Dragon* operates as independently as possible from TSR.

+25: *Fun and More Games*

1. Quoted from *APA-L* #503, as cited in Peterson 2012, 510.

2. Ibid.

3. Quoted from a letter Gary wrote to IFW member George Phillies, as cited in Peterson 2012, 542.

4. As cited and explored in Peterson 2012, 556.

5. From a phone interview with Dave Wesely, April 4, 2014.

6. Quoted from *Alarums & Excursions* #2, as cited in Peterson 2012, 512–13. Gary wrote a number of other similarly pointed responses to APA fanzinists in later issues of the *Dragon* including #16 and #22.

+26: Gary's Other Job

1. This scene and its dialogue is based on details from a phone interview with Elise Gygax on May 11, 2013. Dialogue with corresponding citations is quoted directly from Elise's account.

2. Quoted from an interview with Ernie Gygax, April 27, 2013.

3. Ibid.

4. This scene and its dialogue is based on details from a phone interview with Elise Gygax on May 11, 2013. Dialogue with corresponding citations is quoted directly from Elise's account.

5. Ibid.

6. Ibid.

7. Ibid.

8. Ibid.

+27: It's Like Dungeons and Dragons, but Advanced

1. Royalty figures from Peterson 2012, 573.

2. Quoted from a phone interview with Frank Mentzer, April 16, 2013.

3. Ibid.

4. Ibid.

5. Quoted from Chaosium's *Different Worlds* #3, as cited in Peterson 2012, 75.

6. Royalty figures from Peterson 2012, 573.

+28: Trouble in Paradise

1. This scene is based on details from a phone interview with Tim Kask, September 30, 2014.

2. Sheppard 1979.

3. Quoted from a Gary post in *EN World RPG News & Reviews* 2002.

4. Article titles cited in the *Dragon* #30 and Peterson 2012, 599.

5. Quoted from a Gary post in *EN World RPG News & Reviews* 2003a.

6. William Dear, quoted in the *Dragon* #30 and in Tresca 2011, 191.

7. Ortega 2012.

8. Contemporary reviews of *Little Wars* quoted in Peterson 2012, 269.

9. Ibid.

10. Quoted from a Gary post in *EN World RPG News & Reviews* 2003–2004.

11. Sourced from a post in *EN World RPG News & Reviews* 2007–2008. This was evidently a widespread account as I remember hearing it myself as a child in the 1980s.

12. A 1987 quote by Dr. Thomas Radecki, cited in Scheele 2003.

13. *Entertainment Weekly* 1992 and WTAE 2013.

14. A Gary quote from Rausch 2004a.

15. A notion explored in Peterson 2012, 602–3.

+29: A Devastating Loss

1. Quoted from a phone interview with Mary Jo Gygax-Walker, April 28, 2013. The scene is based on Mary Jo's account and its dialogue is a quote from that account.

2. From an e-mail interview with Mildred Marmur, January 23, 2015.

3. Quoted from a phone interview with Larry Elmore, October 3, 2014.

4. From a phone interview with Mary Jo Gygax-Walker, April 28, 2013.

5. Quoted from follow-up e-mail correspondence with Mary Jo Gygax-Walker, 2014. According to Mary Jo, she and Gary lived at Dragonlands for four years, and she lived there alone for four more after their separation. After the divorce, Gary and Gail moved into the house. Evidently the reason the home was available for only $325,000 in 1979 was that the former owners had a difficult marital split. Regarding the history of broken relationships in the house, Mary Jo wrote, "Those vibrations stayed in that house they had built and those who purchased it from Gary got a divorce and the next purchasers actually had a priest exorcise the house."

6. A quote from Gary from the *Dragon* #35 from Wizards of the Coast 1999.

7. Quoted from a phone interview with Mary Jo Gygax-Walker, April 28, 2014.

8. Quoted from Mills 1980.

+30: The Dictator

1. This scene is based on Gygax and Sacco 2002. Much of the dialogue used here is directly derived from Gary's quotes from that account. The account reads: "I issued some instructions. When Brian heard what I had ordered he shouted loudly for all to hear: 'I don't care what Gary said. I own controlling interest in this company and it will be done the way I say!'"

2. Quoted from a Brian Blume interview in Alsop 1982.

3. Quoted from a Kevin Blume interview in Alsop 1982.

4. Appelcline 2014, 49. According to Paul Stormberg, this was a conflict between the Blume brothers and young members of the Development, Design, and Art Departments who would regularly post humorous sketches and the like around the office. These were often considered inappropriate by the Blumes and escalated to a point where several individuals were fired and several more quit in protest, leaving the art director, Jim Roslof, with an "artistless art department and had to rebuild from scratch." Interestingly, this incident seemingly paved the way for the hiring of some of TSR's greatest artists including Larry Elmore, who started in November 1981, and Jeff Easley, who began in March 1982.

5. Quoted from a Gary post in *EN World RPG News & Reviews* 2002.

6. Ibid.

7. This is a fictionalized letter based on later accounts that Gary had considered resigning around this time. While there is no record of Gary ever drafting a resignation letter, this scene is meant to represent that sentiment. Two such suggestions of resignation occur in Gygax and Sacco 2002, where Gary writes, "I should have parted ways with TSR then and there," when discussing the scene that opens the chapter. Later he writes: "After the reorganization where Brian and Kevin Blume boxed my position as president and CEO into a powerless role, they were evidently not completely satisfied. A part of that possibly stemmed from the fact that by sheer force of personality, along with occasional mutterings about leaving the company, I managed to stop some of their plans . . ."

8. Ibid.

9. From a phone interview with Larry Elmore, October 3, 2014.

10. Gary explains that he didn't resign because "I still had a lot of loyalty to the company and the vision upon which it had been created." See Gygax and Sacco 2002.

+31: Parting Ways

1. This scene and its dialogue is based on a phone interview with Mary Jo Gygax-Walker, April 28, 2013. While Mary Jo couldn't remember all of the exact words used, the fictionalized dialogue captures the essence of the conversation. Dialogue with corresponding citations are direct quotes from Mary Jo's account.

2. Quoted from a phone interview with Frank Mentzer, April 16, 2013.

3. Quoted from a phone interview with Mary Jo Gygax-Walker, April 28, 2013. While Mary Jo couldn't remember all of the exact words used, the fiction-

alized dialogue captures the essence of the conversation. Dialogue with corresponding citations are direct quotes from Mary Jo's account.

4. Ibid.

5. A term Ernie used humorously when describing his parents' relationship during an April 27, 2013, interview. Presumably this refers to both their explosive conflict as well as their high level of sexual activity, as evidenced by five children.

6. The original name of the subsidiary was TSR Entertainment Corp., but quickly changed to Dungeons & Dragons Entertainment Corp. According to Gary, "When I was instructed by the Blumes to move to the West Coast and head up TSR Entertainment, the first thing I noted out there was a distinct dislike of TSR, this from earlier contact with the Blumes, as far as I could ascertain. Thus I immediately requested the BoD for a name change, and I got my way without any real fight." See Gygax and Sacco 2002.

7. From a 2002 written interview with Gary, conducted by Ciro Alessandro Sacco, as well as a Gary post in *EN World RPG News & Reviews* 2005b.

8. Quoted from a Gary interview in Borsuk 1985.

+32: *There's No Business Like Show Business*

1. This scene is based on Gygax and Sacco 2002. Dialogue with corresponding citations is based on direct quotes from Gary's account.

2. Ibid.

3. Quoted from Gygax 1979.

4. This scene is based on Gygax and Sacco 2002. Dialogue with corresponding citations is based on direct quotes from Gary's account.

5. A term Ernie used when discussing their time in Hollywood during an April 27, 2013, interview. Ernie also mentioned that Gary sometimes rented bungalows at the hotel and frequented other swanky establishments such as the Magic Castle and Barney's Beanery.

6. From a phone interview with Luke Gygax, April 5, 2013.

7. Quoted from a Gary post in *EN World RPG News & Reviews* 2004–2005.

8. Quoted from a Gary interview in La Farge 2006.

+33: *The Coup*

1. This scene is based on Gygax and Sacco 2002. Dialogue with corresponding citations are direct quotes from Gary's account. The account reads: "I first heard of

this, TSR being on the block, whilst in California. A friend and business associate called from New York, warned me that «Kevin Blume was shopping TSR on the city streets» and demanded that I get back to Lake Geneva as quickly as possible to find out what was wrong . . . I flew back to Lake Geneva and spent a full week investigating the state of TSR finances, questioning officers and key management personnel under the Blumes. On the following week, a[t] the monthly meeting of the Board of Directors, I presented a rather lengthy paper dealing with the sorry state of corporate finances, the clear mismanagement of TSR by Kevin Blume and concluding with a demand for his resignation. Kevin was livid. Brian demanded how I proposed the company could run without Kevin and I told him the same way it did prior to Kevin's elevation to senior management, by him and me. Brian retorted hotly he could not run the company any more. At that I shrugged and said, 'Very well, in that case I will run it alone because Kevin has proven himself totally incompetent.'"

2. Ibid.

3. Appelcline 2014a, 58.

4. Quoted from Gygax and Sacco 2002.

5. *Milwaukee Journal* 1982. According to Jeff Perren, from the author's April 12, 2015 interview, TSR sought to recover the ship's bell, which was rumored to be made of solid silver—silver that had supposedly been melted down from silverware owned by Antonio López de Santa Anna, who had been captured during the Mexican-American War.

6. Quoted from Alsop 1982.

7. This scene is based Gygax and Sacco 2002. Dialogue with corresponding citations is directly quoted from Gary's account.

8. Ibid.

9. Quoted from Gygax and Sacco 2002.

10. Ibid.

11. Ibid.

12. Ibid.

13. Ibid.

14. Quoted from Gygax and Sacco 2002. This scene is also based on that continued account, which reads: "I fully expected to be dismissed at that time. Instead the 'outside directors' were forced to agree, as there was no question that the corporation was in debt to the bank for about $1.5 million and there appeared to be no way to repay the loan. In the final vote, Kevin voted against my motion for his removal, Brian abstained (which speaks volumes) and the stooges voted for it, so the motion carried four to one."

15. Quoted from a Gary post in *EN World RPG News & Reviews* 2003–2004.

16. Peterson 2014.

17. From Gygax and Sacco 2002. Gary's account reads: "It must be noted that Brian Blume also held a like option and, had he exercised it, control would have reverted to him and Kevin. He did not believe in TSR, so he would not risk the $70,000 cost for option exercise."

18. Quoted from Gygax and Sacco 2002.

+34: Trojan Horse

1. This scene and its dialogue is based on Gygax and Sacco 2002. Dialogue with corresponding citations is quoted directly from Gary's account. The account reads: "She [Lorraine] was in my confidence, but I began to become uneasy about her after two incidents. In one she stated that she held gamers in contempt, that they were socially beneath her. In the other, when I stated that I planned to see that the employees gained share ownership when the corporate crises were passed in recognition of their loyalty, Lorraine had turned to my personal assistant Gail Carpenter (now Gail Gygax, my wife) and said: Over my dead body!"

2. Ibid.

3. Quoted from Gygax and Sacco 2002.

4. Quoted from a Lorraine Williams account, as cited in Ewalt 2013, 169.

5. Ibid.

6. Peterson 2014.

7. A quote from Gary, as cited in Peterson 2014.

8. Peterson 2014.

9. Ibid.

10. Ibid.

11. Quoted from a Gary post in *EN World RPG News & Reviews* 2004.

12. From *EN World RPG News & Reviews* 2004.

13. Quoted from a Gary post in *EN World RPG News & Reviews* 2002.

14. A quote from Lorraine Williams, as cited in Ewalt 2013, 170.

15. A quote from Lorraine Williams, as cited in Peterson 2014.

16. A quote from Gail Gygax in the 2014 trailer for *Dungeons & Dragons: A Documentary*, directed by A. Savini; http://dndadoc.com/trailer-2.

+35: New Beginnings

1. This scene and its dialogue is based on Gygax and Sacco 2002. Gary's account reads: "Baker prepared a plan, complete with banking and legal counsel

components, accounting and assurance of investment capital to the tune of $1–$2 million whenever needed. I was s[k]eptical, but I accompanied Baker to a series of meetings in Chicago. These were impressive and the only hitch came when the investors['] representative failed to meet with us in the offices of the law firm that was to serve as counsel. While in their presence, Baker made a phone call to the investors, spoke at length for all to hear, so we understood it was an oversight, but that all was in line."

2. Quoted from a phone interview with Stephen Chenault, February 13, 2013.

3. Quoted from a phone interview with Paul Stormberg, August 20, 2015.

4. Quoted from a Gary post in *EN World RPG News & Reviews* 2005b.

5. Appelcline 2014a, 101.

6. This how-to RPG book contains some helpful hints about how to effectively run and play in a role-playing game, but notably contains several statements/warnings about separating the real from the imaginary. These include: "Conflict and violence in such games are only simulations, not meant to be translated into real-life experiences" (p. 23); "A master knows the difference between role-playing, role assumption, and real life and never mixes one of these with another" (p. 23); "Master role-playing gamers easily separate the difference between play and reality" (p. 35); and "Remember that the real you and your game persona are different" (p. 37). One must wonder if Gary felt pressured by the publisher to include such warnings.

7. Quoted from Gygax and Sacco 2002.

+36: *Dangerous Journeys*

1. This scene and its dialogue is based on Gygax and Sacco 2002. The phone call itself is fictionalized, as the method in which NEC and JVC delivered their messages is not expressly mentioned.

2. Quoted from a Gary post in *EN World RPG News & Reviews* 2003–4.

3. From Gygax and Sacco 2002. According to Gary, "Three separate law firms reviewed the complaint filed by TSR and assessed it as one of the sort used by a larger company to force a smaller one out of business."

4. A Gary quote from Gygax and Sacco 2002.

5. Ibid.

6. This is a fictionalized conversation—it is not known exactly how the offer to settle was communicated or by whom, but the parties did agree to settle.

7. This scene is based on Gary accounts in *EN World RPG News & Reviews* 2003–2004 and Gygax and Sacco 2002. According to Gary, there were

"many meetings and days of negotiation," so this scene serves as a dramatized composite of those meetings. Lastly, the location of the meetings at TSR's boardroom is fictionalized, as those details are not expressly mentioned in his accounts.

8. From Gygax and Sacco 2002.

9. Quoted from a Gary post in a *EN World RPG News & Reviews* 2004–2005. Ironically, this strategy is not all that different from the one TSR employed when it developed *AD&D*, denying Arneson his royalties.

10. Quoted from Tresca 2011, 64.

11. Quoted from a Gary post in *EN World RPG News & Reviews* 2003–2004.

12. Ibid.

+37: *Justified*

1. Quoted from Fox's *Futurama* episode entitled "Anthology of Interest," 2000.

2. Ibid.

3. Ibid.

4. Ibid.

5. Ibid.

6. Quoted from a Gary post in *EN World RPG News & Reviews* 2003a.

7. Quoted from a Gary post in *EN World RPG News & Reviews* 2002.

8. From an interview with Peter Adkison, December 28, 2014. In an effort to promote goodwill and acquire "clean" intellectual property, similar deals were struck with other estranged TSR employees, including Dave Arneson, Tracy Hickman, Margaret Weis, R. A. Salvatore, and Ed Greenwood. Having uncontested intellectual property was especially important because Adkison already had a sense that Wizards might be sold sooner or later.

9. Quoted from a Gary post in *EN World RPG News & Reviews* 2005b.

10. From a phone interview with Chris Clark, November 21, 2014.

11. A notion explored in Appelcline 2014c, 366.

12. Quoted from a Gary post in *EN World RPG News & Reviews* 2003a.

13. Ibid.

+38: *Silver and Gold*

1. Quoted from a Gary post in *EN World RPG News & Reviews* 2003b. The scene is based on a series of posts around the topic of his sixty-fifth birthday.

2. Quoted from a Gary post in *EN World RPG News & Reviews* 2003c.

3. Quoted from a Gary post in *EN World RPG News & Reviews* 2005a.

4. Ibid.

5. A term Gary used for his friends and collaborators at Troll Lord Games. Quoted from a Gary post in *EN World RPG News & Reviews* 2004–2005.

6. Quoted from a phone interview with Paul Stormberg, August 20, 2014.

7. Quoted from a Gary post in *EN World RPG News & Reviews* 2004.

+39: *King of the Nerds*

1. Quoted from a Gary post in a *EN World RPG News & Reviews* 2006a.

2. Samuel Adams was Gary's favorite American beer while his drink of choice to cool down after a long day of writing was a glass of pure buttermilk. Gary discusses these in *EN World RPG News & Reviews* 2003a, 2003b.

3. A sentiment expressed by author's interviews with Elise (phone interview, May 11, 2013), Ernie (interviews, April 27, 2014, and August 30, 2014, plus follow-up e-mails) and Luke Gygax (phone interview, April 5, 2013).

4. From a Gary post in *EN World RPG News & Reviews* 2007–8. "I use Col Pladoh to poke a bit of fun at myself. The Colonel part comes from my always playing Colonel Mustard in *Clue* games because I like the starting position, and the fact I am a Kentucky Colonel. The Pladoh part is a spoof on the wisdom of Plato and the silliness of Playdoh," he wrote.

+40: *The End of the Road*

1. A favorite term to describe longtime gamers, as used in a Gary post in *EN World RPG News & Reviews* 2002.

2. This scene is based on an account from a phone interview with Frank Mentzer, April 16, 2013.

3. A fond remembrance of Ernie and Luke Gygax. While Gary's love of football is a relatively little-known fact about him, he did write in the *Strategic Review* #4, when talking about how well newly hired Tim Kask fit in, "He even waits for half time during football games to call with various business matters— thus assuring he'll get through to us!"

4. From an interview with Ernie Gygax, August 30, 2014, plus follow-up e-mails.

5. Quoted from a Gary post in *EN World RPG News & Reviews* 2003a.

6. Quoted from a Gary post in *EN World RPG News & Reviews* 2004–2005. Gary regularly used the phrase "Let's pretend," when describing his childhood games and considered *D&D* a formalized version of such games.

7. Quoted from a Gary post in *EN World RPG News & Reviews* 2005a.

8. Quoted from a Gary post in *EN World RPG News & Reviews* 2002.

9. Quoted from a Gary e-mail reposted in Chenault and Gray 2008.

+41: The Legacy

1. Quoted from the March 5, 2008, episode of Comedy Central's *The Colbert Report*.

2. Quoted from a Sam Lipsyte interview in Temple 2013.

3. Quoted from a Junot Díaz interview in Gilsdorf 2014.

4. Quoted from Rogers 2008.

5. Quoted from a phone interview with Tim Kask, February 6, 2013.

6. Quoted from a Jay Lake interview in Staggs 2010.

7. From a Gary post in *EN World RPG News & Reviews* 2002.

8. Quoted from a phone interview with Paul Stormberg, August 20, 2014.

9. Quoted from Gygax 1987.

10. A Gail Gygax quote from the Gygax Memorial Fund website, http://www.gygaxmemorialfund.org.

+42: The Butterfly Effect

1. Quoted from an e-mail interview with Rodney Thompson, October 15, 2014.

2. Quoted from an e-mail and phone interview with Mike Carr, January 11, 2015.

3. Quoted from a Luke Gygax interview in Borrelli 2014.

4. Quoted from the True Dungeon website, www.truedungeon.com.

5. Ibid.

6. From the MagiQuest website, http://magiquest.com/media/downloads/Benefits%20and%20Facts.pdf.

7. Quoted from King and Borland 2014, 22.

8. Quoted from a Richard Garriott interview in Crigger 2008.

9. John Romero, quoted in King and Borland 2014, 120.

10. Quoted from Rogers 2008.

11. Ibid.

12. Quoted from King and Borland 2014, 8.

13. Quoted from a Gary post in *EN World RPG News & Reviews* 2003b.

14. Craig 1986.

15. A Jon Favreau quote from Boucher 2008.

16. Quoted from *Freaks and Geeks* episode "Discos and Dragons" (Dreamworks Television, 2000).

17. Quoted from a phone interview with Luke Gygax, April 5, 2013.

18. Quoted from a phone interview with Chris Clark, November 21, 2014.

19. Quoted from Tresca 2011, 12.

20. Quoted from an e-mail interview with Jay Little, December 15, 2014.

+43: *The Road Goes Ever On*

1. Quoted from a phone interview with Larry Elmore, October 3, 2014.

2. Quoted from an interview with Peter Adkison, December 28, 2014.

3. Ewalt 2013.

4. Quoted from Dancey 2001.

5. Ibid.

6. From an interview with Peter Adkison, December 28, 2014.

7. Ewalt 2013.

8. Quoted from Smith 2014.

9. Quoted from an e-mail interview with Rodney Thompson, October 15, 2014.

10. Quotes from 2010 7th Circuit Court of Appeals decision, as cited in Tresca 2011, 192, and Borelli 2014.

11. Ibid.

12. From a June 20, 2014, complaint filed with the Supreme Court of the State of New York: Westpaw Films Inc., Directly and Derivatively on Behalf of the D&D Production, Plaintiff, against James Sprattley, Michael Andrew Pascal, and Fantasy Game Films LLC, Defendants. Supreme Court of the State of New York County of Kings.

13. As quoted in Yee 2014.

14. An Andrew Pascal quote from Jeffries 2014.

15. Michaud 2014.

+44: *A Man for All Seasons*

1. Quoted from a phone interview with Stephen Chenault, February 13, 2013.

2. Ibid.
3. Quoted from a phone interview with Paul Stormberg, August 20, 2014.
4. Quoted from a phone interview with Tim Kask, February 6, 2013.
5. Quoted from Gygax 1978, 6.
6. A Gary quote from Rausch 2004b.

Index

A Note on the Author

Michael Witwer is a lifelong gamer and gaming enthusiast. He holds degrees from Northwestern University and the University of Chicago, where this book first emerged as the subject of his master's thesis. He is also a film and theater actor and marketing professional, and is the brother of actor Sam Witwer, who originally introduced him to *Dungeons & Dragons*. He lives in Chicago, Illinois, with his wife and two children. For more information, visit his website at www .empireofimagination.com

THE CITY OF LAKE GENEVA

2. OAK HILL CEMETERY

3. TSR GRAY HOUSE – DRAGON MAGAZINE

5. PIONEER CEMETERY

6. GARY'S CHILDHOOD HOME

7. HORTICULTURAL HALL

9. GARY'S LAST HOUSE

10. GENEVA THEATER

11. TSR HOTEL CLAI - THE DUNGEO

12. THE RIVIERA

To Dragonlands

GENEVA LAKE